Elisabeth Donat, Sarah Meyer, Gabriele Abels (eds.)
European Regions

Political Science | Volume 92

This open access publication has been enabled by the support of POLLUX (Fachinformationsdienst Politikwissenschaft)

and a collaborative network of academic libraries for the promotion of the Open Access transformation in the Social Sciences and Humanities (transcript Open Library Politikwissenschaft 2020)

This publication is compliant with the "Recommendations on quality standards for the open access provision of books", Nationaler Open Access Kontaktpunkt 2018 (https://pub.uni-bielefeld.de/record/2932189)

Universitätsbibliothek **Bayreuth** | Universitätsbibliothek der Humboldt-Universität zu **Berlin** | Staatsbibliothek zu **Berlin** | Universitätsbibliothek FU **Berlin** | Universitätsbibliothek **Bielefeld** (University of Bielefeld) | Universitätsbibliothek der Ruhr-Universität **Bochum** | Universitäts- und Landesbibliothek | Sächsische Landesbibliothek - Staats- und Universitätsbibliothek **Dresden** | Universitätsbibliothek **Duisburg-Essen** | Universitäts- u. Landesbibliothek **Düsseldorf** | Universitätsbibliothek **Erlangen-Nürnberg** | Universitätsbibliothek Johann Christian Senckenberg | Universitätsbibliothek **Gießen** | Niedersächsische Staats- und Universitätsbibliothek **Göttingen** | Universitätsbibliothek **Graz** | Universitätsbibliothek der FernUniversität in **Hagen** | Martin-Luther-Universität **Halle-Wittenberg** | Staats- und Universitätsbibliothek Carl von Ossietzky, **Hamburg** | Technische Informationsbibliothek **Hannover** | Gottfried Wilhelm Leibniz Bibliothek - Niedersächsische Landesbibliothek | Universitätsbibliothek **Kassel** | Universitäts- und Stadtbibliothek **Köln** | Universität **Konstanz**, Kommunikations-, Informations-, Medienzentrum | Universitätsbibliothek **Koblenz-Landau** | Universitätsbibliothek **Leipzig** | Zentral- u. Hochschulbibliothek **Luzern** | Universitätsbibliothek **Mainz** | Universitätsbibliothek **Marburg** | Ludwig-Maximilians-Universität **München** Universitätsbibliothek | Max Planck Digital Library | Universitäts- und Landesbibliothek **Münster** | Universitätsbibliothek **Oldenburg** | Universitätsbibliothek **Osnabrück** | Universitätsbibliothek **Passau** | Universitätsbibliothek **Potsdam** | Universitätsbibliothek **Siegen** | Universitätsbibliothek Vechta | Universitätsbibliothek der Bauhaus-Universität **Weimar** | Universitätsbibliothek **Wien** | Universitätsbibliothek **Wuppertal** | Universitätsbibliothek **Würzburg** | Zentralbibliothek **Zürich** | Bundesministerium der Verteidigung - Bibliothek | Landesbibliothek **Oldenburg**

Elisabeth Donat, Sarah Meyer, Gabriele Abels (eds.)
European Regions
Perspectives, Trends and Developments in the 21st Century

[transcript]

This publication has been produced as part of the research project REGIOPARL | Regional Parliaments Lab in cooperation with Forum Morgen.

Bibliographic information published by the Deutsche Nationalbibliothek

The Deutsche Nationalbibliothek lists this publication in the Deutsche Nationalbibliografie; detailed bibliographic data are available in the Internet at http://dnb.d-nb.de

This work is licensed under the Creative Commons Attribution-ShareAlike 4.0 (BY-SA) which means that the text may be remixed, build upon and be distributed, provided credit is given to the author and that copies or adaptations of the work are released under the same or similar license. For details go to http://creativecommons.org/licenses/by-sa/4.0/
Creative Commons license terms for re-use do not apply to any content (such as graphs, figures, photos, excerpts, etc.) not original to the Open Access publication and further permission may be required from the rights holder. The obligation to research and clear permission lies solely with the party re-using the material.

First published in 2020 by transcript Verlag, Bielefeld

© Elisabeth Donat, Sarah Meyer, Gabriele Abels (eds.)

All rights reserved. No part of this book may be reprinted or reproduced or utilized in any form or by any electronic, mechanical, or other means, now known or hereafter invented, including photocopying and recording, or in any information storage or retrieval system, without permission in writing from the publisher.

Cover layout: Maria Arndt, Bielefeld
Proofread by Graeme Currie

Print-ISBN 978-3-8376-5069-3
PDF-ISBN 978-3-8394-5069-7
EPUB-ISBN 978-3-7328-5069-3
https://doi.org/10.14361/9783839450697

Contents

Preface 9

European Regions
Perspectives, Trends and Developments in the 21st Century
Elisabeth Donat, Sarah Meyer 11

I.
Regional Identity – a Citizens Perspective

Regional Identity between Inclusion and Exclusion
Elisabeth Donat 25

Regional Europeans
The Relationship between Social Identities and EU Support in Austria
Katrin Praprotnik 43

Ambiguous Identities at the Rhine border
Failures and Successes of Europeanisation in a Pioneering Laboratory of European Integration
Camille Dobler 59

II.
Regions in a Turbulent EU – Political and Legal Manifestations

Regional Identities in Europe
Their Manifestations in Constitution- and Policy-Making
Karl Kössler 83

Scottish Independence
The Romantic Game
Andreas Rahmatian 99

True Bavarians
The Volatile Identity Politics of Born Regionalists
Roland Sturm 117

III.
Unintended and Intended Consequences of EU Programs on Regional Developement

Can Money Buy Love?
The Impact of EU Cohesion Policy on European Identity
Fabian Landes 129

The EU's Regional Investments After the Financial Crisis
Paradigm Change or Business as Usual?
Moritz Neujeffski 145

Cross-border Cooperation in Central Europe
A Comparison of Culture and Policy Effectiveness in the Polish-German and Polish-Slovak Border Regions
Urszula Roman-Kamphaus 163

IV.
Still Dreaming of a "Europe of Regions"? On the Interplay of Regions in the EU

New Multi-Level Governance in the EU?
The European Committee of the Regions and Regional Diversity
Justus Schönlau 195

Small is Beautiful?
Identity and Placism in Europe
Claire Wallace 211

'Europe of the Regions'
A Genealogy of an Ambiguous Concept
Ulrike Guérot 231

Authors Register 245

Preface

The idea of this edited volume emanated from the conference 'Redefining Regions in Europe', which took place at Danube University Krems (Austria) in January 2019. This conference was the kick-off event to the project 'REGIOPARL I Regional Parliaments Lab', an international research project located at Danube University Krems that is supported by and conducted in cooperation with Forum Morgen. REGIOPARL is a multiannual comparative research project that focuses on the role of regional actors in the EU multilevel system of governance. At the same time, it aims at contributing to the ongoing debate on the future of the EU from a regional perspective.

The conference's main objective was to open the field by gathering various approaches to the definition and study of regions in Europe from several scholarly disciplines. This interdisciplinary perspective was deliberately chosen at the beginning of a project that is mainly located in political science. The various contributions to the conference clearly revealed the importance of questions related to collective identity – and regional identity in particular – when studying the multifaceted role of regions within the larger political and legal framework of the EU governance system. This is the reason why the issue of regional identity also is a key point of reference in many of the contributions to this book.

This edited volume is the third publication within the 'Krems Publication Series on European Democracy', edited by the Department of European Policy and the Study of Democracy at Danube University Krems. We would like to thank Forum Morgen for the cooperation with Danube University Krems and for funding the REGIOPARL project, including this publication. Furthermore, we express our thanks to Graeme Currie for proofreading as well as Michael Heber and Fabian Landes for taking care of formal adaptions of the manuscript. Finally, special thanks go to the authors of the individual contributions to this book, who add some fresh insights and unorthodox thinking to the contemporary study of regions in Europe from an interdisciplinary perspective of political science, sociology and legal studies.

European Regions
Perspectives, Trends and Developments in the 21st Century

Elisabeth Donat, Sarah Meyer

Introduction

In the early 21st century, Europe's regions find themselves on a continent that is facing deep political, social and economic change. The financial and economic crisis has left its mark all over Europe, the ongoing Brexit process is causing unprecedented uncertainty among citizens and in various economic sectors, and migration and climate change are just two examples of policy domains posing a challenge to the unity and cohesion of the EU and its member states.

These upheavals, however, also offer an opportunity to change the role played by regions in the EU's multilevel system of governance. Facing the political vacuum induced by member states' blocking of major decisions at EU level, there are even resurgent calls for a 'Europe of the Regions' – or, as Abels and Battke (2019) suggest it, 'Europe with the regions' –, in the hope that regions might be more rational and reliable partners in EU decision-making processes, as it is in cities and regions where the costs of political inaction will be felt first.

Hence, while sub-state entities could be viewed as declining in importance in an age of globalization and increasing rivalry between EU member states, regions nonetheless frequently have centre stage in European affairs, as was the case, for instance, for Wallonia on the issue of the EU's 'CETA' trade agreement with Canada in 2016. EU political leaders also increasingly acknowledge the importance of taking local and regional perspectives into account more systematically in the EU policy process, as exemplified by the follow-up activities to the 2018 report by the Task Force on Subsidiarity, Proportionality and 'Doing Less More Efficiently'. Though the involvement of regions does not automatically guarantee more effective or better governance, there is a lot of expertise among regional actors in the implementation and application of EU legislation, which often takes place at the regional or local levels within member states – and this is increasingly recognized by EU institutions and member states.

Regions also serve as significant objects of identification to their inhabitants. Due to their (perceived) 'closeness' to the people, regions are often understood as fulfilling an important linking function between citizens and 'upper' levels in the political decision-making process (c.f. Chacha 2013). In this regard, it is easy to understand why many consider regions and regional political actors to be well placed to overcome the EU's democratic deficit by bridging the gap between citizens and 'far-off Brussels'. This seems even more important at a time when citizens (and political elites!) are not easily convinced of the advantages of multilateralism, let alone EU supranational governance. It is not surprising that in recent years much of the political and public discourse on European integration was accompanied by reference to a crisis of legitimacy of the EU political project. It is in this context that regions have yet again received more attention as potential facilitators of European democracy. By strengthening the role of regions in the EU political process, the argument runs, 'higher' levels of governance could profit from the strong levels of identification as well as their expertise in policy implementation, thus boosting the overall legitimacy of the EU (cf., e.g., Panara 2019).

Region as a Fluid Concept

Compared to the rather static construct of 'the state', 'region' is a far more flexible, fluid concept. Rather than being composed of a number of largely undisputed defining features, *region* carries a broad range of different meanings in both scholarly literature and politics. It is used, for instance, to refer to whole continents in international or geopolitical contexts (e.g. Europe as a region) and to particular parts of the world map that cross state borders (e.g. the Balkan region or the EU macro regions) as well as to sub-national political units (e.g. the German *Bundesländer* or Spanish *Comunidades Autónomas*). In addition to these mainly territorial and geographical understandings of region, several recent approaches rearrange the classification of regions according to administrative and economic indicators, including the NUTS regions or regional typologies of what ESPON calls 'functional areas'.[1]

Regions can thus be defined using a range of criteria – territorial, functional, historical, and many others. While this can clearly lead to analytical ambiguity, it is also one of the term's strengths. Battke and Abels (2019: 236), for instance, argue that regions should be defined 'as "soft spaces" that are subject to continued rescaling processes'. By broadening the classical territorial perspective towards a functional understanding of regions, scholars account for the fact that the definition and boundaries of regions are socially constructed and, thus, not static (cf. ibid.)

---

[1] https://www.espon.eu/tools-maps/regional-typologies, 1 September 2019

While a broad understanding of the concept of regions certainly has its merits, the main empirical focus in this volume is very much on regions as *sub-national political units within Europe*. Because they are strongly related to the constitutional order of (EU member) states, the boundaries of regions in Europe as defined above seem to be clear and largely stable. However, European regions have obviously been affected – and continue to be so – by major political changes and 'experiments' in recent decades: The EU's external borders have changed considerably as a result of several rounds of enlargement; and internal borders are still shifting (consider, for example, Brexit or the shifts in the Balkans) or remain contested (e.g., Gibraltar or Piran Bay). Territorial shifts have also been witnessed *within* EU member states, often accompanied by decentralization and/or the re-organization of regional political units (cf. Keating 2013). Finally, regions are not only affected by such territorial dynamics, but often become decisive actors themselves: Some regions (or more precisely: regional political actors) strive for political independence while simultaneously desiring continuity in the form of ongoing EU membership; while some form new conglomerates with their neighbours to strengthen cross-border cooperation, as can be seen in the EUREGIOs, or split up into smaller units to reinforce local economies and culture.

Issues of territory and borders thus remain politically salient – as do questions of identity and 'belonging': Among citizens, there seems to be a steadily growing emotionality not only when it comes to the 'homeland' and its (imagined or desired) borders at state level, but likewise – and sometimes even more importantly – with regard to regional 'belonging'. In line with this, many of the contributions to this edited anthology deal with aspects of regional identity – either by explicitly making it the focus of inquiry or by acknowledging its importance as a contextual variable in political processes. According to this approach, the role of regional identity must not be neglected when analysing the role of regions in EU multilevel governance.

Regions and their role in EU multilevel governance have been subject to intense research in recent years, resulting in a vast body of literature, particularly in the field of political science. This is not least due to the changes that came into force with the Treaty of Lisbon, which rearranged the way regions participate in the EU's political system (e.g., Abels/Eppler 2015; Bursens/Högenauer 2017; CoR 2013; Högenauer/Abels 2017; Tatham 2015). Scholars have, for instance, dealt with regional activity in connection with the Early Warning System (EWS) (Borońska-Hryniewiecka 2015; 2017; Fromage 2016; 2017) and the Regional Authority Index (Hooghe et al. 2016) has become an important source for comparing the influence that regional channels have on the multilevel system both in Europe and worldwide.

This anthology takes a closer look at European regions by providing a multifaceted picture of their innovative abilities as well as the potential perils of 'regional closure'. The various chapters range across questions of regional identification and feelings of belonging; institutional, political and legal structures that enhance or limit regional political endeavours; and questions of cross-border cooperation. Most of the contributions examine examples from various regions throughout Europe and focus on similarities and differences among them. Others take a horizontal perspective by focusing on regional political representation within EU multilevel governance or on EU programmes for regional economic development.

While the dream of a 'Europe of the regions' had clearly lost some of its appeal, the new millennium has so far witnessed a growth in relevance of the regional level – both as a layer of citizens' identity and as an increasingly important political player in EU multilevel governance. This is the underlying notion linking the various chapters in the four sections of this volume, as will be outlined briefly in the remainder of this introduction.

1. Regional Identity – A Citizens' Perspective

While political scientists have recently been busy studying the role of regions in the context of EU multilevel governance, other disciplines in the social sciences seem to be lagging behind. While geographers' interest in spatial orders and their consequences for political, economic and social systems has generated a body of relevant work in the field of regional studies, sociologists have long neglected the role of regions in processes of collective identification.[2] There are still relatively few studies that focus on regional identity as a main dependent or independent variable in sociological analysis. This is rather astonishing, given the vast body of literature on collective identities that exists in the field of political sociology. Meanwhile, however, survey questions on collective identities have been improved, moving, first, from the classic 'Moreno question'[3] to more sophisticated measures and, second, recognizing the importance of 'multiple identities'. The latter is of particular importance in contexts of multilevel governance. On the one hand, the very notion of collective identity – including regional identity – is always Janus-faced, since it guarantees cohesion within social groups not least by defining 'external' boundaries in order to form clear-cut identities (Tajfel 1982). At the same time, concepts of nested and multiple identities (Medrano/Guitérrez 2001) highlight the potential synchronicity of various collective identities, thus integrating regional identities in a larger framework of social/territorial identities.

Several contributions in this volume focus on the tension between openness and closure that is immanent to collective identities. Are empirically observed re-

---

2   Exceptions being the addition of 'identification with the region' as a default category in item batteries and the addition of NUTS regions as standard classifications in multilevel analyses.
3   'What is your national identity?'

gional identities more integrative or more exclusionary in nature? To what extent are sentiments of regional belonging not only exploited by populist movements, but also used by mainstream political actors? And how do regional identities tie in with a European identity that is becoming increasingly important, at least among younger and better educated cohorts within society? While multiple identities seem to be on the rise and are increasingly recognized in scholarly literature, it might be misleading to directly infer a pro-European stance – the existence of multiple identities perhaps only points us to the fact that the act of placement *per se* has become of high importance to some individuals.

The first section of this volume is dedicated to the fundamental question of regional identity. As such, it also sets the scene for many of the contributions in the following sections, given the high salience of questions related to collective identity in the context of both regional and European politics.

Elisabeth Donat gives an example of a very strong regional identity, in the case of Tyrol, with reference to survey data on regional identity. Following the classical approach of attitude theory in applying a tripartite definition of regional identity, she argues that 'Identity' is more than just 'identification'. Alongside the cognitive component of classification, the affective and the connotative components of regional identity are equally important, since they serve as sources of key political attitudes and behaviour.

In her chapter, Katrin Praprotnik focuses on the relationship between various identities. Surveys have long tended to operationalize collective identities as mutually exclusive. Praprotnik addresses an important research gap by dealing with the relationship between regional and European identity. Using Austrian data from the European Value Study, she demonstrates that support for the EU is nearly equal among those who consider themselves solely 'Europeans' and the mixed group of 'regional Europeans'. Her analysis also demonstrates once again the importance of education for such attitude patterns.

Camille Dobler draws a dense picture of the multiplexity of collective identities by using the example of the Strasbourg border region. Her qualitative interviews illustrate the coexistence of various identities but also reveal that European identity is not a particularly significant referent for her interview partners. European identity seems to be more functionally than emotionally integrated in people's stories at the border; it mainly comes to respondent's minds when addressing cross-border activities such as working or education. Her chapter again illustrates the importance of boundaries as a social fact and not merely a geographical matter (Simmel 1903).

2. Regions in a Turbulent EU – Political and Legal Manifestations

While the first section of this volume focusses on regional identities at the individual level of citizens, the contributions in this section analyse their manifestation at the level of the polity and in the dynamics of party politics.

A strong regionalism or even regional nationalism as promoted by various political actors across European regions – rooted in or making use of a pronounced regional identity – always carries the risk of encouraging separatist tendencies. Yet at the same time, advocates of secession sometimes argue that if their region were to become politically independent, it should remain a member of the EU – this is the case in both Scotland and Catalonia. At first glance, this could be interpreted as a sign of genuine support for European integration or a generally pro-European stance. In fact, however, such positioning may simply be instrumental, as the European level together and the notion of a 'Europe of the regions' are seen as means of fostering the desire for political autonomy and independence. Meanwhile, Brexit has also finally brought the issue of 'recovering' political autonomy to the level of the European Union. The fact that the arguments used by Brexiteers and Scottish separatists in their respective referendums were quite similar (see Rahmatian in this volume) tells its own tale.

While separatism is clearly the most extreme political manifestation of regionalism, it is by no means the only one. Federalist arrangements often prove very effective in balancing regional interests and identities within a polity, even in the case of strong regional parties. This is for instance the case in Bavaria (cf. Sturm 2019 and in this volume). Whether and to what extent regionalism manifests in claims for separatism may be influenced by a number of factors, including specific historical events, constitutional arrangements and economic developments. The key significance of shifts in the dynamics of party politics, however, should not be disregarded in this respect: Cleavage theory (Lipset/Rokkan 1967) has already taught us that the existence of social grievances and the formation of a shared collective identity do not necessarily translate into collective political action (cf. Bartolini/Mair 1990). The latter requires organization, i.e. 'someone who can take advantage of political opportunities, develop organizations of some kind, and interpret grievances and mobilize consensus around them' (Tarrow 1992: 177).

The contributions in this section look at legal and political manifestations of regionalism in several EU member states. Though the empirical contexts and analytical settings are diverse, the issue of regional identity appears as an important point of reference in each of the three chapters.

Karl Kössler's contribution deals with manifestations of regional identity at the level of policy and the political system. Taking examples from regions within and beyond current EU territory, Kössler explores how references to regional identities are reflected in constitutional documents and welfare-state policies. When rooted in self-perceptions of regional distinctiveness and identity, he argues, such references are to be understood as 'successful' instances of regions claiming (more) self-government. At the same time, however, they may also affect processes of identity formation at the regional level itself.

The next chapter touches upon the most far-reaching demands for political autonomy, i.e. separatist movements. Andreas Rahmatian discusses calls for Scottish independence in the United Kingdom and challenges the very notion of the concept of 'civic nationalism' as employed by the Scottish National Party. The chapter goes on to identify a number of ironic parallels between the referendums for Scottish independence and Brexit, respectively. Rahmatian further argues that both Brexit and the UK government's stance during the lengthy process of negotiations with the EU can only be understood by taking into account what he calls Britain's legal feudalism, which still serves as the framework for a state without a written constitution.

Roland Sturm takes a closer look at Bavaria, a special case in German politics compared to the other Länder. The population of Bavaria is characterized by a particularly strong regional identity. This is clearly reflected in the political behaviour of its main governing party, the CSU, which is often said to desire more autonomy for Bavaria or a greater decentralization of state powers in Germany. This, however, is not the case, as aptly demonstrated by Sturm. Rather, the CSU's anti-Berlin politics are to be understood mainly as a symbolic gesture and a matter of strategy. Hence, despite heavily relying on regional allegiance in its communications, the CSU clearly sees Bavaria's place as within Germany and the EU.

3. Intended and Unintended Consequences of EU Programmes for Regional Development

European regions held out great hopes for the EU, not only with regard to their desire for increased political influence. Economically disadvantaged regions also expected to catch up rapidly with stronger regions in terms of economic and social development. Such expectations seemed eminently reasonable, given that the EU treaties explicitly set out the goal of strengthening the EU's economic, social and (since the Treaty of Lisbon) territorial cohesion. Many of these hopes, however, have not been fulfilled. First, despite the strengthening of the role of regions in the EU governance system as a result of treaty change, regions have not become participants in the EU legislative process as a 'third level' alongside the Council and the European Parliament. Second, EU cohesion policy programmes by and large seem to show heterogeneous effects (Bachtrögler/Oberhofer 2018).

Against this background, the emergence of a new regional Euroscepticism and even calls for independence cannot be precluded, at least in some European regions and both among citizens as well as regional political actors. Conversely, the (perceived) effectiveness of EU cohesion policy in a given region seems to have at least the potential to reduce anti-EU voting (cf. ibid.).

EU regional investment programmes increasingly require cross-border cooperation between regions and member states. This has resulted in a number of successful projects fostering cross-border infrastructure, culture or educational links. Such cooperation points to an encouraging future for European regions as they manoeuvre beyond the 'national containers' of member states that have undoubtedly blocked many decisions at the EU level in recent years. Regional cross-border cooperation also contains promise in the form of the emergence of multiple collective identities across state borders. This is not limited to privileged social groups that regularly travel across the continent and benefit most from European integration. As things stand, however, this is of course all still up in the air.

The contributions in this section look at EU regional investment programmes from a range of angles, either as the dependent or the main independent variable. They focus on European identity, the question of policy shifts as a result of the global financial crisis, and cross-border cooperation, respectively.

Fabian Landes' contribution presents his research on the effects of territorial investment on European identity. By means of a multilevel analysis, Landes tests the assumption that attachment to the EU is a consequence, at least in part, of economic-utilitarian considerations on the part of citizens. The effects of such investment can be demonstrated for mixed identities (at once national and European) and vary among countries but surprisingly not within them, pointing to the fact that the 'national container' is still the dominant category in politics.

Moritz Neujeffski examines whether regional investment programmes in the EU have undergone a shift in their rationale from redistribution to competitiveness following the global financial crisis. He analyses major reforms within the European Structural and Investment Funds prior to and after the crisis and compares them to the Investment Plan for Europe, a.k.a. the 'Juncker Plan'. Employing the theory of 'discourse coalitions', he identifies a continuous strengthening of market-based instruments and the endorsement of more competitiveness already prior to the crisis, pushed by a stable coalition of a handful of member states.

Cross-border cooperation between regions in Europe are at the core of Urszula Roman-Kamphaus' contribution. Comparing the Polish-German and Polish-Slovak border regions, she highlights the importance of cultural factors for understanding differences in the effectiveness of EU-funded cross-border cooperation. While pre-existing networks and cultural similarities promote successful implementation across the Polish-Slovak border, Roman-Kamphaus argues that policy innovation is higher in the Polish-German case precisely because of the lack of such resources.

4. Still Dreaming of a 'Europe of the Regions'? On the Interplay of Regions in the EU

The concept of a 'Europe of the regions' has at times been popular in both European politics and the scholarly literature, particularly during the 1980s. It has been accompanied by various attempts to strengthen the role of regions within the EU's multilevel governance framework. While the role of regions has indeed been strengthened via EU treaty reforms – beginning with the establishment of the European Committee of the Regions in the Maastricht Treaty – regional political actors have since suffered a degree of disillusionment: EU member states still have the major say at nearly all levels of the EU decision-making process today. Nevertheless, there are gentle signs of a restructuring and re-empowering at the regional level: the Committee of Regions is a vivid example of constructive cooperation among regions within the EU and is greatly valued by its members and partners. Furthermore, several contributions to this volume also provide evidence of a rise in regional identification *together* with identification as European, which suggests a growing interest in European affairs among citizens with a strong regional identity. Some authors even go further in perceiving momentum at the European level towards again granting regions a major stake in the EU governance system: Ulrike Guérot (2016), for example, argues in favour of restructuring the EU political system as a European Republic. Gabriele Abels and Jan Battke (2019) also inquire into the role of regions in EU governance following the failure of a 'Europe of the regions' to emerge, concluding that what actually seems to be in the making nowadays is a 'Europe with the regions' (ibid.: 237).

The contributions in the final section of this volume look at the origins of and the drift away from the dream of a 'Europe of the regions'.

Justus Schönlau takes a closer look at the role of the European Committee of the Regions (CoR) in reinforcing notions of multilevel governance in the EU. Though its institutional role is limited to an advisory function by the EU treaties, Schönlau shows how the CoR managed to expand its impact on EU policy making in various ways while aggregating and balancing the multitude of views and experiences of its heterogeneous member base. Taking the examples of CoR policy action in the field of climate change and the very recent RegHub initiative, he argues that the CoR has indeed become a significant agent in the institutionalization of multilevel governance, thus supporting not only the functioning but ultimately also the legitimacy of the European integration project.

In her contribution, Claire Wallace analyses the end of the 'European dream', which has led to a re-emergence of nationalism. For a long time it was hoped that growing Europeanization would lead to growing cosmopolitanism, but, at least at the beginning of the new millennium, these hopes had to be buried as nationalism and populism grew throughout Europe. Wallace's analysis of Eurobarometer data provides evidence that, alongside growing national identification, regional identification has also increased among citizens. Her text presents examples of this trend in the cases of Latvia and Scotland and leads her to conclude that recent times have seen a growth in 'placism'– a tendency to identify with places in general.

Ulrike Guérot's chapter contains a brief history of the concept of 'Europe of the regions', in which she criticises the dominance of the member states at nearly all levels of EU decision making. Guérot diagnoses a lack of republicanism in the current political system of the EU and argues for both to be integrated in the near future: republicanism and a federal structure that would give more power to the regions. Her innovative approach is to call for a 'European Republic' that would create a common umbrella under which European regions could peacefully coexist and citizens' rights would be managed under the principle of equality before the law.

The field of Regional Studies is multifaceted, multidisciplinary and multilevel. Given the 'sui generis' nature of the EU, it is not surprising that we can observe increasing scholarly interest in the role of regions within the EU context. For regions in Europe, numerous political, economic and societal challenges have come along with the new millennium. The aim of this book is to contribute to the reflection and study of the various regional responses to these challenges across Europe. By collecting contributions from political science, sociology as well as legal studies, this volume reflects the diversity in the field and takes account of the complexity of European regions within a constantly changing environment.

References

Abels, Gabriele/Battke, Jan (eds.) (2019): Regional Governance in the EU, Cheltenham: Edward Elgar Publishing.

Abels, Gabriele/Eppler, Annegret (eds.) (2015): Subnational Parliaments in the EU Multi-Level Parliamentary System: Taking Stock of the Post-Lisbon Era, Innsbruck/Wien/Bozen: Studienverlag.

Bachtrögler, Julia/Oberhofer, Harald (2018): "Euroscepticism and EU Cohesion Policy: The Impact of Micro-Level Policy Effectiveness on Voting Behavior." In: Department of Economics Working Paper No. 273, Wien: Wirtschaftsuniversität Wien.

Bartolini, Stefano/Mair, Peter (1990): Identity, competition, and electoral availability. The stabilization of European electorates 1885-1985, Cambridge/New York: Cambridge University Press.

Borońska-Hryniewiecka, Karolina (2015): "Differential Europeanization? Explaining the Impact of the Early Warning System on Subnational Parliaments in Europe." In: European Political Science Review 9/2, pp. 255–278.

Borońska-Hryniewiecka, Karolina (2017): "Regional Parliamentary Empowerment in EU Affairs. Building an Analytical Framework." In: The Journal of Legislative Studies 23/2, pp. 144–161.

Bursens, Peter/Högenauer, Anna-Lena (2017): "Regional Parliaments in the EU Multilevel Parliamentary System." In: The Journal of Legislative Studies, 23/2, pp. 127–143.

Chacha, Mwita (2013): "Regional attachment and support for European integration." In: European Union Politics 14/2, pp. 206–227.

CoR [Committee of the Regions] (2013): "The Subsidiarity Early Warning System of the Lisbon Treaty – the role of regional parliaments with legislative powers and other subnational authorities" July 20, 2019 (https://publications.europa.eu/en/publication-detail/-/publication/e3818ca2-e63f-4de1-b1eb-5a662fe86667).

Fromage, Diane (2016): "Regional Parliaments and the Early Warning System: An Assessment Six Years after the Entry into Force of the Lisbon Treaty." In: SSRN Electronic Journal 2016/33, pp. 1–49.

Fromage, Diane (2017): "Regional Parliaments and the Early Warning System: An Assessment and Some Suggestions for Reform." In: Jonsson Cornell, Anna /Goldoni, Marco (eds.), National and Regional Parliaments in the EU-Legislative Procedure Post-Lisbon. The Impact of the Early Warning Mechanism. Portland Oregon [US]/Oxford [UK]: Hart Publishing.

Guérot, Ulrike (2016): Warum Europa eine Republik werden muss! Eine politische Utopie, Bonn: Dietz.

Hooghe, Liesbet/Marks, Gary/ Schakel, Arjan/Osterkatz, Sandra Chapman/Niedzwiecki, Sara/ Shair-Rosenfield, Sarah (2016): Measuring Regional Authority: A Postfunctionalist Theory of Governance, Oxford: Oxford University Press.

Högenauer, Anna-Lena/Abels, Gabriele (2017): "Conclusion: Regional Parliaments – A Distinct Role in the EU?." In: The Journal of Legislative Studies 23/2, pp. 260–273.

Keating, Michael (2013): Rescaling the European State. The Making of Territory and the Rise of the Meso, Oxford: Oxford Scholarship Online.

Klatt, Martin (2018): "The So-Called 2015 Migration Crisis and Euroscepticism in Border Regions: Facing Re-Bordering Trends in the Danish–German Borderlands." In: Geopolitics, pp. 1–20.

Lipset, Seymour M./Rokkan, Stein (1967): Party Systems and Voter Alignments: Cross-National Perspectives, New York/London.

Medrano, Juan D./Gutiérrez (2001):"Nested identities: national and European identity in Spain." In: Ethnic and Racial Studies 24/5, pp. 753-778.

Panara, Carlo (2019): "Deconstructing and Reconstructing Good Governance in Relation to Regional and Local Participation in EU Decision-Making Processes."

In: Abels, Gabriele/Battke, Jan (eds.), Regional Governance in the EU, Cheltenham: Edward Elgar Publishing, pp. 3 –51.

Simmel, Georg (1903): "Soziologie des Raumes." In: Eigmüller Monika/Vobruba Georg (eds.) (2016), Grenzsoziologie, Wiesbaden: Springer, pp. 9–18.

Tajfel, Henri (1982): Social identity and intergroup relations, Cambridge.

Tarrow, Sidney 1992: "Mentalities, Political Cultures, and Collective Action Frames. Constructing Meanings through Action." In: Morris, Aldon D./McClurg Mueller, Carol (eds.), Frontiers in Social Movement Theory, New Haven: Yale University Press, pp. 174-202.

Tatham, Michaël (2015): "Regional Voices in the European Union: Subnational Influence in Multilevel Politics." In: International Studies Quarterly 59/2, pp. 387–400.

I.
Regional Identity – a Citizens Perspective

Regional Identity between Inclusion and Exclusion

Elisabeth Donat

Do Regions Provide Cause for Optimism in a Turbulent Europe?

These days, waiting for decisions to be made at EU level requires patience. The EU 28 appear to have lost their fizz. Recently, both 'internal' matters, such as the appointment of a new European Commission, and 'external' questions, such as the EU's ongoing attempts to deal with what is often referred to as 'the migrant crisis', have made one thing very clear: At the level of its member states, the EU is divided – into north and south, east and west, old and new members, and a United Kingdom that, thanks to Brexit, is largely preoccupied for the time being. In many countries, populist movements appear to be determining the direction of government policy; political ideas incubated by these movements are being adopted – more or less willingly – by the political mainstream, thereby sowing the seeds of Euroscepticism among broad swathes of voters. These developments, the political vacuum and the powerlessness currently affecting many EU decision-making processes, have caused many to reconsider the concept of a 'Europe of the Regions' (Ruge 2004) for new ideas and renewed hope. The concept of a 'European Republic' (Guérot 2016) is not the only proposal that includes a greater role for Europe's regions; an anthology recently published in German (Hilpold et al. 2016) explores strategies for enhancing the regions' influence in the European context. But why should we assume that regions would be 'more reasonable', more amenable to uniting in a federal Europe consisting of regions and would not act merely as smaller versions of today's nations, which would find it just as hard to achieve unity among their many particular interests? The formation of regional identity strengthens and supports a political community and is a key variable when considering the reorganisation of regions and their competencies at the EU level. This chapter asks what regional identity means and how much common interest a political community requires. At the same time, it considers the balancing act that needs to be performed between an inclusive and an exclusive (in the sense of exclusionary) regional identity.

Opinion polls periodically reveal that, in terms of territorial reference points, regional identity is one of the most relevant sources of identification, immediately behind national identity, and well ahead of any European identity (Mühler/Opp

2004, Haller 2009, European Commission/European Parliament 2017).[1] Regional identity shows incredible persistence: even though identities are becoming increasingly cosmopolitan, global, hybrid and multiple, regional identity is a consistent key factor in the self-definition of most respondents (Pohl 2001). Interest in regional identity has also grown, not least as a result of the boom in social geography. Conversely, the 'spatial turn' in the humanities and social sciences since the 1980s has also seen the concept of space grow in prominence in analyses of social structures and social action (Schroer 2008). In the 1990s, extensive studies were carried out of the importance of national identity and the distinction between nationalism and patriotism (Fleiss et. al. 2009; Parker 2010; Blank/Schmidt 2003; Weiss/Reinprecht 2004; Kosterman/Feshbach 1989). As the European Union underwent successive major enlargements, research started to focus on questions of European identity. Political scientists are particularly interested in the various levels of identity – regional, national, European and cosmopolitan – because a shared identity is an important aspect of a political community (Herrmann/Brewer 2000; Peters 2005; Meyer 2009; Datler 2012; Galais/Serrano 2019). Nonetheless, little attention has so far been paid to 'regional identity' in the political sciences, and though it is one of the dimensions of 'identity' regularly included in major surveys of opinion, it is rarely analysed in depth (see also the chapter by Praprotnik in this volume).

As a result, our knowledge of the substance and specific forms of manifestation of regional identity is limited. In large international surveys of attitudes, regional identity is most commonly dealt with using the concept of 'attachment' to the region, alongside questions on attachment to town or city, nation and the EU/Europe. Yet this operationalisation covers only one aspect of regional identity, namely the degree of identification with the region. It does not explain what substantive elements regional identity draws upon, whether there is an emotional spectrum of 'attachment', and what forms of planned behaviour (Ajzen et al. 2005) it can motivate. Unfortunately, opinion surveys and research often use the concept of 'identity' hastily and in an unreflective way, a fact that has already been subject to criticism (Brubaker/Cooper 2000). Even if 'identity' can shift in the course of life and is influenced by socialisation processes (Erikson 1974), we can assume that it is not renegotiated each day but is more or less habitually present (on the example of national identity, Deschouwer et. al. 2015) and only becomes salient in a given situation or context (Herrmann/Brewer 2000).

This chapter begins by summarising the findings of research carried out in the social sciences on the measurement of national and European identity and uses this to identify problems of the definition and measurement of regional identity.

---

1   Asked about attachment, 89 percent of respondents answered that they feel attached to their city, town or village, 92 percent to their country, and only 54 percent to the European Union.

Drawing on survey data from a study of regional identity in the Tyrol, it then considers whether the distinction between a constructive identity and a chauvinistic attitude should also be made at the regional level. Finally, it considers the implications for relations between regions in a federation of European regions.

Defining and Measuring Regional, National and European Identity

We use territorial designations quite naturally to describe all kinds of collective identities: thus, we can speak of a local, regional, national and European identity, with reference in each case to a territory that we can easily envisage. As early as 1903, Georg Simmel (Simmel 1903: 15) in his essay on the sociology of space argued that 'This is why consciousness of boundedness is not at its most precise with so-called natural boundaries (mountains, rivers, oceans or deserts) but rather with merely political boundaries which only place a geometrical line between two neighbours.' Simmel was one of the first to stress the social component of the construction of space. Space is no longer a static given fact, but is defined, shaped and transformed by social activity. Relations of objects in space, of people, the organisation of space in general are expressions of existing power relations, because they create hierarchies. By means of 'Spacing' (Löw 2000), the appropriation of space, space is constructed in material and immaterial terms (via values, norms, rules). It only becomes space in itself by means of (re)construction processes that take the form of acts of synthesis. These acts of synthesis encompass the perception, imagination and memory of spaces. In the temporal dimension, spatial relations are reinforced by unchanging routines and (cognitive) reproduction and only called into question when conflicts arise (Keating 2013). Precisely such conflict situations and power struggles make us aware of how spaces are emotionally charged: spatial identity is always also social identity. To speak of purely 'territorial identity' appears to be misleading: social relations are reflected in space and in this way give space meaning. We are not dealing with mere 'place-ism' (i.e. a need for territorial belonging, Lewis 2016; Evans 2012), but also and above all the social relations associated with a given space.

To return to the questions we posed at the start, this raises the matter of whether regional identity can be 'more constructive' per se than national identity, and whether, for example, regions would act 'more reasonably' in a European-level political entity than do nation states. If, however, it is not possible to speak of spatial identity in itself, we can assume that regions are also deeply infused with social identity and emotionalised and undertake the same processes of demarcation and drawing of borders as nations. Since it has so far proved impossible, in the case of nations, to empirically demonstrate the existence of a constructive, collective identity, a constitutional patriotism (Habermas 1993), a rational solidarity community, we may also assume that in the case of regions, attachment always goes hand in hand with processes of demarcation and exclusion. In studies of national identity, it has been observed that individuals who (are said to) embody a patriotic position continually flirt with nationalist attitudes (Wagner et. al. 2012). In concrete terms, this finds empirical expression in the difficulty of distinguishing a nationalist factor from a patriotic, civic 'rational' factor (Schatz et al. 1999): Both constructs (and their measurement errors) exhibit such consistently high correlation that it is hard to distinguish cleanly between them (Fleiss et. al. 2009; Parker 2010; Blank/Schmidt 2003; Weiss/Reinprecht 2004; Kosterman/Feshbach 1989). Nor do the two concepts stand up well to testing via construct validation, since they show similar correlations with external factors. It therefore cannot be said that they represent two distinct attitude patterns.

At the regional level, Chacha (2012) attempts to distinguish between 'inclusive' and 'exclusive' attachment to region, where the former includes identification with the nation alongside identification with the region, and where the analysis also shows a small, positive correlation with European identity. By contrast, exclusive regional identification demonstrates no correlation with European identity – though it is questionable, given the low coefficient, whether the distinction between these two stances can be considered proven. Moreover, it may not be correct to assume that this correlation automatically indicates a pro-European stance: Wallace (2020, in this volume) notes a general increase in the desire to identify with a territory or group. Simultaneously identifying with region, nation and the EU/Europe does not necessarily indicate a cosmopolitan attitude but may merely reflect this general desire to identify with territories and/or groups. To explain this situation requires a more precise determination of substance, emotional content, and potential behavioural consequences, as undertaken, for instance, by Roudometof (2019) with reference to the 'local'. When only a single indicator is applied (the question of attachment), it remains unclear what this attachment consists of, how it may be expressed in terms of emotions, and what kinds of action it might precipitate.

When considering regional identity in a political context, it is particularly important to distinguish it from a 'regionalism' that might bring the agendas of the group in question to the fore (potentially at the cost of others) (Pohl 2001: 12919): 'The line between vague regional identity and active political regionalism is not sharp and the motifs are mixed together.' Models of 'mixed' and 'nested' identities assume that the coexistence of regional and European identity indicates an inclusive and open attitude (Hermann/Brewer 2000; Galais/Serrano 2019; Medrano/Gutiérrez 2001). In light of research on secession and autonomy movements within the EU, however, this extrapolation appears somewhat dangerous: whether such professions of identity are in fact pro-European or merely pay lip service to Europeanism as a means of resisting a restrictive nation state needs to be examined in each individual case: 'Through subsidiarity, regions have come to perceive the EU "as an ally against the central state".' (Jolly 2007: 4)

Research at the level of European identity has also attempted to differentiate between 'cultural' and 'civic' identity, though no tests on representative samples have so far been carried out (Bruter 2003, 2004). Measuring the emotional component of collective identity has proven particularly difficult. Duchesne (2008) and Duchesne & Frognier (2008) have suggested that political identity is adequately operationalised using the concept of 'identification'; the concept of 'citizenship' has been deployed as a means of explaining who respondents include within their own group and who they exclude (Reeskens/Hooghe 2010): however, such analyses remain trapped at the level of 'social categorisation', i.e. the cognitive classification of people into groups. Using this approach tends to mask the consequences of such acts of categorisation: Attitudes always also include affective and connotative components (Allport 1967; Herrmann/Brewer 2000; Kaina 2009). Precisely this positive, emotional relation would be the basis for the legitimation for political action at the regional, national or European level.

Collective identity is generated at the level of the individual (attitudes) and reinforced at the collective level via the social construction of cultural norms (narratives, discourses etc.) (Wiesner 2017). The cognitive components of a constructive identification with region/nation/Europe appear to be relatively clear (at least in theory): it involves a commitment to fundamental democratic values, civil rights, the rule of law and recognition of the constitution (Habermas 1993; Laborde 2002). However, here we are dealing with abstract, postmaterialist structures that many respondents would likely have difficulty in identifying and categorising in an empirical test. The definition of the affective components of such an attitude is unclear (Deschouwer et. al. 2015; Fleiss et al. 2009): Is it a matter of 'pride' at certain constitutional achievements that binds 'patriots' to a certain territory or group? Or does a constructive regional identity consist of a combination of 'love' of a territory together with certain values?

Nor is regional identity immune to preferential evaluation of one's own group and the deprecation of outside groups, in the appropriate context (Tajfel 1982). 'Pride' in one's own region always includes an element of comparison: 'proud' in contrast to whom or what? Even where 'pride' focuses 'merely' on democratic achievements such as constitutionalism or the rule of law, it cannot avoid a degree of idealisation. It is therefore not only worth varying the substantive features used to measure collective identity but also, at the level of affect, to model the nuances of feeling associated with attachment. Weiner's (2004) attribution theory provides a useful framework for analysing the various possible forms of emotional attachment: 'The most basic assumption of an attribution view of emotion is that feelings are determined by thoughts, and specifically by beliefs about causality.' (ibid. 355). Causal beliefs triggered by an event are distributed along the dimensions of causal locus (internal/external), causal stability (stable/unstable) and causal control (controllable/uncontrollable). In accordance with the fundamental attribution error, people tend to attribute events, and particularly successes, to internal qualities rather than situational circumstances. In the case of self-serving bias, for instance, we attribute our successes to our own aptitudes and efforts than to situational factors. Attribution errors of this kind are also committed with regard to groups: group-serving attributional bias describes this phenomenon in relation to the attribution of successes to the internal qualities of the group to which one belongs. If we arrange emotions along these dimensions, focusing in particular on those that are attributed to internal causes, we generate the following classification (Table 1):

Table 1: Attribution, causal dimension, behaviour relations (Weiner 2004: 357)

Outcome	Cause	Relevant Causal dimension	Emotion		Motivational Consequences	
			Self-directed	Other-directed	Achievement	Social
Success	All causes	None	*Happiness*		+	+
	Aptitude	Internal	*Pride*			
	Effort	Internal	*Pride*			
	Others	External		*Gratitude*		+
Failure	Aptitude	Internal	*Shame*		-	-
	Effort	Internal	*Guilt*		+	+
	Others	External		*Anger*		-

In the following analysis of emotional attachment to the region, the focus will therefore lie on the emotions of pride, happiness, gratitude, and shame. As a completely neutral emotion, 'indifference' will also be included. It should be noted that the emotion 'pride', in particular, is attributed to an internal cause in multiple instances: once as a consequence of aptitude and again as a result of effort. By contrast, Weiner classifies happiness as a 'relatively "thoughtless" emotion' (ibid. 357), as it arises independently of any specific cause. Weiner describes 'gratitude' as an emotion that is capable of evoking pro-social behaviour, as it may arouse a desire to 'balance the scales of justice'. While, according to this schema, pride has no effect on the motivational basis for further action, shame leads to withdrawal and inhibits future action. The next section examines these relationships in terms of causal attribution to one's own group for data relating to regional identity in Tyrol.

Survey Results: A Passion for Tyrol

In the following section, which considers the case of regional identity in Tyrol, we consider what elements constitute this identity, what emotional nuances they contain, and whether it is possible to distinguish between inclusive and exclusive (in the sense of exclusionary) attachment. The data discussed here was gathered in 2011 by means of a representative random sample of 500 Tyrolean men and women.[2] Prior to gathering this quantitative data, 29 narrative interviews were carried out with Tyrolean residents, consisting of a biographical component and a problem-centred component focusing on the respondents' regional identity. The qualitative interviews were carried out by trained personnel from Tyrol, i.e. by members of the 'in-group', which proved highly conducive to an open atmosphere for the discussions. These interviews proved extremely helpful when it came to designing the questionnaire, as they indicated just how very strongly Tyoleans identify with their region. These ties are so strong that the attachment is even expressed in terms of physical, corporeal images and metaphors (the heart, the five senses, blood, genes). Detailed descriptions of one's own group with an emphasis on their authenticity (authentic like the miners, authentic like *Tyrolean* sportsmen and women, authentic and committed to solidarity like Tyrolean freedom fighters) contrast with vague descriptions and evasive speculations about other groups. The interview material also provided numerous metaphors for social inclusion and exclusion.

The strong emotional attachment to Tyrol is also evident in the quantitative data. 86 percent of respondents stated that they had deep roots in Tyrol and 87 percent that they love the region. By contrast, only 27 percent answered that they only live in Tyrol because of the high quality of life – a purely functional attachment thus appears to be rare. The data reveals – as do the qualitative interviews – generally very strong attachment to the region on the part of its inhabitants. In accordance with the considerations of the previous section, emotional attachment to the region has been broken down as the result of various styles of attribution in a more detailed manner than is usually the case in studies of this kind. Respondents were asked to choose between five emotional states when considering their attachment to Tyrol. Drawing on Weiner's (2004) attribution theory, the survey covers a full spectrum of emotions of attachment by distinguishing between pride, gratitude, happiness, indifference, and shame. According to this theory, events associated with 'pride' are interpreted as internal, controllable and stable results of sequences of occurrences by those who experience them. By contrast, 'gratitude' is attributed to an external cause – events and successes are caused by other people. 'Happiness' is a weak expression of a positive emotional state, in contrast to 'indifference', which describes

---

2   The survey was made possible thanks to the support of the Tyrolean Science Fund (*Tiroler Wissenschaftsfond*).

a neutral emotional state, and was present above all in the interviews with individuals who considered attribution on the basis of territories or groups to be of little relevance in general. For reasons of balance, an explicitly negative emotion was also included in the survey in the form of 'shame'. To give an example: successes on the part of one's own group – even where one was perhaps not personally involved in an immediate sense – could lead to an increase in self-worth by being experienced in the form of pride, since 'pride' is attributed to internal, stable and controllable causes. This leads to a boost in esteem for one's own group – and simultaneously for oneself (cf. Tajfel 1982).

Around a third of respondents stated that they were 'proud' when they thought of Tyrol; 24 percent felt gratitude; 38.5 percent, happiness; and only 5.7 percent expressed indifference. None of the respondents reported feeling shame in connection with Tyrol (Figure 1). There were no differences in attribution by different age groups or generations, though differences were apparent among respondents with different levels of education and places of birth.

Figure 1 Attachment to Tyrol

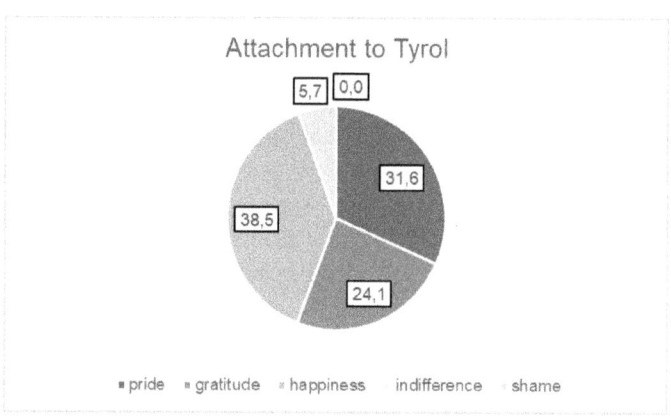

The sociostructural characteristics 'education' and 'place of birth' have a clear influence on emotional attachment to the region. The lower the level of school education, the more likely the respondent is to report feeling the emotion of 'pride' in connection with the region. By contrasts, respondents with higher levels of educational attainment have a more dispassionate stance towards the region (Figure 2) and are more likely to express their emotional connection in terms of 'indifference' or 'happiness'. Higher levels of education thus appear to lead to a 'cooler' relationship to the region or indicate that such attributions are generally less significant for these respondents.

Figure 2: Educational Attainment and Regional Attachment[3]

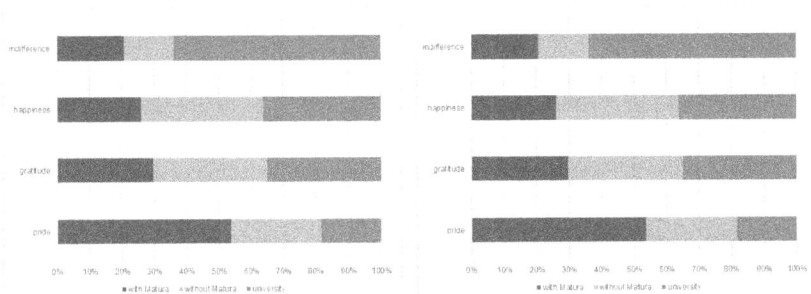

Place of birth naturally plays a large role in determining attachment to the region: respondents who were born in Tyrol were more likely to be proud of the region, while those who moved there later in life were most likely to select the comparatively neutral emotion of 'happiness' (Figure 3).

Figure 3: Place of Birth and Attachment to the Region

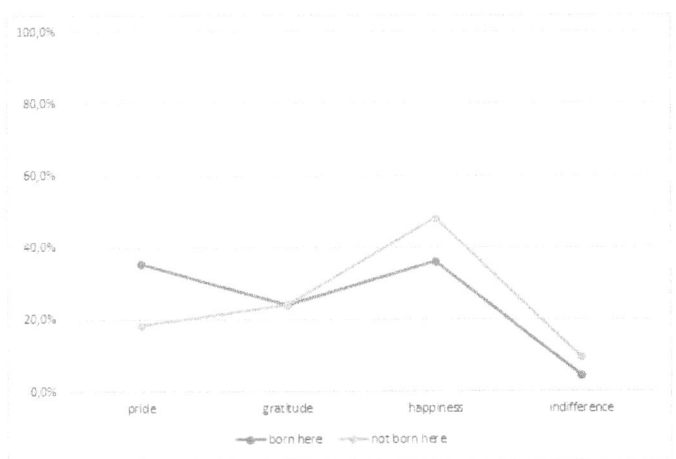

Following this overview of the data and discussion of how emotional attachment varies according to sociostructural characteristics, we will now consider how these emotions correlate with other attitude patterns. The focus here is on which

---

3   The Matura is the highest school leaving certificate in Austria, achieved after usually twelve years of schooling.

emotions, if any, can be linked with exclusionary activities or associated with chauvinism. In a logical regression, the influence of attitudes towards incomers and the correlation with conservative attitudes were examined. Two indexes were constructed: the first models the expectations made of new arrivals, the second consists of conservative values (for the individual items in the indexes, see Table 3 in the appendix). When new residents arrive in Tyrol, they are expected to adapt. More than 80 percent of respondents agreed with the statement that new arrivals should not be given preferential treatment ('strongly agree' and 'generally agree'), and nearly as many respondents agreed that new residents should comply with prevailing norms ('strongly agree' and 'generally agree'). A greater variety of emotional responses were elicited on the question of whether newcomers to Tyrol should bring their own culture and way of life with them: only around half of respondents agreed (strongly) that they should. Respondents also demonstrated a very high level of conservative values (cf. Appendix, Table 3). They were almost unanimous in considering 'security and order' and 'conscientiousness' to be important values. The value 'being hardworking and ambitious' also found the approval of a high proportion of respondents – more than 80 percent considered this to be an important virtue ('important and 'very important'). Only with respect to the value 'sense of tradition' was there a degree of variation in the answers given (cf. Table 3 in the Appendix). We performed a multinomial regression to examine the influence of critical attitudes towards new residents and conservative values on the various categories of emotional attachment (Table 2). 'Indifference' was selected as the reference category. For the model of the variable 'pride', both factors appeared to have a significant influence. In the case of the other two models ('gratitude' and 'happiness'), only conservative values appeared significant. 'Gratitude' and 'happiness' thus appear to have less of an exclusionary character than 'pride'.

Table 2: Multinominal Regression (Reference Category 'Indifference')

		Significance	Exp(B)
Pride	Constant term	0.442	
	Critical attitude towards new residents	0.050	1.205
	Conservatism	0.000	0.375
Gratitude	Constant term	0.384	
	Critical attitude towards new residents	0.929	1.009
	Conservatism	0.001	0.454
Happiness	Constant term	0.770	
	Critical attitude towards new residents	0.341	1.099
	Conservatism	0.016	0.583

It is worth examining the substance of 'pride' more closely in terms of these results. There is a strong sense of pride in belonging, and this is clearly projected towards the 'outside' (Figure 4). Nearly all the respondents stated that they were at least partly proud that Tyrol is so popular among tourists. Almost two thirds were of the opinion that people should use clear 'markers' to indicate their origins to the outside world, and nearly half of respondents answered that it makes them proud when politicians from Tyrol are included in the Austrian national government. Once again, these distributions indicate a strong tendency towards differentiation into ingroups and outgroups on the part of the respondents.

Figure 4: Pride (N= 500)

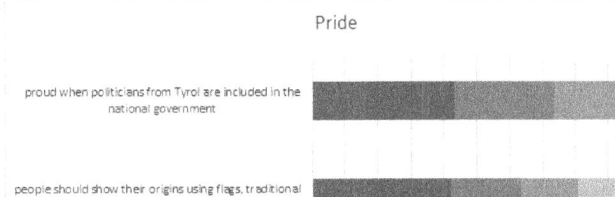

If these items are combined to create a 'pride scale', a correlation with exclusionary attitudes is again revealed. Pride shows a correlation of 0.327** with a critical attitude towards new arrivals, indicating a significant (p=0.01) correlation between pride in one's region and a critical attitude towards incomers.

In summary we can conclude that regional attachment has several emotional dimensions, which entail a variety of implications (for action). The dimension of 'pride' stands out in particular: drawing on Weiner's (2004) attribution theory, it can be argued that an attitude of pride makes one relatively receptive to the promotion of chauvinistic attitudes and prejudices towards other groups. The data also generally indicates a strong attachment to the region. Other analyses (cf. Donat 2020) show that regional pride is also closely associated with an uncritical stance towards history and a sceptical attitude with regard to the modernisation of the region. Conservative positions are also prominently represented throughout the entire sample. The range of opinions revealed by this survey is relatively uniform, which is why it is virtually impossible to apply clustering procedures, and multinomial regression reveals low coefficients and generally weak correlation in a generally homogeneous set of opinions. The respondents reported an almost uniformly high level of attachment to the region, as the qualitative interviews had already shown. The survey reveals a region that is highly 'self-assertive' with high levels of regional attachment in virtually every population group.

Social Closure in a Europe of the Regions

In the results presented here, Tyrol gives the impression of being a self-assertive region. This places high expectations on new arrivals seeking to join Tyrolean society. Tyroleans express their identity to the outside world (with pride) and have a clear understanding of what it means to belong. Their desire to uphold existing norms is evident in their wish for Tyrol to remain as it is (cf. Donat 2020). How would a region that is so self-assertive conduct itself in a 'Europe of the regions'? Although the results presented here certainly do not allow us to draw conclusions about how a regional identity of this kind would influence behaviour in a union with other (strong?) regional identities, nonetheless, they do outline a number of parameters that the processes of demarcation and exclusion associated with a very strong regional identity reveal. It is legitimate to ask how cooperation and the pursuit of a united common interest can be achieved when several self-assured regions of this kind come together. In view of the growing disparities among Europe's regions, the issue of the regional balance of power also arises – and the related matter of who would call the tune. A self-assured region such as Tyrol is certain to see itself as a key player, as the 2019 European Parliament election campaign demonstrated: 'Europe Needs Tyrol', but does Tyrol need Europe?

Figure 5: The 2019 European Parliamentary Election Campaign in Tyrol

(Source: VP Tirol)

Keating (2013) takes the view that the wealthier regions in a European union of regions would also agree to an expansion of resource redistribution among the regions. But this has to be weighed against the existence at the present time of many separatist movements, many prominent examples of which are economically powerful and seek to disengage from national structures that bind them together with economically weaker regions. It would therefore be hasty to make a blanket judgement, and the situation calls for observation of individual cases and detailed analysis of the components of regional identity that would provide further information on processes of demarcation and exclusion.

Alongside the substantive features of regional identity, greater attention should also be paid to emotional components, as they give a particularly useful insight into the fine line that is crossed when collective identities drift into regionalism. Although this research has outlined only some basic elements of one specific regional identity, it is based on a comprehensive sample and extensive preparation in the form of qualitative interviews. In this regard, it has an advantage over large, international comparative surveys: For instance, the 2017 Eurobarometer sought the opinions of only 86 individuals from Tyrol. This is why it is important that detailed surveys of this kind are undertaken in the future.

In a world that is very much structured by the supposedly neutral meritocratic ideal and the notion of singularity (Reckwitz 2017) as the path to social success, it makes sense to apply attribution theory as a model that can explain causal attributions of success and failure. These attributions also apply to groups, particularly when they allow us to raise our self-evaluations. The emotional spectrum of attachment a region's inhabitants have to the region is broad and does not always follow functional and rational considerations. The political situation in Europe in the early 21st century has again revealed the explosive power of such emotions.

References

Allport, Gordon (1967): "Attitudes." In: Fishbein, Martin (ed.): Readings in Attitude Theory and Measurement, NY/London/Sydney: Wiley, pp. 1–14.

Ajzen, Icek/Fishbein, Martin/Lohmann, Sophie/Albarracín, Dolores (2005): "The influence of attitudes on behavior." In: Albarracín, Dolores/Johnson, Blair T. (eds.): The handbook of attitudes, Lawrenc.

Blank, Thomas/Schmidt Peter (2003): "National Identity in a United Germany: Nationalism or Patriotism? An Empirical Test with Representative Data." In: Political Psychology 24/2, pp. 289–312

Brubaker, Rogers/Cooper, Frederick (2000): "Beyond 'Identity'." In: Theory and Society 29/1, pp. 1–47.

Bruter, Michael (2003): "Winning hearts and minds for Europe. The impact of News and Symbols on Civic and Cultural European Identity." In: Comparative Political Studies 36/10 pp. 1148–1179.

Bruter, Michael (2004): "On what Citizens mean by feeling "European": Perceptions of News, Symbols and Borderless-ness." In: Journal of Ethnic and Migration Studies 30/1, pp. 21–39.

Chacha, Mwita (2012): "Regional attachment and support for European integration." In: European Union Politics 14/2, pp. 206–227.

Datler, Georg (2012): "'Europäische identität' jenseits der Demos Fiktion." In: Aus Politik und Zeitgeschichte 4/8, pp. 57–61.

Deschouwer, Kris/De Winter, Lieven/Dodeigne, Jérémy/Reuchamps, Min/Sinardet, Dave (2015): "Measuring [Sub]National Identities in Surveys. Some Lessons from Belgium." Paper presented at The state of the federation 2015, Liege, Belgium.

Donat, Elisabeth (2020): "Regionale Identität(en) in der EU." In: Hermann, Andrea Tony/Ingruber, Daniela/Perlot, Flooh/Praprotnik, Katrin/Hainzl, Christina (eds.): regional.national.föderal – Zur Beziehung politischer Ebenen in Österreich, forthcoming.

Duchesne, Sophie (2008): "Waiting for a European Identity ... Reflections on the Process of Identification with Europe." In: Perspectives on European Politics and Society 9/4, pp. 397-410.

Duchesne, Sophie/Frognier, André-Paul (2008): "National and European Identifications: A Dual Relationship." In: Comparative European Politics 6, pp. 143–168.
European Commission/European Parliament (2017): Eurobarometer 87.1 (2017). TNS opinion, Brussels [producer]. GESIS Data Archive, Cologne. ZA6861 Data file Version 1.2.0.
Erikson, Erik H. (1974): Identität und Lebenszyklus. Drei Aufsätze. 2. Auflage, Frankfurt am Main: Suhrkamp.
Evans, Gillian (2012): "The aboriginal people of England." In: Focaal 2012/62, pp. 17–29.
Fleiss, Jürgen/Höllinger, Franz/Kuzmics, Helmut (2009): "Nationalstolz zwischen Patriotismus und Nationalismus? Empirisch-methodologische Analysen und Reflexionen am Beispiel des International Social Survey Programme 2003 ‚National Identity'." In: Berliner Journal für Soziologie 2009/3, pp. 409–434.
Galais, Carlo/Serrano, Ivan (2019): "The effects of regional attachment on ideological self-placement: a comparative approach." In: Comparative European Politics, pp. 1–23.
Guérot, Ulrike (2016): Warum Europa eine Republik werden muss!. Eine Politische Utopie, Bonn: Diez.
Habermas, Jürgen (1993): "Staatsbürgerschaft und nationale Identität." In: id. (ed.): Faktizität und Geltung. Frankfurt am Main: Suhrkamp, pp. 632-660.
Haller, Max (2009): Die Europäische Integration als Elitenprozess. Das Ende eines Traums?, Wiesbaden: Springer.
Herrman, Richard/Brewer, Marilynn (2000): "Identities and Institutions: Becoming European in the EU." In: Herrman, Richard/Risse, Thomas/Brewer, Marilynn (eds.): Transnational Identities. Becoming European in the EU, Lanham/Boulder/NY/Toronto/Offord: Rowman & Litllefield.
Hilpold, Peter/Steinmair, Walter/Perathoner, Christoph (eds.) (2016): Europa der Regionen, Berlin/Heidelberg: Springer.
Jolly, Seth K. (2007): "The Europhile Fringe?. Regionalist Party Support for European Integration." In: European Union Politics, Vol. 8/1, pp. 109–130.
Kaina Viktoria (2009) "Kollektive Identität und europäisches Einigungswerk – Konzepte und empirische Befunde." In: Wir in Europa. Wiesbaden: Springer.
Keating, Michael (2013): Rescaling the European State. The Making of Territory and the Rise of the Meso, Oxford: Oxford Scholarship Online.
Kosterman, Rick/Feshbach, Seymour (1989): "Toward a Measure of Patriotic and Nationalistic Attitudes." In: Political Psychology 10/2, pp. 257–274.
Laborde, Cécile (2002): "From Constitutional to Civic Patriotism." In: British Journal of Political Science 32/4, pp. 591–612.
Lewis, Camilla (2016): "'Regenerating community'? Urban change and narratives of the past." In: The Sociological Review 64/4, pp. 912–928.
Löw, Martina (2001): Raumsoziologie, Frankfurt am Main: Suhrkamp.

Medrano, Juan D./Gutiérrez (2001):"Nested identities: national and European identity in Spain." In: Ethnic and Racial Studies 24/5, pp. 753-778.
Meyer, Thomas (2009): "Europäische Identität." In: Meyer, Thomas/Hartmann-Fritsch, Christel (eds.): Europäische Identität als Projekt. Innen- und Außensichten, Wiesbaden: Springer, pp. 15–30.
Mühler, Kurt/Opp, Karl-Dieter (2004): Region und Nation. Zu den Ursachen und Wirkungen regionaler und überregionaler Identifikation, Wiesbaden: Springer.
Parker, Chrstopher S. (2010): "Symbolic versus Blind Patriotism: Distinction without Difference?" In: Political Research Quarterly 63/1, pp. 97–114.
Peters, Bernhard (2005): "Public discourse, identity and the problem of democratic legitimacy." In: Eriksen Erik O. (ed.): Making the European Polity : Reflexive Integration in the EU, Routledge Studies on Democratizing Europe, London: Routledge, pp. 84–123.
Pohl, John (2001): "Regional Identity." In: International Encyclopedia of Social & Behavioral Sciences, pp. 12917–12922.
Reckwitz, Andreas (2017): Die Gesellschaft der Singularitäten: Zum Strukturwandel der Moderne, Berlin: Suhrkamp.
Reeskens, Tim/Hooghe, Marc (2010): "Beyond the civic–ethnic dichotomy: investigating the structure of citizenship concepts across thirty-three countries." In: Nations and Nationalism 16/4, pp. 579–597.
Roudometof, Victor (2019): "Recovering the local: From glocalization to localization." In: Current Sociology Review 67/6, pp. 801–817.
Ruge, Undine (2004): "Eine konservative Vision — das 'Europa der Regionen." In: Leviathan, Vol. 32/4, pp. 495–513.
Simmel, Georg (1903): "Soziologie des Raumes." In: Eigmüller, Monika/Vobruba, Georg (eds..) (2016): Grenzsoziologie, Wiesbaden: Springer, pp. 9–18.
Tajfel, Henri (1982): Social identity and intergroup relations, Cambridge.
Taylor, Donald M./Doria, Janet R. (1981): "Self-Serving and Group-Serving Bias in Attributions." In: The Journal of Social Psychology 113, pp. 201–211.
Schatz, Robert T./Staub, Ervin/Lavine, Howard (1999): On the Varieties of National Attachment: Blind versus Constructive Patriotism. In: Political Psychology Vol.20/1, pp. 151-174.
Schroer, Markus (2008): "Bringing space back in. Zur Relevanz des Raums als soziologischer Kategorie." In: Döring Jörg/Thielmann Tristan (eds.): Spatial Turn. Das Raumparadigma in den Kultur- und Sozialwissenschaften, Bielefeld: Transcript, pp. 125–148.
Weiner, Bernard (2004): "The Attribution Approach to Emotion and Motivation: History, Hypotheses, Home Runs, Headaches/Heartaches." In: Emotion Review 6/4, pp. 353–361.
Wagner, Ulrich/Becker, Julia C./Christ, Oliver/Pettigrew, Thomas F./Schmidt, Peter (2012): "A Longitudinal Test of the Relation between German Nationalism,

Patriotism, and Outgroup Derogation." In: European Sociological Review 28/3, pp. 319-332.

Weiss, Hilde/Reinprecht, Christoph (2004): Nation und Toleranz? Empirische Studien zu nationalen Identitäten in Österreich, Wien: Braumüller Verlag.

Wiesner, Claudia (2017): "Was ist europäische Identität? Theoretische Zugänge, empirische Befunde, Forschungsperspektiven und Arbeitsdefinition." In: Hentges, Gudrun/Nottbohm, Kristina/Platzer, Hans-Wolfgang (eds.): Europäische Identität in der Krise?, Wiesbaden: Springer, pp. 21-56.

List of Tables and Figures

Figure 1: "Attachment to Tyrol." Created by Donat, Elisabeth (2020) for this publication.

Figure 2: "Educational Attainment and Regional Attachment." Created by Donat, Elisabeth (2020) for this publication.

Figure 3: "Place of Birth and Attachment to the Region." Created by Donat, Elisabeth (2020) for this publication.

Figure 4: "Pride." Created by Donat, Elisabeth (2020) for this publication.

Figure 5: "The 2019 European Parliamentary Election Campaign in Tyrol." Taken from VP Tirol.

Table 1: "Attribution, causal dimension, behaviour relations." Taken from Weiner, Bernhard (2004): "The Attribution Approach to Emotion and Motivation: History, Hypotheses, Home Runs, Headaches/Heartaches." In: Emotion Review 6/4, p. 357.

Table 2: "Multinominal Regression (Reference Category 'Indifference')." Created by Donat, Elisabeth (2020) for this publication.

Table 3: "Expectations Placed on New Arrivals in Tyrol and Conservative Values." Created by Donat, Elisabeth (2020) for this publication.

Appendix

Table 3: Expectations Placed on New Arrivals in Tyrol and Conservative Values

	Should adapt to prevailing norms	Should bring their own culture and way of life with them[4]	Should keep to themselves	Should not be given preferential treatment
Strongly agree	57.3	28.3	4.9	67.5
Generally agree	24.5	26.5	5.1	15.8
Neither agree nor disagree	15.0	33.5	14.8	11.0
Generally disagree	2.4	8.3	22.8	2.4
Strongly disagree	0.8	3.4	52.4	3.2
	Sense of tradition	Being hard-working and ambitious	Conscientiousness	Security and order
Very important	36.2	41.2	57.4	59.8
Relatively important	32.2	39.4	32.3	30.3
Neither important nor unimportant	20.0	16.8	8.7	9.1
Relatively unimportant	10.1	1.8	1.4	0.8
Not Important at all	1.4	0.8	0.2	0

[N= 500]

Regional Europeans
The Relationship between Social Identities and EU Support in Austria

Katrin Praprotnik

[1]Politics in European countries is multi-level politics. Some decisions are made at the regional level, others at the national level and more and more policies have started to be negotiated at the European level. Whether each layer of the political system is rooted in the heart of its citizens has been subject to scholarly attention. A corresponding social identity is said to be an important prerequisite of public support for a given political level. When it comes to public support for the European Union, scholars have examined the potentially intervening effect of a strong national identity (Carey 2002; Hooghe/Marks 2005, 2004; Kuhn/Stoeckel 2014). These studies revealed that as long as feelings of attachment are not exclusive, a strong national identity does not necessarily preclude positive attitudes towards the European Union. Identity studies that stress the fact that identities are mutually inclusive further corroborated this finding (Marks 1997, 1999; Haesly 2001; Citrin/Sides 2004; Díes Medrano/Gutiérrez 2001).

Quite interestingly, however, these studies have largely neglected the relationship between a *regional* and a European identity (but see Chacha 2012). We know considerably less about people's attachment towards their region and its effect on their feelings towards the European Union. This comes as a surprise, since a regional identity is often equally as strong as a national identity and in some countries even exceeds national attachment (European Commission 2019). Furthermore, the European Union acknowledges the relevance of the regional level in its treaties and political structure. In 1992, the Maastricht Treaty anchored the principle of subsidiarity and established the European Committee of the Regions in the EU's institutional framework.

---

1 This research has been conducted under the auspices of the Austrian Democracy Lab (ADL, Danube University Krems and University of Graz). The ADL is part of the larger cluster democracy.research, a cooperation with Forum Morgen. Please visit www.austriandemocracylab.at for more information.

Thus, the present paper aims to shed light on the relationship between a regional and a European identity and its effect on public opinion towards the EU. To be more specific, my research question asks how a European identity that is coupled with a regional identity affects EU support.

The remainder of this chapter is structured as follows: In the next section, I will elaborate on the theoretical framework. Based on the relevant literature, I expect to see that a European identity has a positive effect on EU support and that a coupled regional/European identity has an equally positive effect on EU support. Following the theoretical section, I present my case selection and data. The analyses will be based on the Austrian data of the European Values Study 2018 (Glavanovits et al. 2019; Kritzinger et al. 2019). The fourth section is devoted to the empirical analyses. The results show that a European identity favours EU support and that an additional regional identity does not hinder a positive attitude towards the EU. In the concluding section, I review this result against the background of current identity literature and its relevance to the ongoing debate about the future of the European Union.

Social Identities and Support for the European Union

Since the formation of the European Coal and Steel Community in 1951 and throughout the history of the European Union, scholarly interest in the factors underpinning public support for this unique political institution has been very high. While earlier studies focused on utilitarian explanations (Eichenberg/Dalton 1993; Gabel/Palmer 1995; Lubbers/Scheepers 2010; Hakhverdian et al. 2013; Vasilopoulou/Talving 2018), more recent studies have considered the connections between European and national social identities and attitudes towards European integration (Carey/Lebo 2001; Carey 2002; Kuhn/Stoeckel 2014). This development of the scholarly debate mirrors the development of the European Union. Since economic effects prevailed at first, scholars tested whether people with a higher socio-economic status who are able to profit from the unification process are supportive of European integration. At least since the Treaty of Maastricht in 1992, the EU represents more than a single market. Scholars then began to include the concept of social identity and the effect of national and European identities in their models. Most commonly, these items were measured as self-reported perceptions of nationality, feelings of pride with respect to one's own country or feelings of attachment to different territorial levels. Both theories proved to be fruitful and helped to paint a better picture of public support towards the European Union (Hooghe/Marks 2004).

If we look at the studies explaining EU support based on European and national identities, there are two lessons that can be learned. First, European identity is a strong predictor of EU support and second, social identities are mutually inclusive. I start by elaborating on the first claim, which will lead me to my first hypothesis.

The identity approach began with an investigation of national identity on EU support. The underlying rationale was that people grew up as nationals or, at least in a context of a strong nation state. The European Union, due to an ongoing integration process, especially since the Maastricht Treaty in 1992, was only present for most people at a later point in time. In order to understand public opinion towards the European Union, scholars saw it as important to understand the linkage between these established national identities and the unification process. It is interesting to note that the relevant studies focussed on a national identity that excluded an additional European one. The scholars reported that feelings of exclusive nationalism reduced support for the European Union (Carey 2002; Hooghe/Marks 2004, 2005; Luedtke 2005; but see Christin/Trechsel 2002). For example, Carey (2002, also see Carey/Lebo 2001) who was the first to promote the identity approach, measured national identity as a binary variable that distinguished between those who feel only as a member of their nation and all others. He even multiplied this survey item by the level of national pride. It does not come as a surprise that these strong and proud nationalists are less supportive of the European integration process.

However, whether someone supports the European Union should depend not only on national but also on *European* identity, i.e. whether someone feels an attachment towards Europe. Some studies did in fact already measure European identity, but the wording of the theoretical claims remained exclusively concerned with the national level. For example, although Kuhn and Stoeckel (2014) were interested in the effect of an exclusive national identity on EU support, they operationalised their independent variable based on a survey item on EU citizenship. Those who reported feeling 'not really' and 'definitely not' European citizens were classified as exclusive nationalists. The results then showed that these exclusive nationalists were less likely to support EU economic governance. If we stick to the original survey item, then it is equally plausible to conclude that people who do not identify with Europe are less likely to be in favour of the European Union.

Studies that measured citizens' identification with Europe and linked it to support for the European Union unanimously highlight the positive effect of identification on public opinion towards the EU. Carey (2002), for instance, ran a second model in addition to the one mentioned above and included an item on attachment to Europe. This coefficient remained positive and significant even when controlling for attachment towards other layers of the political system. The study by Hobolt (2014) presents another convincing and more recent example. She linked attachment towards Europe to public support for a deeper and wider European Union in the future. Again, attachment to Europe explained positive attitudes towards both versions of further integration.

In line with this literature on European identity and EU support, I claim that a strong European feeling should explain positive attitudes towards the European Union. Hence, the first hypothesis reads as follows:

> H1. People with a European identity are more likely to support the European Union compared to people without a European identity.

The second lesson on social identities directly links to the previous discussion on national and European identities. The presence of a European identity should not only be relevant to understanding support for the EU, it is also plausible to *expect* a European identity regardless of the existence of strong national identities. To date we have ample empirical evidence that social identities are mutually inclusive. For example, Marks (1997: 35) refers to 'nested identities', where 'multiple, coexisting identities with local, regional and supranational territorial communities [exist], alongside an identity with the nation'. He supported his claim a few years later with bivariate analyses that showed a positive relationship between national and EU attachment. Similarly, using factor analysis, Haesly (2001) showed that while British EU supporters would claim that their national identity is stronger than their European identity, they nonetheless have a supranational identity, and both of these feelings coexist within these people (in contrast to Eurosceptics who reject having an EU identity). Regardless of the analytical approach and the countries under scrutiny, the empirical studies on social identities conclude unanimously that identity is a mutually inclusive concept (also see Citrin/Sides 2004; Díez Medrano/Gutiérrez 2001; Risse 2010).

While the combination of different identities and the effect of a combined European and national identity on EU support are well established, much less is known about the combination of European and regional feelings on the one hand, and positive attitudes towards the European Union, on the other. A study by Chacha (2012: 222), however, reports that "[s]upport for European integration […] also hinges on the level of inclusive regional attachment among EU citizens."

Based on our knowledge of the effect of European and national identities on EU support and Chacha's (2012) research, I distinguish between regional Europeans and Europeans. While the first group of people holds both a regional and a European identity, the second group are exclusively attached to Europe. If social identities are inclusive, and a European identity explains support of the EU integration process, then positive EU attitudes should equally prevail in both groups.

> H2. People with a European identity AND a regional identity (regional Europeans) are equally likely to support the European Union as people with only a European identity.

The following section presents the data used to test the hypotheses.

Data: The European Values Study

In order to answer the research question and the hypotheses derived from it, I will rely on the European Values Study (EVS). The EVS is a cross-national survey of human values in areas such as family, politics and society. Since 1981, the EVS has conducted five waves of surveys in between 16 and 47 European countries/regions each time. In the present chapter, I examine the relationship between regional/European identity and EU support based on the Austrian data from the most recent EVS, which was carried out in 2018 (Glavanovits et al. 2019; Kritzinger et al. 2019).[2] The population consisted of people aged 18 or older who had their primary private residence in Austria. All interviews were face-to-face and conducted in spring 2018.

The survey provides adequate questions for both my dependent and independent variables. Recall that the dependent variable should reflect people's support for the European Union. I use the following EVS question to operationalise EU support:

> Q38. Please look at this card and tell me, for each item listed, how much confidence you have in them, is it a great deal, quite a lot, not very much or none at all? – The European Union

A simple tabulation provides an overview of the descriptive results of the EVS Austria with respect to this question. The Austrian figures show that 7 percent have a lot of confidence in the European Union and 34 percent have quite a lot of confidence. The remaining have not very much (38 percent) and no confidence at all (19 percent) in the European Union (and 2 percent did not answer). These results are comparable to other data sources such as the Eurobarometer study (with the proviso that the questions are similar, but not identical). In the most recent Eurobarometer wave, Austrians were surveyed about their image of the European Union. Based on a five-point scale, 8 percent reported a 'very positive', 32 percent a 'fairly positive', 37 percent a 'neutral', 18 percent a 'fairly negative' and 4 percent a 'very negative' image (European Commission 2019).

In the multivariate models, I differentiate between people who have a 'great deal' or 'quite a lot' of confidence in the EU and all other respondents. This binary construction of the variable helps to identify EU supporters and is a commonly used approach in the literature (e.g. Hakhverdian et al. 2013; Vasilopoulou/Talving 2018).

---

[2] This sample includes all the respondents from the EVS study in Austria plus an additional sample on people with a migration background. In my multivariate analyses, I use the recommended data weights to guarantee representativeness.

My main independent variables are European and regional identities. I operationalise these variables based on the question on attachment towards the different geographical levels. Hence, in the following I will use the term identity and attachment interchangeably. The corresponding survey item taken from the EVS reads:

> Q45. People have different views about themselves and how they relate to the world. Using this card, would you tell me how close do you feel to...?
> ... your region [v164]
> ... Europe [v167]

In answering this question, people could choose between 'very close', 'close', 'not very close' and 'not close at all'. Again, descriptive statistics provide a first impression of the survey results (see Table 1). When the Austrian participants were asked about their feelings of attachment towards Europe, 20 percent reported that they are 'very close' and 46 percent that they are 'close'. 'Not very' or 'not at all close' were the responses of 27 percent and 6 percent, respectively.

Unsurprisingly, Austrians hold higher levels of attachment towards their region than towards Europe. Almost all respondents feel 'very' (45 percent) or 'fairly' (43 percent) close to the regional level. Only a minority reported that they are 'not very close' (10 percent) or 'not close at all' (1 percent).

Table 1: Attachment towards different geographical levels (row, percent)

	Very close	Close	Not very close	Not close at all	Don't know	Did not answer
Europe	20	46	27	6	1	0
Nation state	46	46	6	1	0	0
Region	45	43	10	1	0	0
City/Town	47	41	11	1	0	0

Notes: Figures do not add up to 100 due to rounding. Source : European Values Study 2018 – Austria (Glavanovits et al. 2019; Kritzinger et al. 2019).

In order to compare these figures, Table 1 additionally includes the corresponding answers to both the national and the local level. We see that these results are quite similar to people's attachment to their region and well above those of the European level.

Again, I collapsed the relevant variables and generated the binary variables *European identity* and *Regional identity*. These variables differentiate between attachment (i.e. 'very close' and 'close') and a lack of attachment to each level (i.e. 'not very close' and 'not close at all'). Next, in order to test H2, I generated the variable

Nested identities. This variable distinguishes people that are solely attached to the regional level from people without any attachment to either level, from people with European attachment only and from those who have both regional and European attachment. If a European identity (and hence attachment) is compatible with a regional identity then I would expect to see equal levels of EU support among Europeans and regional Europeans.

My models will control for both the utilitarian (e.g. Gabel/Palmer 1995) and the cue-taking explanations of EU support (e.g. Hooghe et al. 2002). In line with previous literature, I use education to take the line of argumentation within the utilitarian approach into account. The variable *Education* is incorporated as a categorical variable in the models. In line with the cue-taking approach, I include the respondents' political position measured by a *Left/right self-placement* on a scale that ranges from zero (extreme left) to ten (extreme right). Finally, all models control for *Age* and *Gender* as these two variables are commonly used control variables that showed relevant effects in the past. Younger people are generally found to be supportive of the European idea (Inglehart 1970, Lubbers/Scheepers 2010, Kuhn 2012, but see Defelm/Pampel 1996 and Carey 2002 who found no age effect). The same goes for male compared to female respondents (Inglehart 1970, Lubbers/Scheepers 2010, Defelm/Pampel 1996, Nelsen/Guth 2000, Carey 2002).

Explaining Support for the European Union in Austria

How does a European identity affect support for the European Union? How does a European identity that is supplemented by a regional identity change EU attitudes? In order to provide an answer to these questions, I will first present binary inspections of the variables and then multivariate models that test whether these relationships hold under control of other relevant factors. I begin by comparing support of the European Union among people who feel attached towards Europe and others. The difference is quite remarkable. Among those who have a European identity, 11 percent are strong supporters of the European Union and 40 percent are supporters (38 percent have some support and 11 percent have no support). If we look at the group without a European identity, we see that only 5 percent are strong supporters of the European Union and 26 percent are supporters (44 percent with some and 26 percent with no support). This is a difference of 20 percentage points in EU support between people with and without a European identity and hence in line with the expectation of H1. Table 2 inspects this relationship further and presents a bivariate tabulation of the newly generated variable Nested identities and EU support. Recall that the variable Nested identities reflects a combination of the two survey items on attachment towards Europe and the regional level. The first group of people stated that they feel only attached to their region, the second group reported that they feel neither attached to Europe nor to their region, the third group showed attachment towards Europe and finally, the fourth group revealed both attachment to Europe and to the regional level. Again, we see that European identity is closely linked to EU support. It is interesting to note that EU support is rather similar among Europeans and regional Europeans. Both groups show high figures of EU support. Among Europeans, 13 percent and 44 percent have a lot or quite a lot of confidence in the European Union. Among regional Europeans, 10 percent and 40 percent have a lot or quite a lot of confidence in the European Union. This is in line with H2, and the multivariate models will show whether there is no significant difference in EU support among Europeans and regional Europeans.

Table 2: Nested Identities and EU support (row percent)

	A great deal of confidence in the EU	Quite a lot of confidence in the EU	Not very much confidence in the EU	No confidence at all in the EU
Regional attachment only	6	29	44	21
No attachment	2	12	40	46
EU attachment only	13	44	27	16
EU and regional attachment	10	40	39	11

Source : European Values Study 2018 – Austria (Glavanovits et al. 2019; Kritzinger et al. 2019).

These multivariate models are binary logistic regression models. Recall that the dependent variable differentiates between people who have confidence in the European Union and all other respondents; i.e. EU supporters vs. EU critics. Model I presents the multivariate test of H1. The first hypothesis expects that a European identity will be shown to be positively linked with support for the European Union. Model II presents the multivariate test of H2. The second hypothesis holds that regional Europeans, i.e. people that identify with both the EU and their region, are just as likely to support the European Union as Europeans, i.e. people that identify only with the EU.

Table 3: Binary logistic models: Explaining EU support in Austria

	Model I (H1)		Model II (H2)	
European identity	3.791***	(7.54)		
Regional identity	1.150	(0.65)		
Nested Identities				
Regional identity only			0.267***	(-3.92)
No identity			0.111***	(-5.23)
European identity only			Reference category	
Regional and European identities			0.901	(-0.35)
Education				
Secondary education or Lower	Reference category		Reference category	
Apprenticeship or vocational middle school	0.783	(-1.15)	0.775	(-1.19)
Higher school certificate or advanced vocational training	1.119	(0.45)	1.102	(0.38)
University degree	1.712*	(1.95)	1.682*	(1.87)
Left/right self-placement	0.843***	(-4.11)	0.843***	(-4.02)
Age	0.992*	(-1.72)	0.992*	(-1.81)
Female	0.895	(-0.77)	0.881	(-0.88)
Pseudo R2	0.106		0.110	
N	1,685		1,683	

Note: Dependent variable: EU supporters (0/1); Exponentiated coefficients; t-statistics in parentheses; * $p < 0.10$, ** $p < 0.05$, *** $p < 0.01$. Source: European Values Study 2018 – Austria (Glavanovits et al. 2019; Kritzinger et al. 2019).

The multivariate tests confirm hypothesis 1. There is a positive relationship between European identity and support for the European Union. The coefficient EU identity in Model I is greater than one and highly significant. If people identify with the European Union, then they are more likely to support the EU as well. In order to interpret the magnitude of the effect, I predict the probabilities of EU support. If a person does identify with the European Union, then the probability that he or she supports the EU is 0.53. This figure drops to 0.23 if identification with the EU is absent. The predicted probabilities and their respective confidence intervals are plotted in Graph 1.

Figure 1:. Predicted Probabilities of EU support: European Identity

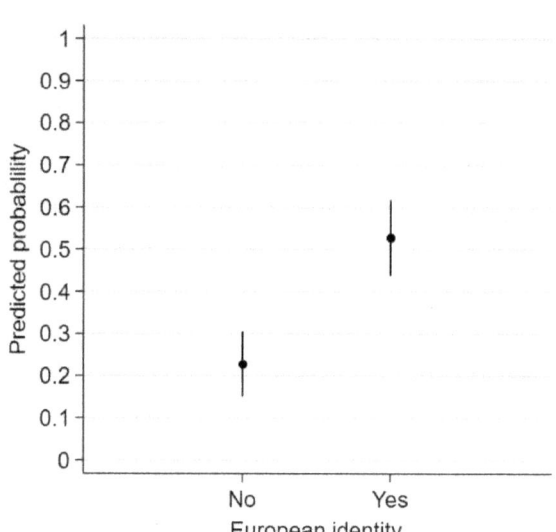

Note: Predictions are based on Model I in Table 3.

Furthermore, there is no significant difference between people with only a European identity and people with a European identity AND a regional identity. Both Europeans and regional Europeans are supporters of the European Union. This is in line with Hypothesis 2, which expected regional Europeans to be equally likely to support the European Union compared to people with only a European identity. In Model II, people with only a European attachment are taken as the reference category. Compared to this group, the coefficient Regional and European identities is not significant, and hence I conclude that there is no statistical difference between these groups. Note that both people who do not identify with either level or who are only attached to their region are less likely to support the European Union compared to the reference category Europeans. These coefficients are significant and smaller than one. Again, I will look at expected probabilities of EU support to interpret the magnitude of the effects. Model II predicts Europeans to be supportive of the EU with a factor of 0.55 and regional Europeans by a factor of 0.52. In comparison to these two types, people with no attachment reach a predicted probability of EU support of 0.12 and people with an attachment only to their region of 0.24 (see Graph 2).

Figure 2: Predicted probabilities of EU support: Nested Identities

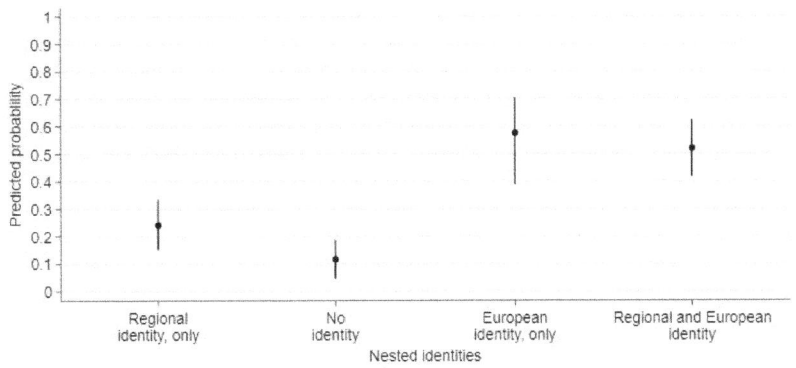

Note: Predictions are based on Model II in Table 3.

In terms of the control variables, the models yield results that are in line with expectations and partly statistically significant. First, the significant coefficient Education re-confirms the explanatory power of the utilitarian approach (Gabel/Palmer 1995; as well as Lubbers/Scheepers 2010; Hakhverdian et al. 2013; Vasilopoulou/Talving 2018, for more recent studies). If people hold a university degree, then they are more favourable towards the European Union.

Second, the variable Left/right self-placement equally shows a relevant finding and corroborates the cue-taking approach. People that place themselves more towards the right of the political spectrum are more Eurosceptic compared to people that tend towards the left. In contrast to other recent studies (van Elsas/van der Brug 2015; König et al. 2017), there is no U-shaped relationship between ideological position and EU position. These authors have argued that both extremes of the political spectrum tend to oppose the EU integration process, albeit for different reasons. While left-wing parties fear a loss of their social security systems, right-wing actors are afraid of jeopardising their own national sovereignty (also see van Elsas et al. 2016; Lubbers/Scheepers 2010). This finding is not surprising for a country like Austria, in view of the country's party system. The most left-wing party, the Greens, is a pro-European party and its supporters share these positive attitudes towards the European Union. The most right-wing party, the Freedom Party of Austria, is the only Eurosceptic party in the spectrum and its supporters agree with its critical stance on integration. The lack of an extreme left wing party (at least in the national parliament) and hence the absence of Eurosceptic left-wing cues explains the linear relationship further. There is no evidence of support for European unification by the political right due to their support of free trade policies, as found in earlier studies such as Defelm and Pampel (1996).

With respect to Age, I find that younger people are more pro-European. This is in line with some previous studies (Inglehart 1970; Lubbers/Scheepers 2001; Kuhn 2012). However, others have reported no effect (Defelm/Pampel 1996; Carey 2002).

Finally, the coefficient Female shows no statistically significant results in either model. With respect to Female, I expected to see men as more favourable of the European Union than their female counterparts (Inglehart 1970; Lubbers/Scheepers 2010; Defelm/Pampel 1996; Nelsen/Guth 2000; Carey 2002). At least in the case of Austria 2018, the models do not support this conclusion.

Regional Europeans in Austria: Conclusion

In this chapter, I examined the effect of identity on EU support among Austrian residents in 2018. My focus was to look at EU identity together with regional identity. Although the number of studies acknowledging the identity component in their explanations of public opinion towards the European Union has mushroomed in recent decades (Carey 2002; Hooghe/Marks 2005, 2004; Kuhn/Stoeckel 2014), they still largely overlooked the relevance of regional identity (but see Chacha 2012). While we know that people may feel themselves to be Europeans and nationals of their country at the same time, our knowledge of regional identities – i.e. whether strong ties at this level are equally inclusive – is still limited.

Based on the relevant literature, my hypotheses expected to see a positive relationship between an EU identity and a pro-European attitude as well as an equally positive attitude among Europeans and regional Europeans. While Europeans identify only with the European level, regional Europeans' hearts beat for both the EU and their region. The empirical analyses based on the Austrian data of the European Values Study 2018 corroborated the hypotheses. In addition, they showed that people with higher education are more pro-European (in line with the utilitarian approach, e.g. Gabel/Palmer 1995) and that a more right-wing political position favours Euroscepticism in Austria (in contrast to a U-shaped relationship in other countries, but still in line with the cue-taking approach, e.g. Hooghe et al. 2002).

These findings provide a positive outlook for future cooperation among the EU member states. Especially since regional attachment tends to be strong, the finding that a European and regional identity are inclusive is promising.

The present paper followed a classical approach to explain the role of identity on EU support. Already researchers like Hooghe and Marks (2004), however, have concluded that while the identity approach proves to be empirically powerful (maybe even more than the utilitarian approach) its theoretical underpinnings still fall short of the latter approach. Future research should tackle this issue in order to strengthen the theoretical reasoning behind the identity hypothesis as well as the operationalisation of the identity variables.

References

Carey, Sean (2002): "Undivided Loyalties: Is National Identity an Obstacle to European Integration?" In: European Union Politics 3/4, pp. 387–413.

Carey, Sean/Lebo, Matthew (2001): "In Europe, but Not Europeans: The Impact of National Identity on Public Support for the European Union." In: Paper Presented at the European Consortium for Political Research Joint Sessions of Workshops April 2001 in Grenoble, pp. 6-11.

Chacha, Mwita (2013): "Regional Attachment and Support for European Integration." In: European Union Politics 14/2, pp. 206–227.

Christin, Thomas/Trechsel, Alexander H. (2002): "Joining the EU?: Explaining Public Opinion in Switzerland." In: European Union Politics 3/4, pp. 415–43.

Citrin, Jack/Side, John (2004): "More than Nationals: How Identity Choice Matters in the New Europe." In: Herrmann, Richard K./Risse-Kappen, Thomas/Brewer, Marilynn B. (eds.), Transnational Identities: Becoming European in the EU, Lanham, MD: Rowman & Littlefield, pp. 161–185.

Deflem, Mathieu/Pampel, Fred C. (1996): "The Myth of Postnational Identity: Popular Support for European Unification." In: Social Forces 75/1, pp. 119–143.

Díez-Medrano, Juan/Gutiérrez, Paula (2001): "Nested Identities: National and European Identity in Spain." In: Ethnic and Racial Studies 24/5, pp. 753–778.

Eichenberg, Richard C./Dalton, Russell J. (1993): "Europeans and the European Community: The Dynamics of Public Support for European Integration." In: International Organization 47/4, pp. 507–534.

European Commission (2019): "Eurobarometer Interactive", June, 26 2019 (http://ec.europa.eu/commfrontoffice/publicopinion/index.cfm/Chart/index).

Gabel, Matthew/Palmer, Harvey (2006): "Understanding Variation in Public Support of European Integration." In: European Journal of Political Research 27/1, pp. 3–19.

Glavanovits, Josef/Aichholzer, Julian/Hajdinjak, Sanja/Kritzinger, Sylvia (2019): "The European Values Study 2018 – Austria Edition". Vienna: AUSSDA.

Haesly, Richard (2001): "Euroskeptics, Europhiles and Instrumental Europeans: European Attachment in Scotland and Wales." In: European Union Politics 2/1, pp. 81–102.

Hakhverdian, Armen/van Elsas, Erika J./van der Brug, Wouter/Kuhn, Theresa (2013): "Euroscepticism and Education: A Longitudinal Study of 12 EU Member States, 1973-2010." In: European Union Politics 14/4, pp. 522–541.

Hobolt, Sara B. (2014): "Ever Closer or Ever Wider? Public Attitudes towards Further Enlargement and Integration in the European Union." In: Journal of European Public Policy 21/5, pp. 664–680.

Hooghe, Liesbet/Marks, Gary (2004): "Does Identity or Economic Rationality Drive Public Opinion on European Integration?" In: PS: Political Science and Politics 37/3, pp. 415–420.

Hooghe, Liesbet/Marks, Gary (2005): "Calculation, Community and Cues: Public Opinion on European Integration." In: European Union Politics 6/4, pp. 419–43.

Hooghe, Liesbet/Marks, Gary/Wilson, Carole J. (2002): "Does Left/Right Structure Party Positions on European Integration?" In: Comparative Political Studies 35/8, pp. 965–89.

Inglehart, Ronald (1970): "Cognitive Mobilization and European Identity." In: Comparative Politics 3/1, pp. 45–70.

König, Thomas/Marbach, Moritz/Osnabrügge, Moritz (2017): "Left/Right or U? Estimating the Dimensionality of National Party Competition in Europe." In: The Journal of Politics 79/3, pp. 1101–1105.

Kritzinger, Sylvia/Aichholzer, Julian/Glavanovits, Josef/Hajdinjak, Sanja/Klaiber, Judith/Seewann, Lena (2019): "The European Values Study 2018 Austria (SUF Edition)". Vienna: AUSSDA Dataverse. doi:10.11587/8A4CWK

Kuhn, Theresa (2012): "Why Educational Exchange Programmes Miss Their Mark: Cross-Border Mobility, Education and European Identity." In: JCMS: Journal of Common Market Studies 50/6, pp. 994–1010.

Kuhn, Theresa/Stoeckel, Florian (2014): "When European Integration Becomes Costly: The Euro Crisis and Public Support for European Economic Governance." In: Journal of European Public Policy 21/4, pp. 624–41.

Lubbers, M./Scheepers, P. L. H. (2010): "Divergent Trends of Euroscepticism in Countries and Regions of the European Union." In: European Journal of Political Research 49/6, pp. 787–817.

Luedtke, Adam (2005): "European Integration, Public Opinion and Immigration Policy: Testing the Impact of National Identity." In: European Union Politics 6/1, pp. 83–112.

Marks, Gary (1997): "A Third Lens: Comparing European Integration and State Building." In: Klausen, Jytte/Tilly, Louise A. (eds.). Europe, the Search for European Identity., pp. 23–43. Lanham: Rowman and Littlefield.
Marks, Gary (1999): "Territorial Identities in the European Union" In: Anderson, Jeffrey J./Marks, Gary (eds.), Regional Integration and Democracy: Expanding on the European Experience, Lanham: Rowman & Littlefield, pp. 69–91.
Nelsen, Brent F./Guth, James L. (2000): "Exploring the Gender Gap: Women, Men and Public Attitudes toward European Integration." In: European Union Politics 1/3, pp. 267–291.
Risse, Thomas (2010): "A Community of Europeans?: Transnational Identities and Public Spheres". Ithaca: Cornell University Press.
van Elsas, Erika/van der Brug, W. (2015): "The Changing Relationship between Left-Right Ideology and Euroscepticism, 1973-2010." In: European Union Politics 16/2, pp. 194–215.
van Elsas, Erika J./Hakhverdian, Armen/ van der Brug, Wouter (2016): "United against a Common Foe? The Nature and Origins of Euroscepticism among Left-Wing and Right-Wing Citizens." In: West European Politics 39/6, pp. 1181–1204.
Vasilopoulou, Sofia/Talving, Liisa (2019): "Opportunity or Threat? Public Attitudes towards EU Freedom of Movement." In: Journal of European Public Policy 26/6, pp. 805–823.

List of Tables and Figures

Figure 1: "Predicted Probabilities of EU support: European Identity." Data taken from Glavanovits et al. (2019); Kritzinger et al. (2019).
Figure 2: "Predicted probabilities of EU support: Nested Identities." Data taken from ibid.
Table 1: "Attachment towards different geographical levels (row, percent)." Data taken from ibid.
Table 2: "Nested Identities and EU support (row, percent)." Data taken from ibid.
Table 3: "Binary logistic models: Explaining EU support in Austria." Data taken from ibid.

Ambiguous Identities at the Rhine border
Failures and Successes of Europeanisation in a Pioneering Laboratory of European Integration

Camille Dobler

Introduction

Autumn is certainly one of the best seasons to enjoy the picturesque streets of Strasbourg. A fresh breeze blows around the millennial cathedral; geraniums are still blossoming at the windows of the famous half-timbered houses, and tourists become sparser, leaving café terraces to locals. In the autumn of 2018, in addition to posters announcing the traditional Christmas market to come, onlookers may also notice two advertisement campaigns on giant electronic billboards. At bus stops, a worrisome campaign from the municipality is inviting residents to 'register and vote, this time', on 26 May. A large blue star garnished with 15 smaller gold stars covers the face of American president Donald J. Trump. Nearby, at crossroads and parking lots, a stately red poster from the regionalist party Unser Land is calling for the region to 'break free' from the new administrative division of regions, and to take its fate into its own hands. A few hundred meters away, the Louise Weiss building of the European Parliament emerges from behind trees and bell towers. Such scenery might seem bizarre, yet, along the Rhine border, such things are part of the ordinary landscape. On both riversides, antagonistic aspirations of closure and openness towards national and supranational communities exist in a state of cohabitation. In a local context marked by the 2008 economic crisis, territorial restructuring and increasing engagement of regional political and societal actors in transnational cooperation, it is assumed that identification with the EU has evolved positively in recent years, together with a pro-regionalist feeling, to the detriment of identification with national capitals. Part of a larger comparative research project, this chapter seeks to test this assumption empirically with a focus on the French side of the river. The argument proceeds in four steps. The first section conceptualises identities through citizens' discourses and behaviours. The second section sets the scene by reviewing the systemic integration of the borderland where the research was carried out. The third describes and justifies the research design as well as the use of group interviews. The fourth section presents qualitative findings. The chapter concludes with a discussion of the resilience of boundaries in a turbulent EU.

Conceptualising Identity through Citizens' Discourses and Behaviour

Models of identity

In 2000, Martin Kohli saw in borderlands a promising battleground for the development of a European identity (Kohli 2000). In border areas, memories of past struggles, historical traumas and socio-economic rifts between asymmetrical nations (Wilson/Donnan, 1998) might lead to a hardening of national identities. Or maybe daily interactions and fuzzy territorial attachments invite the inhabitants of such areas to renegotiate their identities (Hierro/Gallego 2018). the characteristic blurred heritage that arises from blended roots often results in strong territory-based identities, and a complex emotional relationship with the nation state (Keating 1998; Medeiros et al. 2015). The different socio-political layers – local, regional, national, European – make up unique and fluid constructions of multiples identities (Meinhof 2004). But how do these layers interrelate? A whole array of different competing conceptual models exists. It is not in the scope of this chapter to review them all, and I would like to elaborate on just three that are well-known in the field of EU studies.

The first model derives from the literature on social identity, which has long tended to see identities as incompatible. The exclusionary model conceives of identities as potentially destructive to one another. According to this view, national identities would be threatened, from above, by the development of a European feeling of belonging, or from below, by a strong regional identity, as in the case of Basque nationalism (Carey 2002; McLaren 2006). If individuals remain free to choose to which group they identify with, irreconcilable contradictions between identities do not permit multiple political allegiances.

A second model, by contrast, suggests that individuals are capable of negotiating between multiple identities, from the local up to the supranational, in concentric circles fashion: "people who identify strongly with local communities also identify strongly with nations, and with Europe" (Herrmann/Brewer 2004: 12). In the case of Spain for example, most Catalans and Basques see themselves as both Catalans or Basques and Spaniards (Diez Medrano/Gutiérrez 2001). This 'Russian-doll' model is based on theories of nested identity (Brewer 1993; Calhoun 1999), according to which sub- and superordinate identities can cohabit, as both fulfil different roles: of differentiation and inclusion, respectively. However, one problem with this model is that it fails to explain the 'indeterminacy as to the relationship between lower- and higher-order nested identities' (Diez Medrano/Gutiérrez 2001: 759). How can we explain than in some regions with strong regionalist feelings, the middle-layer of national identity is bypassed, as, in the case of Scotland, for example (Grundy/Jamieson 2007)? Or that a new kind of regional Euroscepticism is developing, as in Flanders?

A third alternative suggests that the multiple components making up an individual's identity cannot be separated into inferior or superior layers. They are not nested or cross-cutting but rather highly entangled. This is known as the marble-cake model (Risse 2003; Risse 2010). Its most important corollary is twofold: since EU membership interacts with different national and local identity constructions, then there are potentially as many 'European identities' as there are European regions. And reciprocally, enmeshment with the supranational level implies a fluid and continuous (re)construction of local and national identities, which might allow contradictory positions within each component.

Identity through Discourses

If people 'choose' their identities rather than naturally possessing them, the question arises of how they are constructed. Symbolic interaction is certainly the most important perspective in sociology that provides theoretical underpinnings for the understanding of identity construction. Its basic premise is that individuals attach symbolic meaning to behaviours, objects, others and themselves and share those meanings through interaction among each other (Mead 1934). In line with the interactionist literature on identity, we assume that the key agent of these negotiations of who people are, of who the 'Other' is, is language. In other words, individuals produce identity through their *talk*. But the words we use do not only reflect the beliefs of the given social context we develop in, they deconstruct and reshape our social environment as well. Language plays a constitutive role in generating social relations: "language provides – as a metaphor puts it – the grammar of social life" (Eder 2007: 403)

The discursive construction of identity can explain the existence of contradictory positions and attachments as conceptualised in the Russian-doll and marble-cake models. This derives from the understanding of identity as a never-ending process of self-identification and assignment of in-groups and out-groups. It is near borders that on-going negotiations of boundaries between different ethnic groups are at their most salient (Barth 1969).

Negotiations and Inter-dependency at the Border

With 28 member countries in the European Union, 14,000 km of external land borders neighbouring 20 countries, and 26 countries within the Schengen area, borderlands make up a substantial percentage of the European Union's territory. One EU citizen in three lives in these border areas, which are home to 36 trans-border agglomerations and two million cross-border workers. The highly-integrated Rhine border between France and Germany is one of many examples. From a natural boundary, the river was framed over centuries as a social boundary, strengthening social orders on each side of the river and eventually crystallising into two national borders. By crossing the river, local populations construct, de-construct and re-construct those symbols of political identities (Simmel 1997). And the corollary holds, too: as does any institution, borders in return change social contexts and alter local populations' perception of social boundaries. This ability of citizens to participate in the (un)making of borders, through language but also through their everyday actions, as 'banal' as they might seem, constitutes 'borderwork' (Rumford 2009). Thus, in borderlands more than anywhere else, what local populations *say* about themselves, their region and their nation-state, Europe, and the 'Other', should be contrasted with what they *do*. Because the borderland is administratively and logistically integrated, because it separates a region with high unemployment from another with many work opportunities, borders are crossed and contacts occur. Can this prefigure a supranational identity? Cross-border mobility has been shown to be positively correlated to the development of a post-national mindset (Favell/Recchi 2009; Howard 2000; Sigalas 2010), and indeed, the 'contact hypothesis' proposes that interpersonal relations are one of the most effective ways if not the most effective way to overcome conflicts and negative stereotyping between two social groups (Allport 1954). Yet, Gordon Allport also restricted such positive correlation in terms of the qualitative nature of the contact, its context, as well as socio-economic and cultural characteristics of the two social groups that meet. With the French side of the Rhineland border changing nationality four times in 75 years (between 1870 and 1945), few regions in Europe are as likely to develop the feeling of supranational belonging as Martin Kohli called for in this case. Legal and administrative support is another of the criteria needed for positive contact, according to intergroup contact theory. As a matter of fact, it is in the Rhine Basin that local cross-border cooperation was pioneered in the 1950s (Schelberg 2001).Transnational political, economic and cultural structures have since been strengthened under the stimulus of the European Union and the Council of Europe, to encourage the border population to see beyond the 'national container' (Beck 2000)

A European Microcosm in an Integrated Borderland

The last two decades have seen a 'new regionalism' emerging on the multi-level European geopolitical and geo-economic scene, with regions gaining significant relevance in the concrete work of shaping the EU itself (Paasi 2009). If Alsace does not have secessionist desires that exist in Corsica or the Basque-country, it does have a regionalist party, and it is not so uncommon to see discrete *"Elsass Freie"* graffiti and stickers decorating street signs alongside the Rhine. Since the 2015 French territorial reform erased Alsace from the map, those have flourished. As a gesture of appeasement to hurt local pride, the Philippe government put on the table a legislative proposal for the creation by 2021 of a *Collectivité européenne d'Alsace* [European community of Alsace] and the provision of specific competences, in particular a leading role in transboundary cooperation within its geographical boundaries.[1] The forthcoming creation of this new administrative framework endorsing so adamantly a supranational dimension is illustrative of the decisive role played by European regions in giving flesh and bones to European integration. This regional gaze turned towards the Rhine rather than Paris is nothing new. In 2010, after 50 years of transnational collaboration, the creation of the Metropolitan Trinational Region of the Upper Rhine was legally enshrined,[2] gathering the former region of Alsace together with North and South Baden, South-East Palatinate and North-West Switzerland.[3] The latest developments in the area also include the signing of the Aachen Treaty between France and Germany in January 2019, which significantly increased the competences of the Trinational Region's four Eurodistricts. Amongst them, the Eurodistrict of Strasbourg-Ortenau brings together in a 'pilot European territory' 61 French and 51 German municipalities, with 940,000 inhabitants, shaping a former conflict-riven border into a 'laboratory for European integration' (Schultz 2002). In this regard, the launch in 2017 of the binational tramway joining Strasbourg and Kehl was emblematic of the systemic integration of the borderland; the last time a tram had crossed the river being during the Second World War.

---

1 The legislative proposal for a *Collectivité européenne d'Alsace* was presented by the French government on 27 February 2019 and adopted by the Senate at first reading, with modifications on 4 April 2019. Review of the proposal started on 24 June in the *Assemblée nationale*. The proposed *collectivité* is set to couple the two *departements* of the former region of Alsace, Haut-Rhin and Bas-Rhin, by 1 January 2021 in a unique administrative scheme with enhanced prerogatives, in particular regarding road network and border management as well as defence of bilingualism.
2 *Région Métropolitaine Trinationale du Rhin Supérieur/* Trinationalen Metropolregion Oberrhein
3 An Upper Rhine Franco-Germano-Swiss Council made of 71 elected politicians is tasked to represent the six million inhabitants of the borderland. This Council acts as the 'Parliament' of the Trinational Region.

Yet, for the *Eurométropole de Strasbourg*, the binational tramway line is not only symbolic, but also instrumental in securing its title as a 'European capital', in the controversies surrounding the seat of the European Parliament. Strasbourg is home to three major European institutions: the European Parliament, the Council of Europe and the European Court of Human Rights. It is also the home of the European TV-channel ARTE, the European Pharmacopoeia, the European Ombudsman, the Secretariat of the Assembly of European Regions and EUROCORPS. At the heart of the city's 'European district', the *Lieu d'Europe* [Place of Europe] education centre aims at bringing European citizens closer to each other and to European institutions.

Intense Europeanisation of the border seems to have had positive effects. Previous research conducted in this borderland has shown that Rhineland inhabitants on both sides are more likely to support European integration than their compatriots (Schmidberger 1998). The resilience of Europhile feelings in the region to political, social and economic changes remains, however, hypothetical. On the one hand, the existing literature on the impact of major exogenous events such as economic shocks, refugee crises or terrorism on secessionist aspirations converges towards a positive correlation (Orzechowska-Waclawska 2017; Rico/Liñeira 2014). On the other hand, empirical studies have long stressed that regional identity is an important predicator for how likely citizens are to identify with the EU (van Spanje/de Vreese 2011). Overall, there are compelling reasons to believe that European identification in the region has varied. Building on a sample of 15 group discussions with French families carried out in the Strasbourg area, this chapter offers to make sense of the 'identity mix' of one of Europe's most integrated borderland areas.

Operationalising the Identity-Mix: Comparing Family Interviews

In light with the theoretical approach presented above, it was essential to get local populations *talking*. Research in the fields of EU and border studies endorsing a similar conceptualisation have produced valuable insights based on original ethnographic fieldwork and in-depth interviews (see, for examples relating to the German-Polish border; Asher 2005; Meinhof/Galasiński 2010). In this chapter, we are less interested in individual narratives than in understanding the negotiations of meanings in the formation of collective cultural identities.[4] Group interaction

---

4   By cultural identity, I refer in this chapter to what Michael Bruter defines as 'a citizen's sense of belonging to a human community' (Bruter 2013: 36) – as opposed to citizens' identification with a political system as an institution – with which they believe they share a certain heritage, regardless of so-called objective reality. This can include any form of history but also

is one way to gather such insights. Face-to-face interviews have been a successful method of collecting not only personal narratives, but also patterns of common sense and structural views. Here, however, we are also interested in the transmission of these views and potential contagion of affects between citizens. In contrast to qualitative in-depth interviews, group interviews provide data on intra- and interpersonal debates. They are also useful for contextually exploring 'the gap between what people say and what they do' as when participants know each other, they can contradict and correct each other (Conradson 2005: 131).

The 15 group interviews conducted in autumn 2018 each gathered families of three to eight members belonging to two to three generations (parents and children, and grandparents where possible) for a total of 78 participants. Working with families does not guarantee diverse political ideologies within one group to the same extent at artificial sampling. However, low polarisation of opinions is mitigated by mutual trust between participants and generational differences within each group. Conflicting political opinions, particularly regarding European integration, were freely expressed and clearly evident. As numerous research projects have shown, citizens' attitudes towards European integration are divided along social lines (Hobolt 2016; Kuhn 2015; van Spanje/de Vreese 2011), as well as national ones (Diez Medrano 2003; Herrmann et al. 2004). Since the research only focused on France, sampling of participants had to reflect the ethnic diversity of a historical country of immigration. Families were therefore recruited to enable comparison of discussions in these two dimensions: along social lines and according to nationality. Three categories of five families each – to ensure diversity of political ideologies in the sample – were constituted accordingly: the first group consisted of working-class families, the second of upper-middle class families, both holding only French nationality, and the final category of middle-class families holding multiple nationalities (French nationality *and* an additional EU/non-EU nationality). Recruitment was initially undertaken using a snowballing technique and later by direct solicitation as based on theoretical sampling, made easier thanks to the help of respected individuals from local associative outreach programmes. The theme of the discussion was kept deliberately vague so as to limit selection bias, and participants were offered a voucher for their participation in the study (cf. appendix 1).

Standardisation of the discussion was supported by the development of a unique interview scenario. All discussions were moderated by the researcher herself

---

moral or religious traditions, as well as values, philosophical and political norms. A cultural identity is therefore a social identity and can encompass a territorial one. Cultural identities can also turn into political identities 'when governments become parties to them' (Tilly 2003: 609). Here, we are considering a 'we-feeling' loosely defined, a sense of commonality expressed by participants.

and lasted ca. two hours. They were organised around four openly formulated questions only, one using vignettes, a second asking for active participation through free pictorial expression. This helped to make sure that participants enjoyed enough freedom to take the discussion in the directions that are most relevant to them, and to limit research biases. The four questions touched upon different aspects of European integration in the Strasbourg area: regionalism, the border and the figure of the 'Other', EU institutional design and policies, the 'crisis' of European integration, and the meaning of European identity (cf. appendix 2). Each room layout was unique, as the discussions were held in the comfort of each family's living room, but family members were invited to form a semi-circle, with the researcher sitting within this circle, as opposed to chairing from the centre.

Balancing Blurred Allegiances

In the remaining parts of this chapter, I present some of the preliminary results obtained from field research conducted between October and December 2018 in the Strasbourg agglomeration. I draw on extracts from five of the 15 group discussions; all 15 were used for the analysis, and those five extracts were chosen because they are illustrative of patterns that emerged in the overall sample.[5] In the transcriptions below, all names have been changed; // refers to cut-off speech, ... to brief pauses and (...) to longer ones. Italics indicate that words have been left in their original language.

Choosing the 'Other': an Uneasy Task

In constructing cohesive social identities for themselves, individuals rely on opposition to an 'Other', using mechanisms such as stereotyping and flattened categorisations to build social boundaries. Negative stereotyping in particular plays an important role in self-identification, and typical topics for such process include fear as well as dislike. If fear did not appear as a recurrent theme in the discussions – at least in reference to neighbouring French and German communities – dislike and disapproval of behaviours – and occasionally the more extreme form, disgust – were central to all 15 discussions. What appeared as the most intriguing pattern, however, was the absence of a clear 'Other' between *and* within the 15 families. Half of the negative strategies of out-grouping relied on regional differentiation, while

---

5   Qualitative data are difficult to generalize, as samples cannot perfectly match the socio-demographic characteristics of the population. Results should be treated with care and extracts presented in this chapter were chosen because they were illustrative of clearest patterns in our sample.

the other half relied on nationalist discourse. The extract below is derived from a discussion between a family of four, two parents, Véronique and François, with their daughters, Lucie and Julie. Julie left Strasbourg for the neighbouring former region of Lorraine to attend university. The conversation had shifted from their cross-border habits to their support for the French team during the 2018 Football World Cup, when Véronique said that the family also decorated their house with the European flag. She then went on to talk about self-identification.

Extract 1: Middle-Class French Family

Véronique: "Me, I feel closer to Germans.
Julie: Well, for us (looking at her sister) it is a bit different since we live... in fact, no, I do not feel close to Lorrains at all.
(the entire family laugh)
Lucie: No, me I would still say Lorrains. We are closer to Lorrains in mentality. We still have a common history against the... well, between quotation marks, the Germans //
Véronique: Yes, but if you forget //
François (talking to Veronique): Yes, yes, yes, but yes, she is right //
Véronique: No, for me, we have to forget this side of history. For me, regarding the question, I believe that, looking at how we are, regarding work habits, regarding work expectations, well, even me, I would feel closer. How many times did I say, as a joke, 'Well, I think Alsace would be better off as a, how to say this, as a German region or département!' I find us to be closer.
Julie: I would also say Germans rather than Lorrains. Meeting Lorrains every day, I do not share at all the same way of thinking, the same mentality, not the same way...even the way of talking. There are too many things that are changing. The way of driving... Well, too much stuff.
Lucie: Now that I am thinking about it, when I was in Lorraine, I met more with people from Alsace than with Lorrains... because it is true that I take it badly, I get quite offended when a friend, who is not Alsacienne at all, she came to Strasbourg for her studies, and she told me 'No but you, you are résidus d'Allemands [residues of Germans]'. And it is true that, for me, this is the kind of thoughts that are offensive. No, we are not Germans, we remain French. Then yes, there is a proximity with Germany, you cannot deny that, but I do not like it when people call us and say 'No but you are quasi-Germans.'"

In this family, reference to national frames were not obvious, and the choice appeared to be rather between the two neighbouring regions, Lorraine and Baden-Württemberg, as later in the conversation, the distinction was made by mother and daughter between Germany and the *Länder*. The negative stereotyping of *Lor-*

rains as a general category by Julie takes the form of typically vague disapproval of their behaviour: their way of talking and driving. Among each generation, the outgroup strategies differ. Lucie' initial uneasiness at labelling Germans as 'Others' disappears at the memory of an encounter. When she recalls her experience of being out-grouped herself by a friend, only then does she invoke the French national frame, in a typical example of looking-class self (Cooley 1902). Despite clear contradictions, she later expressed strong identification with her region, and then to the supranational, bypassing national identification.

How powerful social interactions are in building the regional self with both French and German nationals alike was palpable in all families, even in those who share a second extra-European nationality. In the case of middle-class French families, this was further strengthened by family memory of war(s). The abstract below comes from a discussion between a family of eight, bringing together three generations: grandparents (Joseph and Madeleine), parents (Christian and Françoise), uncle and aunt (Patrick and Marie) and two teenage boys (Jean and Thomas). In this extract, negative stereotyping targets Germany, while the French, as a general category, are kept at a good distance.

Extract 2: Middle-Class French Family

> Marie: "Me, I think it is because of school that I do not like Germany. All we were seeing, it was factory workers, unemployment, pollution...it was just that...all the Erzählungen in German, it was that, so then, I had a vision of Germany, an Eastern country, the horror you know? It was a bit like...the bottom of Eastern Germany, you know... (she laughs)
> Patrick: Yes. An industrial country.
> Jean: Well, I think for me it is different because I speak as good German as French, almost...well... I speak good German so I feel just as good in France and in Germany. It is as easy to order at a table in France or there. And, actually, I even go more often than you to Germany, I think. Me and Anna, we go to Germany //
> Thomas: every two days.
> Joseph: It is maybe mean what I am going to say, or idiotic, but if I do not go there, it is out of respect for my parents. And if I do not go there, I did my military service in Ackern, nearby.
> Jean: Yes?
> Joseph: Back then, when you were taking a walk with the French uniform, you should have seen the face that old Germans were making!
> Françoise: Ah yes, that....
> Joseph: Ah yes, you got that right! In France, à l'intérieur, we were called 'boches' and then in Germany, we were called 'sales Français' [French scums]!

Jean: Yes, but all this is over now papi! Me, I feel closer to Germans than to ceux de l'intérieur [those from the inside], clearly; I feel better in Berlin than in Paris. (Joseph laughs)
Madeleine: Me, I feel better with les gens de l'intérieur [the people from the inside].
Christian: With my dad, it is not worth discussing, I mean, they are the casques à pointes [spiked helmets]. For us it is funny, because me, personally, I rarely go in Germany. But we put the two of them in bilingual schools and for them, Germany, it is just a continuity of France //
Françoise: Me, I find that Germans are still closer to us than les Français de l'intérieur, still. Culturally, we need to say what needs to be said //
Patrick: Ah! that is funny, that you say we! Because, you, you are a rapatriée [repatriated] anyway!"

In this second abstract, negative constructions are labelled in terms of regional distinctions: generalisation and stereotyping of Germans and Germany, and distancing work from the French national frame by the systematic grammatical use of *"gens de l'intérieur"* to refer to French nationals, and the word *"rapatriée"* to refer to Françoise, who was not born in Alsace. Here, the strong vocabulary used, far from being merely anecdotal, materialises a frontier between the former Alsace region and the rest of France, perceived as such even by those who feel close to France. Generational patterns are made visible through the contrasting interpretations made by Joseph and his grandson concerning the family memory. In-grouping strategies do not follow a clear pattern; with the exception of the grandparents, who express strong regionalist sentiments, the two adult couples and two teenagers disagree in their primary political allegiance. Jean was one of the rare participants in our sample to express a European identity 'first', which he defined as a *"manière de vivre"* [way of living] rather than a feeling.

Europe between Daily Border-Crossing Habits and Great Unknown

It was no surprise that all families were involved in borderwork. But surprisingly, it was among those who did not speak German, namely working class and French families with an immigration background, that borderwork was the most intense. Typical border-crossing activities did not only included occasional hikes or weekly grocery shopping, but daily ice-creams and walks in Kehl, as well as regular afternoons at German swimming-pools. The third extract is taken from a discussion amongst Franco-Turkish local residents. It is exemplary of the appropriation of the border by the local population, but also of the reminiscence of the frontier as an axis of socio-economic inequality in the narratives of the local population.

Extract 3: working-class Franco-Turkish family

Ela: "We go to do grocery-shopping, to eat ice-cream //
Melis: We are just nearby.
Feride: Yes, this is really nice.
Azra: And even more now, with the tram that goes directly //
Feride: and the gardens to take a walk in the summer.
Melis: Yes, we do not have that chez nous [at home].
Feride: In fact, we have a link with Germany, that is the thing that is good. Just the bridge, it binds us...
Feride: and financially, we notice the difference when we shop.
Melis: Oh yes, when it comes to prices...it seems to me it is easier there...there is like a sort of facility...
Halim: Me, I have the feeling that, when you cross the border, it is a bit more developed...the buildings...I like the nature there...it looks clean...We go there with mum, we eat ice-cream. It is nice.
Azra: and with my friend, we go there, to the swimming pool and to do shopping. We could stay here, but it is more (...)
Melis: The mentality of Germans is different than chez nous, too. For people who wear the veil, we are not looked down upon, but in France, we feel it //
Azra: At the swimming pool, we all go there because we have the right to enter dressed.
Halim: There are more freedom there. And fewer unemployed..."

Calls are growing for the reconceptualisation of European identity as a way of *doing*, rather than being (Favell, 2005). Enjoying EU citizenship, crossing borders to go shopping or take a quick swim, not noticing EU logos on tramways on the way: those are signs of a banal Europeanism (Cram, 2001). But if it is clear in our sample that the presence of institutions and opportunities offered by infrastructures have enhanced European behaviours, is it enough to spur emotional identification beyond borders? The abstract below derives from a conversation between six family members. Emilie, the oldest daughter, expresses discomfort at the confusion between the Rhine border and Europe.

Extract 4: Upper-Middle Class French Family

Emilie: "But really, this is not Europe, this is Germany...
Théo: Yes, it is mostly Germany.
Emilie: how to say this...Alsaciens, they are going to speak about Europe, but they are just talking about Germany in reality. Because, I remember, when I was singing at the conservatory, we participated in a concert for the new countries joining the

European Union //
Christine (the mother): Ah yes, I remember!
Emilie: Yes. And that...that was a powerful moment, but still...for.... well, it is not that we do not hear about it, but just that, for Alsatians, in Strasbourg, Europe, it is just about going on foot or with the tram to Germany. Voilà. That is also a bit (...)
Louis (the father): It is true that we are a little bit //
Théo: No, but it is true, I also find that, when there are cultural projects, which are a bit bigger, it is often France, Germany, Switzerland, but well, you never hear about France Norway or even France Spain.
Mathilde: Yes...but then first, the fact that France and Germany are the countries that are a bit.... the authors?
Louis: The founders.
Emilie: Well, but.... what are we, how are we, us, close to Europe, what do we know about it, at the end...except, concretely, our relationships with our close neighbours..."
(silence, then laughs)

The Europeanisation of the border and her family's many border-crossing habits are undermined by Emilie's unease and feeling of discomfort in the face of her own lack of knowledge about the EU. For many respondents in the sample, intense borderwork and banal Europeanism did not automatically equal closeness to Europe, illustrating the clash between concrete and abstracts experience of Europe. Their active European citizenship is balanced by apparent indifference to European integration, and to my surprise, their full awareness of this contradiction. This resulted for many participants in unease regarding their own lack of strong emotional attachment to Europe as a polity. A more direct question about the meaning of a European identity at the end of the discussion was an opportunity for participants to try to 'make sense' of it. The last extract below brings together three sisters and one of their daughters at the kitchen table.

Extract 5: Working-Class French Family

Christine: "We still feel European, right?
(silence)
Nathalie: ...But you, what are you?
Catherine: Well, French first of all...I mean (...)
Nathalie: Me my region...At the beginning, I am Alsacienne. I would put my region first, that yes! I am Alsacienne, then French, and European after.
Catherine: Ah yes! You see, me, European, I would not have thought about it. I would have put Alsacienne and French.
Christine: Me I would almost put France and then Alsace...

> Nathalie: Ah yes? ...and you (she turns towards her daughter) what would you have put first? French or Alsacienne?
> Rose: Bah Alsacienne.
> Christine: Well, it is not that obvious.
> Rose: No, for me, it is logical.
> Nathalie: Even Fogo [the family's dog], on its European passport, it is written 'dog, Alsacien, Français'!
> Catherine: Voilà!"
> (laughs)

As illustrated in this extract, in-group constructions are multi-layered and variable between members of a single family. From the three models of identity presented previously, we can exclude the exclusionary model. Although identification to the region was strong, it should not be confused with regional closure (with the exception of Joseph). For most participants, identification with the region and the nation state follows the strategies of differentiation and inclusion of the nested identity model: French in Germany and *Alsacienne* in France. Yet, it is when looking at the salience of attitudes that the ambiguity – and not simply hybridity – surrounding multiple political identities more clearly emerges. While hybridity refers to a logically composed coherent identity-mix made of different realities, ambiguity as a concept better stresses the context-dependent character of attitudes on identities (Bachleitner et al. 2010). In particular, in our border context, a European attitude only emerges when provoked, either by the moderator or by a provocative family member, despite regular border crossing, so much so that European identity does not appear as a particularly significant referent. Contrary to other regions such as Scotland where a regionalist attitude spurs pro-European feelings, it does not seem to be the case here, despite the immediate proximity of European institutions.

Discussion

To some extent, cross-border regions mirror the working of the EU itself. They share with the EU a complex multi-level governance involving European institutions, nation states, regional authorities, as well as a strong civil society made of non-governmental agencies and citizens' initiatives. The cross-border context has created the potential for peaceful negotiations of social identities between ethnic groups, despite linguistic and cultural differences. I have justified the focus on the Strasbourg agglomeration for the opportunity to study (a) hybrid identities in a pioneering borderland of cross-border cooperation, and (b) a symbolic border of European integration and the seat of several European institutions. In the concluding remarks of this chapter, I would like to go back and sketch two thoughts on the future of regional boundaries in Europe.

Ambiguous Identities, Faded Borders?

People construct their political identities in relation to a range of political and cultural factors, as well as out of their own experiences. In borderlands, those factors vary and clash as the rhythm of everyday life is determined by encounters and border-crossings, but also by difficult memories and stereotypical beliefs. In-group and out-group constructions are continuously re-negotiated. As exemplified above, this happens within families, but more disturbingly, cutting across generational patterns (thus in contradiction to Hipfl et al. 2003; Meinhof 2004). Out-grouping strategies from younger participants with only French nationality were barely more likely than their parents' to be based on supranational and national identification. Strong regional identification was expressed by a majority of participants, distinct from but not in opposition to both France and Germany, as results show that the frontier subsists in border narratives as an axis of contemporary socio-economic inequality. Interestingly, it is only when confronted with the geographical determinism of the border with Germany that the national referent is then reinvoked and gains in legitimacy, with participants leaning towards a concentric circles identity-mix.

Laboratories of European Social Integration

In this multi-layered construction, 'Europe' is not a self-chosen category of identification, which contrasts with the intense usage inhabitants of Strasbourg make of their European citizenship. In the scenario for our discussion, families were invited to order pictures of the city's iconic landmarks from those they were most attached to to those they were least attached to. Interestingly enough, the two pictures illustrating European institutions were, in a majority of cases, placed last. When asked if this was deliberate, to my surprise, many shared that they had already visited the European Parliament: for Europe Day on 9 May, celebrating the anniversary of the 1950 Schuman Declaration, on school trips, or because they used to work as cleaning staff, delivering newspapers, or in the catering service of the European Parliament. "Euro-indifference" alone then fails to explain the detachment that many participants have shown. Despite intensive integration of the borderland and the presence of European institutions, and in full awareness of the resulting political and socio-economic they enjoy, local populations expressed strong mixed feelings towards European integration as a whole. While it is beyond the scope of this chapter to explore the various aspects of Euroscepticism and what is 'going on' behind apparent indifference towards European integration, it appears clearly that borderlands are not only valuable research field to enhance our understanding of the European project in terms of systemic integration, they also offer a unique basis to grasp European unification from below.

Acknowledgement

The research leading to these results stems from the PLATO project (The Post-Crisis Legitimacy of the European Union), which has received funding from the European Union's Framework Programme for Research and Innovation Horizon 2020 under the Marie Skłodowska-Curie Grant Agreement No. 722581.

References

Allport, Gordon W./Mazal Holocaust Collection. (1954): The Nature of Prejudice. Cambridge, Mass.: Addison-Wesley Publishing Company.

Asher, Andrew D. (2005): "A Paradise on the Oder? Ethnicity, Europeanization, and the EU Referendum in a Polish-German Border City." In: City & Society 17/1, pp. 127–152.

Bachleitner, Reinhard/Weichbold, Martin/Aschauer, Wolfgang (2010): "Empirische Befunde zu Raum-, Zeit- und Befindlichkeitseffekten bei Umfragen." In: Bachleitner, Reinhard/Weichbold, Martin/Aschauer, Wolfgang (eds.), Die Befragung im Kontext von Raum, Zeit und Befindlichkeit, Wiesbaden: Springer, pp. 77-136.

Barth, Frederik (1969): Ethnic Groups and Boundaries: The Social Organization of Culture Difference, Oslo: Universitetsforlaget.

Beck, Ulrich (2000): "The Cosmopolitan Perspective: Sociology of the Second Age of Modernity." In: The British Journal of Sociology 51/1, pp. 79–105.

Brewer, Marilynn B. (1993): "Social Identity, Distinctiveness, and In-Group Homogeneity." In: Social Cognition 11/1, pp. 150–164.

Bruter, Michael (2013): "Measuring the Immeasurable?" In: Bruter, Michael/Lodge, Martin (eds.), Political Science Research Methods in Action, London: Palgrave Macmillan UK, pp. 25–46.

Calhoun, Craig (1999): Social Theory and the Politics of Identity, Oxford: Blackwell.

Carey, Sean (2002): "Undivided Loyalties: Is National Identity an Obstacle to European Integration?" In: European Union Politics 3/4, pp. 387–413.

Conradson, David (2005): "Focus Groups." In: Flowerdew, Robin/Martin, David (eds.), Methods in Human Geography: A Guide for Students Doing Research Projects, London: Longman, pp. 128–143.

Cooley, Charles Horton (1902): Human Nature and the Social Order, New Brunswick: Transaction.

Cram, Laura (2001): "Imagining the Union: A Case of Banal Europeanism?" In: Wallace, Helen (ed.), Interlocking Dimensions of European Integration, London: Palgrave Macmillan UK, pp. 233–246.
Díez Medrano, Juan (2003): Framing Europe: Attitudes to European Integration in Germany, Spain, and the United Kingdom, Princeton, N.J.: Princeton University Press.
Díez Medrano, Juan/Gutiérrez, Paula (2001): "Nested Identities: National and European Identity in Spain." In: Ethnic and Racial Studies 24/5, pp. 753–778.
Eder, Klaus (2007): "Cognitive Sociology and the Theory of Communicative Action: The Role of Communication and Language in the Making of the Social Bond." In: European Journal of Social Theory 10/3, pp. 389–408.
Favell, Adrian (2006): "Europe's Identity Problem." In: West European Politics 28/5, pp. 1109–1116.
Favell, Adrian/Etore, Recchi (2009): Pioneers of European Integration. Citizenship and Mobility in the EU, Cheltenham: Edward Elgar Publishing Limited.
Grundy, Sue/Jamieson, Lynn (2007): "European Identities: From Absent-Minded Citizens to Passionate Europeans." In: Sociology 41/4, pp. 663–680.
Herrmann, Richard K./Brewer, Marilynn B. (2004): "Identity and Institutions: Becoming European in the EU" In: Herrmann, Richard K./Risse-Kappen, Thomas/Brewer, Marilynn B. (eds.), Transnational Identities: Becoming European in the EU. Oxford: Rowman & Littlefield, pp. 1-22.
Herrmann, Richard K./Risse-Kappen, Thomas/Brewer, Marilynn B. (2004): "Transnational Identities: Becoming European in the EU." Oxford: Rowman & Littlefield.
Hierro, María José/Gallego, Aina (2018): "Identities in between: Political Conflict and Ethnonational Identities in Multicultural States." In: Journal of Conflict Resolution 62/6, pp. 1314–1339.
Hipfl, Brigitte/Bister, Anita/Strohmaier, Petra (2003): "Youth Identities along the Eastern Border of the European Union." In: Journal of Ethnic and Migration Studies 29/5, pp. 835–848.
Hobolt, Sara B. (2016): "The Brexit Vote: A Divided Nation, a Divided Continent." In: Journal of European Public Policy 23/9, pp. 1259–1277.
Howard, Judith A. (2000): "Social Psychology of Identities." In: Annual Review of Sociology 26/1, pp. 367–393.
Keating, Michael (1998): The New Regionalism in Western Europe: Territorial Restructuring and Political Change, Cheltenham: Elgar.
Kohli, Martin (2000): "The Battleground of European Identity." In: European Societies 2/2, pp. 113–137.
Kuhn, Theresa (2015): Experiencing European Integration: Transnational Lives and European Identity, Oxford: Oxford University Press.

McLaren, Lauren (2006): Identity, Interests, and Attitudes to European Integration, New York: Palgrave Macmillan UK.

Mead, George H. (1934): Mind, Self, and Society: From the Standpoint of a Social Behaviorist, Chicago: University of Chicago Press.

Medeiros, Mike/Gauvin, Jean-Philippe/Chhim, Chris (2015): "Refining Vote Choice in an Ethno- Regionalist Context: Three-Dimensional Ideological Voting in Catalonia and Quebec." In: Electoral Studies 40/December, pp. 14–22.

Meinhof, Ulrike H. (2004): "Europe Viewed from Below: Agents, Victims and the Threat of the Other" In: Herrmann, Richard K./Risse-Kappen, Thomas/Brewer, Marilynn B. (eds.). Transnational Identities. Becoming European in the EU, Oxford: Rowman & Littlefield, pp. 214–224.

Meinhof, Ulrike H./Galasiński, Dariusz (2002): "Reconfiguring East-West Identities: Cross-Generational Discourses in German and Polish Border Communities." In: Journal of Ethnic and Migration Studies 28/1, pp. 63–82.

Orzechowska-Wacławska, Joanna (2017): "Naród, Narodowość, Nacjonalizm We Współczesnej Europie. Baskijskie i Katalońskie Narracje Tożsamościowe." In: Politeja 14/January, pp. 49–70.

Paasi, Anssi (2009): "The Resurgence of the 'Region' and 'Regional Identity': Theoretical Perspectives and Empirical Observations on Regional Dynamics in Europe" In: Fawn, Rick (ed.), Globalising the Regional, Regionalising the Global: Volume 35: Review of International Studies, Cambridge: Cambridge University Press, pp. 121–146.

Rico, Guillem/Liñeira, Robert (2014): "Bringing Secessionism into the Mainstream: The 2012 Regional Election in Catalonia." In: South European Society and Politics 19/2, pp. 257–280.

Risse, Thomas (2003): "The Euro between National and European Identity." In: Journal of European Public Policy 10/4, pp. 487–505.

Risse, Thomas (2010): A Community of Europeans?: Transnational Identities and Public Spheres, Ithaca: Cornell University Press.

Rumford, Chris (2009): Citizens and Borderwork in Contemporary Europe, London: Routledge.

Schelberg, Wim L. G. (2001): "EUREGIO: Pioneer in the Practice of European Cross-Border Co-Operation." In: Administration 49/2, pp. 23–34.

Sénat (2019): "Collectivité européenne d'Alsace" December 6, 2019 (https://www.senat.fr/dossier-legislatif/pjl18-358.html).

Schmidberger, Martin (1998): "EU-Akzeptanz und Europäische Identität im Deutsch-Französischen Grenzgebiet." In: Aus Politik Und Zeitgeschichte B 25-26, pp. 18–25.

Schultz, Helga (2002): "Twin Towns on the Border as Laboratories for European Integration." In:F.I.T. Discussion Paper 4/2.

Sigalas, Emmanuel (2010): "Cross-Border Mobility and European Identity: The Effectiveness of Intergroup Contact during the ERASMUS Year Abroad." In: European Union Politics 11/2, pp. 241–265.
Simmel, Georg (1997): "The Sociology of Space." In: Frisby, David/Featherstone, Mike (eds.): Simmel on Culture: Selected Writings, pp. 137–170. London: Sage.
Tilly, Charles (2003): "Political Identities in Changing Polities." In: Social Research 70/2, pp. 605–620.
van Spanje, Joost/Vreese, Claes de (2011): "So What's Wrong with the EU? Motivations Underlying the Eurosceptic Vote in the 2009 European Elections." In: European Union Politics 12/3, pp. 405–429.
Wilson, Thomas M./Donnan, Hastings (1998): "Border Identities: Nation and State at International Frontiers". Cambridge: Cambridge University Press.

List of Tables and Figures

Figure 1: "Example of advertisement for participants: Strasbourg." Created by Dobler, Camille (2020) for this Publication.

Appendix 1 – Advertisement for Participants

Figure 1: Example of advertisement for participants: Strasbourg

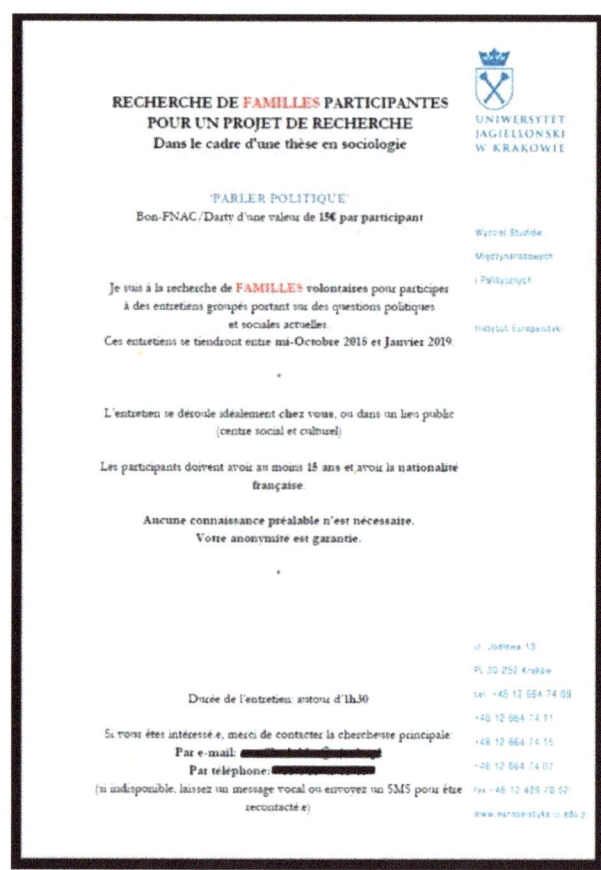

Source: own figure

Appendix 2 – Family Discussion Schedule

Presentation of the session (researcher) & introduction roundtable ~ *10min*
I am giving each of you a few stickers, and I would like to ask you to think about

what summarizes best the region you live in. It can be anything, one thing, several things, you can draw something or write a word. Think a little moment and then I would like you to show your stickers to the others, and to explain to us what you meant and why you picked this. ~ 20min

I am now shuffling your stickers with 7 pictures. I would like you to, together as a group, rank them from what is the most important to you personally (what you are the most attached to), to what is the least important. You can add or remove stickers.

7 photographs include (without legends): European Parliament Louise Weiss building, Council of Europe with European Court of Human Rights, Europe bridge with binational tram over the Rhine, Two riversides Garden, Rhine Palace in the Neudorf district, Strasbourg cathedral, Petite France neighbourhood with Vauban barrage ~ 15min

Now, I would like you to draw something on the stickers: a smiley face! I would like you to think about your current state of mind about the European Union. How do you feel about the European Union right now (if you feel anything at all)? What is the first smiley (or smileys) that come to you mind? I leave you to think for a few seconds. Then please show it one by one to each other and express what you meant and why you chose this smiley face. ~ 20min

Would you have drawn the same smiley a few years ago? How so? ~ 15min

Would you have drawn the same smiley if I had asked you about France right now, and not the EU? ~ 15min

Lately, we often talk about crisis when we talk about Europe. For you what crisis does this refer to? Why do you think about this? Is there anything you want to say about it? ~ 20min

I have a final question. What does it mean to be European? ~ 15min

END – Open floor for remarks & free discussion ~ 30min

II.
Regions in a Turbulent EU – Political and Legal Manifestations

Regional Identities in Europe
Their Manifestations in Constitution- and Policy-Making

Karl Kössler

Introduction

For a certain period of time, starting in the early 1980s, the notion of a 'Europe of the regions' (Keating 2008: 630) generated a lot of support and even enthusiasm, as it became a political slogan used by ardent promotors of regionalism and, for a while, also the European Commission. Around the turn of the millennium, however, the idea of regions as a genuine 'third level of government' within the EU suffered a setback for several reasons, among them the acknowledgement that realising this idea is bedevilled by the enormous diversity of European regions in terms of both legal status and political influence (Weatherill 2005: 15). This chapter is decidedly not about the EU-focused 'Europe of the regions' in the above sense. Instead, it explores European regional identities in broader terms and asks how such identities may manifest themselves, especially in case of regions demanding greater autonomy in both constitution- and policy-making. Section 2 provides a working definition of 'region' and how it relates to autonomy claims and processes of identity formation. Section 3 then explores how the constitutional entrenchment of regional identities interacts with these processes and how such identities may be reflected in policy-making. Section 4 concludes.

European Regions, Autonomy and Regional Identity

The 'Region' as a Contested Term: A Working Definition

As we shall see in this section, the term 'region' has rapidly gained importance in recent decades in politics, academia and in the arenas of both international and constitutional law. It does not come as a surprise, therefore, that understandings of this term have proliferated. In such a context, it is evident that a working definition is needed of what this chapter takes 'region' to mean.

First, the focus is exclusively on regions in a *legal-political* sense. However, as the etymological origin in the Latin word *regio* merely refers to a boundary line, and to the territory between boundaries, the distinctiveness of this territory may manifest itself in a range of quite different ways (Gamper 2004: 3). Depending on the criteria used to set one area apart from others, we may distinguish, for example, historical, cultural and economic regions, which can make it appear that talk of legal-political regions is nothing more than the bias of lawyers and political scientists. There appears to be an emerging consensus, however, that regions should be considered as social constructions rather than natural entities in any case, irrespective of which criteria are used (Keating 1997: 390).

Secondly, we need to narrow the focus within the wider category of legal-political regions. What this chapter looks at are *subnational* regions defined as 'an intermediate territorial level, between the state and the locality' (Keating 1998: 9). This definition does not require, of course, that such intermediate entities are explicitly and literally called regions in constitutional texts, as was the case arguably for the first time with the *regiones* mentioned in Art. 8 of the 1931 Spanish Constitution as autonomous components of the *Estado Integral*. Subnational regions according to this interpretation can be called provinces, cantons, etc. However, the regions addressed in this chapter are certainly not those above the state, i.e. entities bound together by political, economic or military cooperation between states. Until the 1960s, this was arguably the only understanding of 'region' that had common currency, and it is still reflected in terms such as 'macro geo-economic regions' (Ortino 2005: 282) or APEC or ASEAN. While recent decades have witnessed the beginning of a shift towards a more open conception of regions that also includes subnational entities (Keating 1998: 9), Europe has in the meantime seen the emergence of new understandings of legal-political regions. A case in point are cross-border regions, which have been established through sustained bilateral or multilateral cooperation across international boundaries. These regions, often deliberately termed 'Euroregions', which typically follow a functional rationale and/or symbolic rationale of (re-)connecting territories that share some common historical or ethno-cultural identity but are separated by international boundaries, are inherently political in nature. But cross-border regions also have a legal dimension, for instance, under EU law as a consequence of the 2006 EU Regulation on a European Grouping of Territorial Cooperation,[1] in the national law of numerous countries in post-communist Central and Eastern Europe and, importantly in the age of Brexit, under Strand 2 of the 1998 Belfast Agreement. 'Macro-regions' within the EU are an even newer form of legal-political region, albeit one with far weaker legal institutionalisation. With a focus mainly on the economy, they have resulted from

---

1   See Regulation (EC) No. 1082/2006 of the European Parliament and the Council (2006) of 5 July 2006 on a European Grouping of Territorial Cooperation, OJ L210/19, 31 July 2006.

the EU's adoption of macro-regional strategies since 2009 (European Commission 2014). This final kind of region is based on certain common interests and challenges and is itself merely a relatively loose 'network, a modus operandi or, rather, a form of joint action' involving actors from various levels of government levels, not least the subnational regions that this chapter focuses on (Committee of the Regions 2012).

Dynamics of Autonomy and Dynamic Autonomy

As far as the establishment and extension of regional autonomy is concerned, one may distinguish between two basic dynamics that I have explained in more detail elsewhere (Palermo/Kössler 2017: 22–25): a top-down approach of granting limited autonomy primarily for the delivery of regional development policies, as in several European countries such as France during the early post-war period, and bottom-up dynamics with regions themselves claiming distinctiveness and arguing on this basis for some autonomous status. The latter dynamics grew strongly in prominence from the 1970s onwards with the advent of what has been aptly called (Western) Europe's 'regional revolution' (Hopkins 2002: 39). Notable reforms or reform attempts during this decade that involved bottom-up dynamics included the start of a process in Belgium that has so far seen six consecutive state reforms (1970–2011); the adoption in Spain in 1978 of the constitutional framework for the establishment of autonomous communities; and, in the United Kingdom, the (at least attempted) devolution projects for Scotland and Wales (Mény 1982).[2] As this chapter aims to explore the manifestations of regional identities in constitution- and policy-making, it concentrates on cases of autonomy that are characterised by bottom-up dynamics. In other words, it concerns identity-related claims for (more) self-government.

Such demands then typically reflect a dynamic understanding of regional autonomy according to which self-government is a process rather than an outcome. This point relates to a classic controversy on the nature of federalism – a phenomenon that is, despite different views on the exact relationship, closely linked with regional autonomy (Palermo/Kössler 2017: 13–61). After a long period during which Kenneth Wheare's vision of federalism as something inherently static (Wheare 1947: 11) had prevailed, this was challenged in the 1960s, particularly by Carl Friedrich's arguments that federalism should be seen as a dynamic process of federalising

---

2   Both projects eventually failed after post-legislative referendums in 1979. In Wales, only 20.3% voted for devolution, while 51.6% did so in Scotland. But as the latter figure represented merely 32.9% of the registered Scottish electorate, the required threshold of 40% was not reached.

rather than the final outcome of this process. In short, Friedrich pioneered an understanding of federalism as process (Friedrich 1962: 528). For him, federalism was not a 'a fixed and unalterable plan' or 'a static pattern, as a fixed and precise term of division of powers between central and component authorities' (Burgess 2006: 35). The downside of such an approach is of course the uncertainty about when this federalisation process started and where it will end. This point can be illustrated by the way labels of autonomy have been used in the South Tyrolean political discourse over the last three decades. Once the implementation of the reform package agreed upon in 1969 was completed in 1992, a new vision was needed. This was first labelled 'dynamic autonomy', implying bilateral negotiations for additional competences, and then, after 2011, 'full autonomy'. The latter was vaguely defined in a position paper produced by the ruling party, the South Tyrolean People's Party, as reducing national government powers to only a few matters and achieving comprehensive financial authority. Yet, similar to the above-mentioned process of Belgian state reforms, this process remains open-ended and its outcome unclear. What 'full' means in terms of the scope of autonomy of course lies very much in the eye of the beholder.

Regional Identity

Historically speaking, regional identities have often been regarded with a certain disrespect, not least among liberal political theorists. The following quotation from John Stuart Mill testifies to this: 'Nobody can suppose that it is not more beneficial for a Breton or a Basque of French Navarre to be a member of the French nationality than to sulk on his own rock, the half-savage relic of past times. The same remark applies to the Welshman and the Scottish Highlander.' (Mill 1861: 293) The underlying assumption of such disparaging remarks is the belief of traditional liberalism that a nation state built on a monolithic national identity is a necessary prerequisite for democracy. In order to put this monolithic idea of both the nation and the state into practice, the liberal-democratic nation state in this tradition pursues a project of *producing* ex post the uniform national identity, for instance 'Frenchmen' and 'Italians',[3] that its theory of democracy actually *presupposes*. Even though this school of thought has been challenged since its heyday in the 19th century by several movements, especially since the 1990s by the 'liberal nationalism' of Charles Taylor and Will Kymlicka, it continues to exert influence (Norman 2006: 1–3). This is epitomised by the widespread portrayal of national identity formation as something normal and neutral, when it is in actual fact based on a liberal myth

---

3   Regarding France, see Weber (1977). For Italian identity, see Massimo D'Azeglio's often-cited *bon mot*: "We have made Italy, now we have to make Italians", quoted in Hobsbawm (1992: 44).

of neutrality (Kymlicka 2002: 343–347) and on the 'identity fiction' that constructs such identities from the dominant collective identity 'based on power relations and/or the magic of the greater number' (Marko/Constantin 2019: 130). This context is relevant for regional identities in two important ways.

First, the construction of a uniform national identity by 'extending' the dominant collective identity makes it (almost) inconceivable for members of the dominant group that identities other than this fused nationalised one may exist. For instance, 'English Canadians outside Québec largely think of themselves as Canadians-who-happen-to-speak-English, rather than as a distinct national group within Canada' (Miller 2001: 314). And this inability to imagine multiple identities for oneself often entails that regional identities, let alone claims for regional autonomy that are based on such identities, are considered to be something inherently suspicious. Even if national identities tend to dominate in many countries, multiple group attachments at different levels are of course possible and it is increasingly recognised, for instance, 'that European identity can be seen as complementing rather than replacing or conflicting with national and regional identities' (Mendez/Bachtler 2017: 7). Secondly, and something that is often forgotten by movements of regional identity formation, the 'identity fiction' of inflating the dominant identity and simultaneously suppressing others is likewise a problem at the regional level. If autonomy is understood as a tool to empower – whether exclusively or at least largely – the dominant group at the regional level and to reinforce its identity as that of the region as a whole, this replicates the dynamics of 19th-century identity formation in the nation state only on a smaller scale, that is in a 'nation-region' (Kössler 2018). The schizophrenic attitude of reinforcing a supposedly uniform regional identity vis-à-vis the national identity and simultaneously downplaying other identities *within* the region is just as problematic for a vibrant democracy as exclusive identity formation at the national level. At both levels, these processes must demonstrate some degree of pluralism and openness, as they otherwise go against democracy's core idea of multiple claims to representation, i.e. against a notion of a (national or regional) political community 'whose identity will constantly be open to question, whose identity will remain forever latent' (Lefort 1988: 304).

Regional Identities in Constitution- and Policy-Making

Constitutional Entrenchment of Regional Identity

A constitution is 'less something we *have* than something we *are*' (Pitkin 1987: 167) because it is shaped to a significant extent by a distinctive history before the actual process of constitution-making and always inextricably linked with questions of identity. In countries characterised by the presence of both national and regional identities, the constitutive function of a constitution at the national and (where existent) the regional level, i.e. to forge a political community, is equally important as its regulatory function regarding the exercise of public power.

While numerous issues of constitutional design are relevant and indeed fiercely contested where competing identities exist, with territorial demarcation and power-sharing arrangements being only some examples (Kössler 2016), this chapter focuses on the image of the above-mentioned political community, as reflected in constitutional preambles or other programmatic provisions. Importantly, comparative evidence demonstrates that there is an emerging trend for preambles to be granted greater binding force, either independently, as sources of rights, in connection with other constitutional provisions or as guidelines for constitutional interpretation (Orgad 2010; 715–718). In this context of increasing relevance, it is all the more important to recognise that, rather than static images, preambles are better understood as only setting the initial topography upon which the image of the political community is shaped (Jacobsohn 2010: 12). This is because the distance between the preamble and the people for whom it purports to speak always inevitably tends to grow over time (Tushnet 2010: 671). For instance, the preamble of the 1937 Irish Constitution famously still invokes 'the Most Holy Trinity, from Whom is all authority and to Whom, as our final end, all actions both of men and States must be referred', which creates a pronounced dissonance with the reality of an increasingly secular country.

Statements of identity in preambles and other programmatic provisions of national constitutions have been increasingly complemented, during the post-Cold War period, by equivalents at the subnational level. In fact, the processes of shaping the image of the political community at both levels are closely interconnected, sometimes contradictory, and therefore need to be explored in an integrated manner through a multilevel perspective. Regional identities interact with these processes in two ways. First, they often define the creation of a certain image of the political community. Secondly, a constitutional imagination of an identity that had not previously existed may in turn have repercussions on identity formation.

As for the first scenario, pre-existing regional identities were constitutionally entrenched and thus rigidified, for example, in Bosnia and Herzegovina. A good example is the former Article 1 of the 1992 Constitution of the Republika Srpska, which reflected a monistic conception of the identity of this constituent unit in a way that favoured ethnic Serbs over regional minorities. This programmatic article at the very beginning of a constitution adopted on the eve of the Bosnian War (1992-95) defined the Republika Srpska as 'a State of the Serb people and of all its citizens'. Importantly, that statement did not only reflect a certain exclusive conception of identity, privileging one ethnic group, it also had far-reaching institutional repercussions, as it formed the rationale and justification for eschewing power-sharing and entrenching instead highly majoritarian decision-making of the legislative and executive branches of government to the benefit of the Serb majority population. Part of Article 1, the wording 'a State of the Serb people and', was in 2000 eventually declared unconstitutional by the Constitutional Court because it violated the constitutional principle of 'collective equality' of Bosnia's three constituent peoples (Bosniaks, Serbs and Croats).[4] But other legal battles concerning the constitutionalisation of (an exclusive) regional identity have followed. Cases in point are the renaming of municipalities by adding the prefix 'Serbian'[5] or, very recently, the upholding of a National Day of the Republika Srpska considered discriminatory against non-Serbs.[6]

In the second scenario mentioned above, the constitutionalisation of a certain image of regional identity, which had not existed before, in turn influences identity formation. A case in point in this regard is Article 2 of the 1978 Spanish Constitution, a programmatic and ambiguous provision characterised as 'a veritable synthesis of all the contradictions looming during the constitution-making process' and an 'authentic point of encounter between different conceptions of the Spanish nation'.[7] This provision balances 'the indissoluble unity of the Spanish Nation, the common and indivisible homeland of all Spaniards' with the 'right to self-government of the nationalities and regions', thus laying the constitutional basis for what then became known as the state of autonomies (*Estado de las autonomías*) and for the creation of regional identities alongside pre-existing ones such as Catalan and Basque identities. The establishment of the Autonomous Communities (1979-1983) created political spaces for regional parties, which were either newly founded or consolidated under these conditions and proved instrumental in the production and reproduction of regional identities in Spain (Martínez-Herrera 2002). Of course, the regional governments used their new powers in areas such as culture or language to different extents and with varying degrees of success to shape distinctive regional identities. Yet, it can be said that on the whole '[i]rrespective of their relative artificiality or historical depth, all of the autonomous communities embarked on a process of boundary building, which included the invention of symbols as well as the rediscovery and rewriting of regional cultures' (Convers 2000: 130). This process of regional identity-formation eventually again found constitutional expression. Between 2006 and 2011, many Autonomous Communities adopted new statutes, which, despite their subordination to the national constitution, are clas-

---

4   Constitutional Court of Bosnia and Herzegovina (2000), Partial Decision U5/98 III of 1 July 2000.
5   Constitutional Court of Bosnia and Herzegovina (2004), Partial Decision U 44/01 of 27 February 2004.
6   Constitutional Court of Bosnia and Herzegovina (2015), U3/13 of 26 November 2015.
7   Jordi Solé i Tura, one of the framers of the constitution, quoted in Conversi (2000: 126).

sified as constitutional documents in a material sense.[8] These included numerous references to historical kingdoms and traditions, to 'indigenous languages' of the region or flags, monuments and anthems (Delledonne/Martinico 2012). However, in its seminal ruling of 2010, the Constitutional Court famously placed certain limits to identity affirmation in the case of the Catalan statute. The judges held that the national symbols and historical rights mentioned in this statute must be read as referring to the (Catalan) *nationality* as part of the indivisible Spanish *nation* and that Catalonia may be a national reality 'in an ideological, historical or cultural sense' but, unlike Spain, not in legal-constitutional terms.[9]

Regional Identity and Policy-Making

Processes of regional identity formation are reflected in policy-making in a number of areas. But they are arguably intertwined with social welfare policies in a particularly strong way. Apart from redistribution and political legitimation, a third key function of such policies is the creation and/or consolidation of identity(ies) (Palermo/Kössler 2017: 347). While historically 'the welfare state served to "crystallize" the nation-state' (Moreno/McEwen 2005: 2) by engendering a feeling of nationhood, competing regional identity formation has led a number of subnational governments to engage in social welfare. Irrespective of the government level that pursues policies in this area, there is a dialectic relationship between welfare-state policies, on the one hand, and identity and solidarity, on the other: 'Not only does a sense of common identity help sustain the values of mutual help, but the welfare state itself helps foster national [or regional] identity and unity.' (Keating 2001: 40)

Scotland, Flanders and the Basque Country are good examples of the interplay between regional identities and social welfare policies. In the third case, the regional government introduced a minimum income scheme as part of its 1988 Plan to Fight Poverty. This was a pioneering initiative in Spain and mainly inspired by the French *Revenu minimum d'insertion* (Moreno/Arriba 1999). This programme was the fruit of a marriage between identity politics and social policy, as embodied by the coalition government of the Basque Nationalist Party (PNV) and Basque Socialist Party (PSE). With the minimum income, the coalition deliberately and decidedly aimed at strengthening social identity and cohesion within the Autonomous Community.

In Belgium, the economic rise of Flanders (and parallel demise of Wallonia), as ports, service and foreign investments gradually became more important than the coal and steel industry, was soon accompanied by calls for decentralisation of functions including social policy. After this process began with the first state reform of

---

8   Spanish Constitutional Court (2010a), STC 31/2010 FJ 3.
9   Spanish Constitutional Court (2010b), STC 31/2010 FJ 12.

1970, 'autonomous' Flemish social welfare policies came to the forefront of the political agenda and were eventually enabled by another state reform in 1980. While the national government remained responsible for the most important social insurance schemes (e.g. old-age pensions and unemployment insurance), 'social assistance' to individuals was to some extent decentralised (Cantillon 2006). This enabled the Flemish Community, for instance, to complement in 1999 the national programme providing assistance for elderly people with the Flemish Care Insurance, which the Court of Arbitration upheld as constitutional.[10] After the decentralisation of family allowances with yet another state reform in 2011, further transfers of powers regarding social security schemes remain at the heart of efforts to strengthen Flemish identity today – for some, this has been so much at the expense of Belgian identity that these transfers are seen as a key step in gaining independence. That is why further decentralisation of social welfare is looked at in the rest of the country with utmost concern (Swenden 2013: 370).

The link between the assertion of a distinct regional identity and striving for social welfare policies 'of one's own' is particularly evident in the case of Scotland. It is important to note that the creation of the UK welfare state occurred in a post-World War II context in which it was supposed to serve as a powerful new manifestation of common British nationhood, replacing the then-declining Empire in this function (Williams 1989: 162). It was therefore natural that relevant institutions were (re)named the Ministry of *National* Insurance or the *National* Health Service. It was only in the 1960s, when the UK-wide welfare state started to lose its unifying force, that this provided a fertile ground for Scottish parties to pursue an agenda of welfare nationalism. This agenda saw Scotland and not the UK as the primary locus of solidarity. Moreover, the portrayal of Scotland as more socially minded, particularly in comparison to England, became a hallmark of identity formation and underpinned both the thrust in the 1990s for devolution (of certain social welfare policies) and opposition in the 2000s to the privatisation and marketisation of public services (Keating 2012: 221). More than in the Basque Country and Flanders, however, Scottish welfare nationalism has been balanced since the start of devolution in 1998 by a strong counter-current of welfare unionism, which emphasises the need for a common policy framework to equity and a broadly common social citizenship across the UK (Hazell/O'Leary 1999: 43).

Conclusions

'It is fair to claim that no clear account of the concept of autonomy is available.' (Wiberg 1998: 43) This often-quoted statement refers to *territorial* autonomy of re-

---

10   Belgian Court of Arbitration (2001), Judgment No. 33/2001.

gions and not to *non-territorial* autonomy of groups, which is on the whole a much less powerful instrument (Kössler 2010: 265–272). But in addition to 'autonomy' the term 'region' also lends itself to a myriad of different understandings. While there is indeed a proliferation of such conceptions, this contribution has focused exclusively on the *subnational* region and how identities of such regions in Europe are related to constitution- and policy-making.

Regional identity formation is linked with both these dimensions of autonomy in a dialectic relationship. While such identities inspire constitution- and policy-making, these political processes in turn aim at and often succeed in reinforcing regional identities. A certain image of the regional political community, in the above example of the Republika Srpska an exclusive one, not only found its expression in constitutional preambles and other programmatic provisions, it also influenced the subsequent processes of identity formation and provoked resistance from non-Serbs who successfully challenged several constitutional provisions in court. This case illustrates a critical issue for the development of collective identities, especially in the context of power-sharing arrangements for divided societies, which has recently attracted increasing attention, i.e. the systematic exclusion of smaller groups, often referred to as 'others' (Agarin et al. 2018). What has been termed the exclusion-amid-inclusion (EAI) dilemma effectively includes the main groups involved in the previous (but often only frozen) conflict, but at the same time excludes certain 'others'. Going far beyond institutional exclusion, this also has repercussions on perceptions of collective identities. In Spain, the recognition in Article 2 of the Constitution of both a national identity and regional identities, as well as the opportunity for the Autonomous Communities to legally define the latter in their statutes, enabled the reinforcement and sometimes even the initiation of processes of regional identity formation. These processes culminated in the 2000s with several Autonomous Communities revising their statutes. Similar to the Bosnian case, however, the court interpreted and reinforced the national Constitution, especially in the case of Catalonia, as a clear limit. It thus demonstrated the interconnectedness of identity formation in constitutional terms at the national and subnational levels of government.

Not unlike constitution-making, policy-making is also linked with regional identities formation in a dialectic relationship in several areas. This seems to hold true in particular for social welfare policies, which are facilitated by the solidarity bonus generated through a common identity while fostering such an identity at the same time. Yet looked at in detail, this relationship works differently from case to case and has different underlying rationales in each instance. In Flanders, the early but still ongoing calls for the decentralisation of more and more social welfare policies appear to have been inspired in part by a more general desire to 'downsize' the repertoire of powers of the national government. In other words, they seem to some extent instrumental, which is exactly what makes them suspicious to opponents of decentralisation. In comparison, in the case of Scotland, claims for 'ownership' of social welfare policies are arguably far more intimately linked to a continuous narrative on egalitarianism as part of a Scottish (and particularly not English) identity. But even in this case, welfare nationalism, a political force at least since the 1960s, has been faced with a deliberate counter-reaction towards welfare unionism. This once again demonstrates the limits that regional identity formation is typically confronted with, be they legal or political in nature.

While the focus of this paper has been decidedly on regional identities, many of the considerations above regarding the links between constitution- and policy-making, on the one hand, and the formation of collective identities, on the other, are reminiscent of the cumbersome process of developing a European identity. A case in point is the treatment of identity in the Treaty on European Union (TEU), which is central to the EU's constitutional law. Both the preamble and Article 1 of the TEU refer repeatedly the 'peoples of Europe' in the plural, even if reference is made to an 'ever closer union' between them. But on the other hand, Article 9 of the TEU regulates common EU citizenship (in addition to member state citizenship), which was agreed upon in Maastricht in 1992 precisely with a view to the creation of a European political community with a distinctive identity (Kostakopoulou 2007). Moreover, the new Article 2 introduced with the 2007 Lisbon Treaty, aims to establish a community based on shared European values as elements of a common identity. However, the real existence of this community and the enforcement of these values through the procedures of Article 7 have become, in relation to the governments of Hungary and Poland, fiercely debated issues (Halmai 2019). These instances of constitution-making are aimed, as are several other fields of EU policy-making (Prutsch 2017: 18–23), at strengthening a common European identity that can eventually complement national, regional and local identities. At the same time, of course, it needs to be taken into account that 'increasing re-nationalisation tendencies and growing alienation from the "European project"' (Prutsch, 2017: 39) mean this endeavour is now a far greater challenge than it was a few years ago.

References

Agarin, Timofey/McCulloch, Allison/Murtagh, Cera (2018): "Others in Deeply Divided Societies: A Research Agenda." In: Nationalism and Ethnic Politics 24/3, pp. 299–310.
Belgian Court of Arbitration (2001): Judgment No. 33/2001.
Burgess, Michael (2006): Comparative Federalism: Theory and Practice, New York: Routledge.

Cantillon, Bea/Maesschalck, Veerle de/Rottiers, Stijn/Verbist, Gerlinde (2006): "Social Redistribution in Federalised Belgium." In: West European Politics 29/5, pp. 1034–1056.
Committee of the Regions (2012): "Opinion on 'Territorial Cooperation in the Mediterranean through the Adriatic-Ionian Macro-Region'." (Own-Initiative Opinion), 2012/ C 9/03.
Constitutional Court of Bosnia and Herzegovina (2000): Partial Decision U5/98 III of 1 July 2000.
Constitutional Court of Bosnia and Herzegovina (2004): Partial Decision U 44/01 of 27 February 2004.
Constitutional Court of Bosnia and Herzegovina (2015): U3/13 of 26 November 2015.
Conversi, Daniele (2000): "Autonomous Communities and the Ethnic Settlement in Spain." In: Ghai, Yash (ed.), Autonomy and Ethnicity: Negotiating Competing Claims in Multi-Ethnic States, Cambridge: Cambridge University Press, pp. 122-144.
Delledonne, Giacomo/Martinico, Giuseppe (2012): "Legal Conflicts and Subnational Constitutionalism." In: Rutgers Law Journal 42/4, pp. 881-912.
European Commission (2014): "Report from the Commission Concerning the Governance of Macroregional Strategies", COM (2014) 284 Final.
European Parliament/The Council (2006): Regulation No. 1082/2006 of the European Parliament and the Council of 5 July 2006 on a European Grouping of Territorial Cooperation, OJ L210/19, 31 July 2006.
Friedrich, Carl J. (1962): "Federal Constitutional Theory and Emergent Proposals" In: Macmahon, Arthur W. (ed.), Federalism: Mature and Emergent, pp. 528-541, New York: Russell & Russell.
Gamper, Anna (2004): "Regions and Regionalism(s): An Introduction" In: Grabher, Gudrun M./Mathis-Moser, Ursula (eds.), Regionalism(s): A Variety of Perspectives from Europe and the Americas, Vienna: New Academic Press, pp. 3-24.
Halmai, Gábor (2019): "The Possibility and Desirability of Rule of Law Conditionality." In: Hague Journal on the Rule of Law 11/1, pp. 171–188.
Hazell, Robert/O'Leary, Brendan (1999): "A Rolling Programme of Devolution: Slippery Slope or Safeguard of the Union" In: Hazell, Robert (ed.), Constitutional Futures: A History of the Next Ten Years, Oxford: Oxford University Press, pp. 21–46.
Hobsbawm, Eric. J. (1992):"Nations and Nationalism since 1780: Programme, Myth, Reality".Second. Book, Whole. Cambridge/New York: Cambridge University Press.
Hopkins, John (2002):"Devolution in Context: Regional, Federal and Devolved Government in the Member States of the European Union". Book, Whole. London: Cavendish.

Jacobsohn, Gary J. (2010): Constitutional Identity, Cambridge, Mass: Harvard University Press.
Keating, Michael (1997): "The Invention of Regions: Political Restructuring and Territorial Government in Western Europe." In: Environment and Planning C: Government and Policy 15/4, pp. 383–398.
Keating, Michael (1998): The New Regionalism in Western Europe: Territorial Restructuring and Political Change, Cheltenham: Elgar.
Keating, Michael (2001): Nations against the State: The New Politics of Nationalism in Quebec, Catalonia and Scotland, New York: McMillan.
Keating, Michael (2008): "A Quarter Century of the Europe of the Regions." In: Regional & Federal Studies 18/5, pp. 629–635.
Keating, Michael (2012): "Intergovernmental Relations and Innovation: From Co-Operative to Competitive Welfare Federalism in the UK." In: The British Journal of Politics and International Relations 14/2, pp. 214–230.
Kössler, Karl (2015): "Conclusions: Autonomy Beyond the Illusion of Ethno-Culturally Homogeneous Territory" In: Malloy, Tove H./Palermo, Francesco (eds.), Minority Accommodation through Territorial and Non-Territorial Autonomy, Oxford: Oxford University Press, pp. 245–272.
Kössler, Karl (2016): "Beyond Majoritarian Autonomy? Legislative and Executive Power-Sharing in European Regions" In: Matteo Nicolini/Francesco Palermo/Enrico Milano (eds.), Law, Territory and Conflict Resolution, Leiden/Boston: Brill-Martinus | Nijhoff, pp. 39–66.
Kössler, Karl (2018): "Hegemonic or Shared Autonomy? Two Approaches and Their Implications for Constitutional Design" In: Gagnon, Alain-G/Burgess, Michael (eds.), Revisiting Unity and Diversity in Federal Countries : Changing Concepts, Reform Proposals and New Institutional Realities, Leiden/Boston: Brill-Martinus | Nijhoff, pp. 399–423.
Kostakopoulou, Dora (2007): "European Union Citizenship: Writing the Future." In: European Law Journal 13/5, pp. 623–46.
Kymlicka, Will (2002): "Multiculturalism" In: Kymlicka, Will (ed.), Contemporary Political Philosophy: An Introduction, Oxford: Oxford University Press, pp. 343–347.
Lefort, Claude (1988): Democracy and Political Theory, Cambridge: Polity Press.
Marko, Joseph/Constantin, Sergiu (2019): Human and Minority Rights Protection by Multiple Diversity Governance, London: Routledge.
Martínez-Herrera, Enric (2002): "From Nation-building to Building Identification with Political Communities: Consequences of Political Decentralisation in Spain, the Basque Country, Catalonia and Galicia, 1978–2001." In: European Journal of Political Research 41/4, pp. 421–453.
Mendez, Carlos/Bachtler, John (2017): "European Identity and Citizen Attitudes to Cohesion Policy: What Do We Know?" In: COHESIFY Research Paper 1, pp. 1-43.

Mény, Yves (1982): Dix Ans de Régionalisation En Europe : Bilan et Perspectives, 1970-1980 / Publié Par Yves Mény, Avec La Collaboration de Bruno de Witte, Paris: Editions Cujas.

Mill, John Stuart (1861): Considerations on Representative Government, Auckland, New Zealand: Floating Press.

Miller, David (2001): "Nationality in Divided Societies" In: Gagnon, Alain-G./Tully, James (eds.), Multinational Democracies, Cambridge: Cambridge University Press.

Moreno, Luis/Arriba, Ana Gonzalez-de (1999): "Decentralization, Mesogovernments, and the New Logic of Welfare Provision in Spain." In: Instituto de Estudios Sociales Avanzados Working Papers 1, pp. 1–20.

Moreno, Luis/McEwen, Nicola (2005): "Exploring the Territorial Politics of Welfare" In: McEwen, Nicola/Moreno, Luis (eds.), The Territorial Politics of Welfare, London/New York; Routledge, pp. 1-40.

Norman, Wayne (2006): Negotiating Nationalism: Nation-Building, Federalism, and Secession in the Multinational State, Oxford: Oxford University Press.

Orgad, Liav (2010): "The Preamble in Constitutional Interpretation." In: International Journal of Constitutional Law 8/4, pp. 714–738.

Ortino, Sergio (2005): "Functional Federalism between Geopolitics and Geo-Economics" In:

Ortino, Sergio/Žagar, Mitja/Mastny, Vojtech (eds.), The Changing Faces of Federalism: Institutional Reconfiguration in Europe from East to West, Manchester: Manchester University Press, pp. 274–298.

Pitkin, Hanna (1987): "The Idea of a Constitution." In: Journal of Legal Education 37/2, pp. 167–169.

Prutsch, Markus (2017): "Research for CULT Committee – European Identity." In: European Parliament, Policy Department for Structural and Cohesion Policies, pp. 1–44.

Spanish Constitutional Court (2010a): STC 31/2010 FJ 3.

Spanish Constitutional Court (2010b): STC 31/2010 FJ 12.

Swenden, Wilfried (2013): "Conclusion: The Future of Belgian Federalism—Between Reform and Swansong?" In: Regional and Federal Studies 23, pp. 369–382.

Tushnet, Mark (2010): "How Do Constitutions Constitute Constitutional Identity?" In: International Journal of Constitutional Law 8/3, pp. 671–76.

Weatherill, Stephen (2005): "The Challenge of the Regional Dimension in the European Union" In: Weatherill, Stephen/Bernitz, Ulf (eds.), The Role of Regions and Sub-National Actors in Europe, London: Hart Publishing, pp. 1–32.

Weber, Eugen (1977): Peasants into Frenchmen: The Modernization of Rural France 1870-1914, London: Chatto & Windus.

Wheare, Kenneth C. (1947): Federal Government, New York: Oxford University Press.

Wiberg, Matti (1998): "Political Autonomy: Ambiguities and Clarifications" In: Suksi, Markku (ed.), Autonomy: Applications and Implications, Leiden: Brill | Nijhoff, pp. 43–57.

Williams, Fiona (1989): Social Policy: A Critical Introduction, Cambridge: Polity Press.

Scottish Independence
The Romantic Game

Andreas Rahmatian

Introduction

The European Union has recently had to face increased assertions of national identity and regional autonomy in several member states. The 'identitarian' far right is on the rise in a number of countries and is strongly opposed to the idea of the European Union.[1] Growing authoritarian nationalism also pretends to be an answer to global capitalism (Bloom 2016: 50–51). Furthermore, certain regions within EU member states, such as Scotland or Catalonia, are also demanding greater autonomy ever more loudly. It is noticeable that, although both movements (i.e. identitarian politics associated with nation states, and movements for greater autonomy within a state) derive from the same root – nationalism (see Gellner 1998: 3–4, 61) – they can be (but are not always) quite different in their position towards the European Union and in their stance to immigration politics. In Scotland, for example, a rise in nationalism and calls for Scottish independence from the UK (effectively: from England) since the 1960s is evident in the fact that the Scottish National Party (SNP) has held power in the regional (devolved) government of Scotland since 2007. And yet, at least the present leadership of the SNP proclaims to have a rather social-democratic political position[2] and is opposed to a far-right anti-immigration

---

1 This is, however, not really a new development in the EU, see Schlesinger (1994: 325) for a description of this phenomenon about 25 years ago.
2 See, for instance, the speech by the then newly elected SNP leader Nicola Sturgeon on 15 November 2014: 'But in the SNP, the people of Scotland will always know they have a party of true social democracy.' Cited in Sparrow (2014), 'SNP conference – Nicola Sturgeon's speech: Politics Live blog', *The Guardian*, 15 November 2014: https://www.theguardian.com/politics/blog/live/2014/nov/15/snp-conference-nicola-sturgeons-speech-politics-live-blog (accessed 8 March 2019). Historically, the SNP was a conservative party, and from 1934, when it was founded, and at least until 1937 some of its founders, for example Andrew Dewar Gibb, flirted with fascism, albeit rather coyly. See, e.g., Hanham (1969: 163–166).

agenda.[3] It also declares its adherence to a concept of 'civic nationalism' (Kiely et al. 2005: 150). Whatever that may be, it is ostensibly a rejection of a nineteenth and twentieth century-style traditional ethnic and homogeneous mono-cultural nationalism (Gellner 1998: 2–3, 72–73). Such 'traditional' nationalism sees itself as universal, which is incorrect as such, because cultural diversity where nationalism did not play a significant role has inevitably also existed. Furthermore, nationalisms in different nations are necessarily confrontational and in a state of rivalry (Gellner 1998: 6–8, 95). By contrast, the SNP leadership is supportive of membership of the European Union and the EU's anti-nationalist values. It reflects the mood of the Scottish people in this regard: in the EU referendum on 23 June 2016, Scotland voted in all its constituencies and with 62% overall for remaining in the European Union (overall turnout in Scotland: 67.2%).[4]

The following is a perhaps idiosyncratic discussion by a European about Scotland's drive for – and largely already achieved – autonomy within the UK, with an emphasis on the legal perspective. As it concerns the UK, the discussion cannot be divided from 'Brexit', the UK's impending departure from the EU. This chapter concerns the development of autonomy within a country that positioned itself *outside* Europe as a cultural space, and that would not have changed, even if the legal withdrawal from the EU according to Art. 50 TEU had not gone ahead or had been delayed further.

Autonomies Inside and Outside the European Union: The English-Scottish United Kingdom and Brexit

In England, the majority of the English people do not consider themselves part of 'Europe'. British, especially English, people refer to themselves as 'British' in contrast to, and not as a subset of, an identity as 'European'. Furthermore, and possibly in reaction to mounting Scottish nationalism in the context of the 2014 independence referendum, many would also stress that they are 'English'. For them 'Europe' is 'the Continent'. The outcome of the EU referendum was therefore no great surprise; in fact, it was fairly astonishing that the result in favour of Brexit in England was rather weak (53.4%),[5] given the populist anti-immigration and xenophobic agitation, fuelled by the British tabloid press, which characterised the EU referendum campaign.

---

3   See, for instance, Carrell & Watt (2013), 'Nigel Farage and Alex Salmond clash over protesters', *The Guardian*, 17 May 2013.
4   BBC News: 'EU Referendum Results': https://www.bbc.co.uk/news/politics/eu_referendum/results (accessed 8 March 2019).
5   See e.g. BBC website: 'EU Referendum Results':

The Scots generally feel, and usually are, more 'European', but are part of a union with a country that, by contrast, has a non-European orientation. Whether the kingdoms of England and Scotland will remain united, especially in the aftermath of a potentially disastrous 'no-deal Brexit', remains to be seen. Many Scots are sympathisers or supporters of a separatist nationalist movement that seeks Scottish independence but (generally, though not always) sees the future of an independent Scotland in the EU, that is, in a political and economic union of nation states that is designed to overcome nationalism. Thus, the Scottish nationalists largely adhere to a non-nationalist EU. In contrast, other, more traditional right-wing nationalists, such as in France, Germany, Austria or Italy share a similar level of disdain for the EU, but it is precisely this commonality of political perspective that prevents them from cooperating. The idea of 'nationalists of the world, unite!' is a contradiction in terms. This shows two important aspects of nationalism: national identity is not 'natural', but constructed and invented at will, and nationalism involves irreconcilable paradoxes.

The paradoxes of nationalism are also evident in the Brexit debate. Brexit is indeed a peculiarly British, or rather English, problem and is really a matter for the British, with their pathological obsessions with Europe, to sort out.[6] Self-contradictory views are quite common. Even 'remainers', that is, those who oppose Brexit, are not free from nationalistic contradictions. The remainer position combines a nationalistic attitude that emphasises autonomy and uniqueness with a pro-European position. This is true in both England and Scotland individually, and in the UK as a whole. One can draw certain conclusions about developments inside the EU from the experiences around autonomy in a country that will soon be outside the EU.

Unacknowledged Federalism Without a Written Constitution

Are Scottish devolution and the Scottish independence movement really models for the idea of autonomous regions in Europe? This question can be answered immediately with a resounding 'no'. The principal reason is that Scottish devolution is based on a unique constitutional framework that could not, and should not, be followed anywhere else. Any modern federal system with relatively autonomous regions, states, *Länder* or cantons requires a written constitution that sets out the competences of the federation vis-à-vis the separate federal states. Federalism can have a democratising effect by preventing excessive centralisation of political power, but this can only operate properly where there is a constitutional system that distributes powers and has a judicial review system, either through a specialised constitu-

---

6   Fintan O'Toole, 'The paranoid fantasy behind Brexit', *The Guardian*, 16 November 2018.

tional court or (particularly in common law systems) through the ordinary courts assuming the role of a constitutional court.

Britain has no written constitution; that is undisputed. However, what may be controversial is my own interpretation after having lived and worked as a lawyer (mostly as an academic) in both England and mainly Scotland for some twenty years: the United Kingdom has no constitution at all as a modern political and legal system would understand it. What Britain has, is a feudal constitution in the spirit of an *ancien régime*, as in France before the French Revolution of 1789 and before the US Constitution (1787, in force since 1789). The term '*ancien régime*' is characteristically not used by British political scientists, lawyers or historians, because there has been no revolutionary rupture, for England since the Glorious Revolution of 1688-89, and, for Scotland, since the Act of Union of 1707, which formed the Kingdom of Great Britain. The current British system is thus '*ancien*' in substance, at least from a continental European viewpoint (Rahmatian 2018: 620).

The feudal system is part of everyday life in the UK, although ordinary people will often not be aware of it. Every instance of land ownership in England and Wales is technically a feudal tenure in law, whereby the Crown, at the apex of the feudal pyramid, is the only owner of the land, while the user and perceived owner of the individual plot of land or house is actually a vassal or feudal tenant (nowadays usually a tenant-in-chief with no intermediate superiors). Every conveyance of immoveable property in England and Wales today is officially a substitution of vassals – the seller is substituted by the buyer according to the Statute *Quia Emptores* of 1290, which is still in force. Scotland only abolished this system of feudal landholding in 2004. This legal, not only sociological, feudalism is ultimately still the framework of a state that does not have a written constitution (Rahmatian 2018: 620–621 on the legal technicalities): the feudal pyramid, based on landholding and property – mirrored in the ubiquitous and unabated power of the English class system today – is the skeleton of the structure of the British 'state'. It is also characteristic that the term British 'state' is unfamiliar (Loughlin 1999: 35); in Britain one refers rather to the 'Crown' or 'Government' or 'Parliament', as the case may be. Naturally the constitutional and administrative structure of the British 'state' also rests on the feudal system; it could not rest (in law) on a founding constitution, because there is none. The legislative, executive and judicial powers were and are rooted in the feudal structure. The Crown and the British Parliament in particular, including the highest court of the land until 2009, were historically, and still are, creatures of feudalism. The court of final appeal was formerly the House of Lords (technically 'The Appellate Committee of the House of Lords'), whereby the judges or Law Lords were also members of the House of Lords, the Upper House of Parliament. In 2009, a separate Supreme Court was established, which finally achieved proper separation of powers.[7] This features a characteristic of (otherwise historical) feudal systems: the fusion of private law (land ownership) and public law (state institutions), which political theorists of the early modern period so carefully sought to distinguish by conferring sovereignty on the state, the prince, and later the people (public law), and by conferring property on the individual (private law).[8]

I said before that 'naturally' the British constitutional and administrative system rests on the feudal system, but there is almost no reflection on that fact among British public lawyers, and I cannot see much difference between English and Scottish lawyers in this regard. What I have presented is certainly a heretical account of British constitutional law. Legal historians would probably be more forgiving and would remember the statement of the distinguished legal historian Frederic Maitland that 'our whole constitutional law seems at times to be but an appendix to the law of real property' (Maitland 1909: 538).[9] But it would probably not be accepted by traditional British constitutional lawyers. Nevertheless, my understanding has been proven in the course of the Brexit negotiations.

The British system of an unwritten feudal constitution can be interpreted in such as a way as if Britain had a modern democratic constitutional system. In this way, the old feudal *ancien régime* framework is laced with constitutional conventions that emulate a modern constitutional system of the type that emerged following the French Revolution, and as is found in every other EU member state, and as is the tacit assumption underlying the legal and constitutional framework of the EU itself. Recently, British politicians of both principal political parties, have, however, chosen to depart from that method of emulation and pursue a different path. This may be a specific form of English democracy, or it may turn out not to be even that. The feudal constitution itself has (again, naturally) no democratic safeguards enshrined within it (Rahmatian 2018: 624–626). Since the imitation of modern European constitutional democracies is no longer sought, British membership of the EU is incompatible also for this reason, and, for that reason alone, the Brexit negotiations were largely negotiations for their own sake.[10]

Developments in the Brexit process in early 2019 are but a symptom of this conceptual gap. The former British Prime Minister Theresa May could apparently not understand why EU leaders did not agree to a reopening of the negotiations of the withdrawal agreement,[11] after it had been voted down spectacularly in the British

---

7   Constitutional Reform Act 2005, s. 23, and SI 2009/1604: Supreme Court of the United Kingdom: The Constitutional Reform Act 2005 (Commencement No. 11) Order 2009, sch. 2.
8   Montesquieu, *De l'esprit des lois*, book 26, chapter 15 (1995 : 876).
9   'Real property' is the legal term in England for land, immoveable property, which is feudal.
10 I have always made that point in Rahmatian (2017): 'Brexit: Verhandeln um des Verhandelns Willen?' *Der Standard* (Austria), 24 August 2017.
11 Peter Foster, 'Theresa May leaves diplomats in "disbelief" after presenting EU leaders with unchanged Brexit demands', *The Telegraph*, 18 January 2019.

Parliament by 230 votes on 15 January 2019,[12] the worst defeat for any British government in at least 100 years, and then voted down again twice and decisively on 12 and 29 March 2019. The then Prime Minister's stance was the result of a notion of British exceptionalism combined with a complete misunderstanding of the principles of the EU that are based not on some feudal structure with ever-changing constitutional conventions but on a modern constitutional statutory framework which the constitutions of the member states in aggregate and the EU Treaty itself provide. The new UK Prime Minister since 24 July 2019, Boris Johnson, seems to carry this misunderstanding to a new extreme.

However, despite the string of reputation-harming performances in the course of the Brexit debacle, most British politicians still fantasise about the UK being the oldest and best functioning democracy in Europe, with the best legal system in the form of the Common Law. It would not cross their minds that the EU, although it limited British parliamentary sovereignty, acted as a kind of framework that helped the ancient British feudal constitutional system emulate a modern democratic state and ensured that the British constitution continued to be interpreted in the light of a modern liberal and pluralist parliamentary democracy (Rahmatian 2018: 626).

Where does that leave Scotland? Actually, nowhere, but that is partly also self-inflicted. As explained earlier, the British constitutional system is, in essence, still a feudal system. Such a system does not contain any concept of federalism, but provides effectively a centralist state structure. Although Jean Bodin[13] and later Thomas Hobbes[14] developed the modern idea of sovereignty as a clear departure from the late medieval feudal system,[15] they took over the inherent centralism in the feudal system in which any political and legal relation – including the personal element of feudalism, the *homagium*, as well as the proprietary element, the *beneficum* (Ganshof 1964: 72, 75, 106) – ultimately focused on a single vanishing point, the king. This was the case under the French feudal system (and France would became the classic example of a centralist state) and the English system, which imported essentially the (Norman) French feudal system, albeit in a more tightened way (Stenton 1979: 60-61, 64–65). It was only Johannes Althusius (1614) who proposed, against Bodin, the idea of federalism (Althusius 1965: 99). In modern British political and constitutional theory, Althusius is entirely unknown, and Bodin fares little better. Whether greater familiarity with these thinkers would make any change is doubtful, because the concept of federalism, considered rather as an American or German idea, is in any case still unpopular in the UK. Furthermore, for UK politicians and much of

---

12 For a breakdown of results according to political parties and constituencies, see e.g. Antonio Voce and Seán Clarke, 'How did my MP vote on May's Brexit deal?', *The Guardian*, 15 January 2018.
13 Bodin, *Six Books of the Commonwealth*, book 1, chapter 8 (1955: 25–36).
14 Hobbes, *Leviathan*, chapters 18, 22, 26 (1985: 228-239, 274-288, 312–314).
15 Bodin, *Six Books of the Commonwealth*, book 1, chapter 9 (1955: 37–38).

the English people, the idea of a 'federal Europe' or an 'ever-closer' European Union is almost horrific (Schlesinger 1994: 319) – something that contributed to the Brexit result.

Nonetheless, in 1999 the Scotland Act 1998 established the Scottish Parliament.[16] This Act introduced to the UK what is usually called 'asymmetrical devolution', and could more prosaically be termed 'unrecognised limping federalism'.[17] It is limping because there is no equivalent English Parliament; the British Parliament in Westminster covers English affairs, and there is little indication of a political will to change that. It is unrecognised because, rather than laying out a federal structure in a written constitution, these arrangements were rather grafted ad hoc onto the centralist unwritten constitution of the whole of the UK. The Scotland Act 1998 that devolved certain powers to Scotland, a federalisation in all but name, is, however, still an Act of the UK Parliament. According to classical British constitutional doctrine (the theory of parliamentary sovereignty), Parliament cannot bind subsequent Parliaments, which can thus amend or abolish any Act, including the Scotland Act, at will at any time and thereby eliminate the Scottish Parliament and end Scottish devolution. There are no higher-ranking constitutional norms. Recent legislation has nevertheless emphasised that, in this particular case, such a move would not be possible,[18] and the key constitutional decision of the Supreme Court in *Miller* confirmed that in 2017.[19] However, though that may be the law, politics may take a different view. The Scotland Act and Scottish devolution are based on a self-imposed limitation of parliamentary sovereignty by the Westminster Parliament in London. This self-limitation is the same legal construct that made Britain's EU membership and acceptance of supranational EU law possible, and exactly this is in the course of being dissolved. The cited case of *R. (Miller)* incidentally stresses the foundational centralism of the UK: it makes clear that neither the Scottish Parliament, nor the Welsh and Northern Irish Assemblies have a legal veto on the UK's withdrawal from the EU.[20] Whatever Scottish nationalists may want to believe, ultimately Scottish devolution can only exist as long as it secures the grace of the British Parliament in London. This is different from a proper written federal constitution, which all Parliaments, national and regional, would be subjected to.

Many Scots may cherish their devolution, but what Scotland has done with its devolved status has so far been unimpressive. The legislative competence of the

---

16   Scotland Act 1998, s. 1.
17   Scottish nationalists often see devolution as a defective compromise, see e.g. Maxwell (2013: 38–39).
18   Scotland Act 1998, s. 63A.
19   R. (on the application of Miller) v. Secretary of State for Exiting the European Union [2017] HRLR 2, para. 149.
20   R. (on the application of Miller) v. Secretary of State for Exiting the European Union [2017] HRLR 2, para. 150.

Scottish Parliament is actually rather wide,[21] but a look at the titles of the fifteen Acts of the Scottish Parliament passed in 2018 may give an idea of the problems that seem primarily to concern the Scottish legislature: they do not strike one as having a particularly nation-building quality, but are typical of a regional assembly.[22] It is true that the Scottish Parliament has no competence to legislate on Brexit-related matters,[23] but it is astonishing that the SNP, which has formed the Scottish Government since 2007 and has Scottish independence as its declared political aim, has so far not made any serious attempts at preparing for a possible independent Scotland outside the existing legislative constraints. That could include establishing independent informal foreign relations with smaller EU member states (and learning foreign policy from them), or developing greater economic autonomy, for example, by encouraging IT and other high-skills service industries to settle in Scotland, and so forth. An unsympathetic analysis may regard the idea of Scottish independence as a case of romantic political irrationalism or a strategic political dream, and it is not clear whether it is intended that the dream should ever genuinely be fulfilled. Scotland undoubtedly has a separate national identity, expressed by – or made up by – a range of cultural features: education, language (Scots and Gaelic), a different legal system partially based on the historical continental European *ius commune* deriving from Roman Law (White et al. 2013: 21), a cultural outlook generally more directed to Europe, but at the same time influenced

---

21 Scotland Act 1998, ss. 29-30, and on retained EU law after Brexit, see s. 30A.
22 Prescription (Scotland) Act 2018 (asp 15), Historical Sexual Offences (Pardons and Disregards) (Scotland) Act 2018 (asp 14), Housing (Amendment) (Scotland) Act 2018 (asp 13), Islands (Scotland) Act 2018 (asp 12), Land and Buildings Transaction Tax (Relief from Additional Amount) (Scotland) Act 2018 (asp 11), Civil Litigation (Expenses and Group Proceedings) (Scotland) Act 2018 (asp 10), Social Security (Scotland) Act 2018 (asp 9), Forestry and Land Management (Scotland) Act 2018 (asp 8), Offensive Behaviour at Football and Threatening Communications (Repeal) (Scotland) Act 2018 (asp 7), Budget (Scotland) Act 2018 (asp 6), Domestic Abuse (Scotland) Act 2018 (asp 5), Gender Representation on Public Boards (Scotland) Act 2018 (asp 4), Wild Animals in Travelling Circuses (Scotland) Act 2018 (asp 3), Writers to the Signet Dependants' Annuity Fund Amendment (Scotland) 2018 (asp 2), Edinburgh Bakers' Widows' Fund Act 2018 (asp 1).
23 See the Supreme Court Decision The UK Withdrawal From The European Union (Legal Continuity) (Scotland) Bill - A Reference by the Attorney General and the Advocate General for Scotland (Scotland), [2018] UKSC 64, para. 52: '... An enactment of the Scottish Parliament which prevented ... subordinate legislation from having legal effect, unless the Scottish Ministers gave their consent, would render the effect of laws made by the UK Parliament conditional on the consent of the Scottish Ministers. It would therefore limit the power of the UK Parliament to make laws for Scotland ... The imposition of such a condition on the UK Parliament's law-making power would be inconsistent with the continued recognition, by section 28(7) of the Scotland Act, of its unqualified legislative power.' This subordinate legislation would particularly be legislation following the withdrawal of the UK from the EU.

by Presbyterianism as a distinctive variant of Protestantism.[24] However, it appears that blaming the central government in London and insisting on autonomy when it suits the Scots is politically easier[25] than a well-planned, reasonable (and perhaps non-nationalistic) and systematic preparation for full political independence. That may even apply after Brexit: Scottish allegiance to the UK may prevail over allegiance to the EU.

Parallels between the 2014 Scottish Independence Debate and the UK Brexit Debate of 2016

The 2014 Scottish independence referendum also revealed a contradictory attitude. It was never quite clear whether the governing SNP was doing more than indulging in a romantic fantasy. The main disturbing feature of this referendum campaign was not so much the possibility of independence of Scotland from the UK, but rather the complete and naïve unpreparedness of the Scottish Government for this step, shrouded in self-centred nationalistic rhetoric.[26] First, and, for a lawyer, fundamentally important, there was neither a draft constitution for the envisaged new independent state nor even any advanced preparations (Rahmatian 2018: 630).[27] It was claimed that nothing would change much for Scotland after independence, especially not as far as the economy is concerned.[28] It was said that after independence, Scotland would retain the (English) pound as its currency.[29] Scotland, being in the EU via the UK, would remain in the EU as an independent country as well. The last claim should be remembered by Scots who now (rightly) accuse the UK Government of incompetence in legal matters during the Brexit negotiations. The position of the Scottish SNP Government about EU membership of Scotland after

---

24   On the tense relationship between the Presbyterian communities and the Roman Catholicism of the Irish immigrants in the nineteenth and early twentieth centuries, see, e.g. Hanham (1969: 19–20).
25   In the words of one Scottish Nationalist: 'Scotland's subordinate political status' frustrates 'Scottish initiative' in relation to its own welfare and economic policy, see Maxwell (2013: 55). When this was published, the Scottish Parliament had existed for over twelve years.
26   Rahmatian (2014) 'Schottland: Das hässliche Gesicht des Nationalismus', *Die Zeit Online*, 16 September 2014.
27   It is telling that nobody, apart from myself, raised this point as an essential issue, which shows that Scots lawyers are also totally socialised in the deficient concept of the unwritten constitution of the UK.
28   Salmond (2014): 'St. George's Day Speech: Full Text', *New Statesman*, 23 April 2014.
29   For example, S. Carrel, 'It's Scotland's pound and we're keeping it, says Alex Salmond: First minister indicates independent Scotland would use sterling even if formal sterling zone was rejected by UK government', *The Guardian*, 7 August 2014. On the – rather grotesque – effects of such a decision (if approved by England, which seemed very unlikely), see Rahmatian (2012: 337).

independence was not only unquestionably wrong under international law and the rules on state secession (Crawford 2007: 383; Rahmatian 2012: 336), the EU itself also pointed out several times that this view is incorrect, and an independent Scotland would have to reapply for EU membership.[30] The Scottish SNP Government, now very EU-friendly, then rejected out of hand statements made by the EU that other member states could block Scotland's accession to the EU.[31] Since there are many conspicuous parallels between the lofty and disingenuous declarations made during the Scottish independence referendum in 2014 and in the Brexit process from 2016 onwards, one can conjecture that the current pandemonium around Brexit gives a good indication as to how the Scottish independence process would have been if the referendum result in 2014 had been in favour of independence (Rahmatian 2018: 633). However, maybe the Scottish Government did not quite want to win it anyway, just as the proponents of Brexit within the ruling Conservative Party in the UK did not quite want to win the Brexit referendum, either, but only sought political gain in a personal gamble.[32]

In Brexit Britain, Scotland is now probably one of the calmer parts of the country, but that should not make one forget the period of the run-up to the Scottish independence referendum. There was a highly nationalistic atmosphere at that time, no trace of the purported civic nationalism. Furthermore, an inclusive identity-creating nationalism is in any case a contradiction in terms: the making of identity (expressed in an independent Scottish state) always involves inclusion and exclusion, a distinction between 'them' and 'us' (Schlesinger 1994: 321). Accordingly, the whole country was rather engulfed in the usual traditional, hostile and toxic nationalism, and a few elements showed obvious parallels to fascism,[33] though the Scottish Government did not associate itself with these dark forces. This nationalism was then primarily directed at the English – for no justifiable reason – but, if the referendum result had been in favour of independence, it could have turned

---

30 For example, European Parliament, Parliamentary Questions, Subject: Status of the United Kingdom if Scotland leaves, 29 October 2012, available at: http://www.europarl.europa.eu/sides/getDoc.do?type=WQ&reference=P-2012-009862&language=EN (accessed 8 March 2019). See also: *Letter of the then EU Commission President José Manuel Barroso to Lord Tugendhat, House of Lords*, 10 December 2012.

31 Jim Pickard and Mure Dickie, 'EU Commission president says Scotland membership not automatic', *Financial Times*, 16 February 2014.

32 Hinsliff, (2016): 'A pyrrhic victory? Boris Johnson wakes up to the costs of Brexit', *The Guardian*, 24 June 2016.

33 On historical interchanges between Scottish Nationalists and the Nazis in the 1930s and 40s, see Bowd (2013: 138–181). However, even during that time, only a small number of Scots associated themselves with fascism. An outline of the current weird curiosities of Scottish Nationalism is contained in Bowd (2013: 265–267).

quickly against Europeans and other perceived non-Scottish elements as well.[34] This demonstrates again that kindred nationalists – here English and Scottish nationalists – may merge in a nuclear fusion, with the emission of deadly energy as a result, but are unable to work together constructively.

Against the Mainstream of the EU Integration Agenda: Regionalisation as a Non-Nationalistic Approach

Scottish devolution in the UK, which has now left the EU, is not a convincing model for the development of autonomous regions within the EU, but perhaps rather an example of how not to do it. A negative example of this kind can also give guidance points. Furthermore, the Brexit process has unintentionally strengthened the position of the EU as the better political and economic entity for Europe in principle: not even the most brilliantly devised EU-advertising campaign could have made a better case for the EU than has the chaotic British Brexit disaster. The most pallid and uncreative EU-apparatchik in Brussels need only point to the UK after Brexit as a possible alternative to the EU and will have won the argument at once. In this regard, Europeans can be grateful to the British.

However, if the EU wants to survive in the coming decades, it cannot rely on an unexpected boost accidentally provided by the inabilities of a parting member. Rather it is necessary for the EU to adopt a more flexible approach to the process of political and economic integration. Sometimes further integration is expedient, sometimes not, and even a certain reversal must be possible if necessary. The constitutional body of the EU must allow these adaptabilities. In the same way as the ribs must be flexible to allow the body to breathe in and out, otherwise it cannot live, the constitutional and political framework of the EU must allow the EU to breathe as an entity, otherwise it cannot live. Nobody wants to destroy the ribcage, but a static ribcage is a statue, not a living being. A sclerotic EU is a dying EU, a danger that we face now.

For that reason, legal and economic integration in the EU must happen in phases that are, at least in principle, partly reversible. This is a good basis for increased regionalisation in Europe, and that, in turn, allows for a better recognition of autonomous regions within the EU. Pressure for further legal and economic integration still underpins the official agenda of the EU administration, but this could actually

---

34 An insight is provided by the views of Jews in Scotland at the time: 'For now they [the Scottish nationalists] are restricting themselves to propaganda and signposts in Gaelic that no one really needs. But as a Jew who has relatively short roots in Scotland, and with friends and family in England and Israel, as much as I feel Scottish on the outside, I fear that one day people will start asking: "How Scottish are you?"', quoted in Pfeffer (2012): 'Jews on Scottish independence: More faintheart than Braveheart', *Haarez*, 26 October 2012.

lead to the destruction of the fundamental European idea: the prevention of war between France and Germany and between EU member states generally. This is the essence of the EU, and the four freedoms are supposed to contribute to the realisation of this ideal (an aspect that is rarely understood in the UK, hence the Brexit calamity). The more one pursues legal and economic integration and unification across Europe, the more one impedes and endangers the fabric and framework of a union of European states. Further legal unification prompts a tendency of the EU member states to move away from one another. Further (imposed) unity causes further diversity, and, at the same time, a certain level of diversity effects and strengthens unity. This process appears somewhat dialectical, but is actually an ultimately unresolvable paradox, a phenomenon that I have called the 'Herderian paradox', after Johann Gottfried Herder (1744-1803). It applies in relation to already harmonised areas of the law in the EU, such as copyright, and to areas where there is more national diversity, as in the case of European private law (Rahmatian 2016: 919–920) or regulatory rules for the economy. The unity through, and within, diversity is then indeed what Herder saw as the overarching humanist culture that unites mankind, not only in Europe. Unity is actually created and made possible through diversity. Herder does not advocate a value relativism, but a co-existence of different values in different cultures (Berlin 1991: 84).

For Herder, there a distinctive 'national character' ('*Nationalcharakter*') of peoples (Herder *Ideen*, II, 9, iv, 1989: 369–370), which he explained in his philosophy of history, particularly in his *Ideen zur Philosophie der Geschichte der Menschheit* ('Ideas on the Philosophy of the History of Mankind') (1784–1791) (see also Rahmatian 2016: 915-917). Herder's 'national character' is the outcome of a mystical combination of history and tradition, education and civilisation, but also of nature and climate.[35] However, despite the dissimilarity of peoples in their seemingly irreconcilable plurality there is still a 'general spirit of Europe' ('*Allgemeingeist Europas*'), which will gradually extinguish the national characters (Herder *Ideen*, IV, 16, vi, 1989: 705–706). Herder even once uses the term 'European Republic' (*Europäische Republik*) (Herder *Ideen*, IV, 16, 1989: 678). But, contrary to Herder's view, a 'national character' does not derive from nature, culture and tradition, language, education and art. National character is rather deliberately created, a social construct of politics, economics and the media, and frequently consciously fabricated for political ends. It is also often given some irrational mystical spiritual force, which allows it to avoid rational critique.

Humans create the various national characters by behaving as if they were real. In this way the national character can become an important political factor. Britain is a case in point: it is, also culturally, not really a part of Europe, because it chooses not to be, particularly England. However, that may change, and it has indeed been

---

35   Herder *Ideen*, II, 7, iii (1989: 268–270); II, 7, v (1989: 280–281); II, 8 (1989: 298–299).

different in the past. A 'national character', as with individual identities, ought not to be a concept that is fixed and imposed from above ('them' and 'us' as a self-definition against 'them'); for example, a Jew may not be concerned much about his or her Jewishness, but the anti-Semites will be, and that forces him or her into a certain role. The identity of people and peoples should rather be an ever-changing performative act of the self and can therefore only work in democratic systems which allow free discourse and exchange in a stable political space as a prerequisite. This is an aspect of the Herderian paradox of the European 'unity in diversity' of different nations with their different 'characters'. The nations may seek to define and reassess their (imagined and created) identities as they see fit in an ongoing debate.

This concept can also be a model for the regionalisation of Europe in the European Union in a way that does not depend on ethnicities and languages; it is therefore not nationalism in the traditional sense of the past two centuries. Under such a design, nation states would provide the constitutional and legal framework of the regions, particularly in relation to constitutional and social security rights, which would also have to be transportable across the EU. The idea of autonomous regions as a separate concept would gradually dissolve in an all-encompassing regionalisation of Europe.

Nationalists in autonomous regions in Scotland and Catalonia, for example, unconsciously apply this idea already. When nationalist movements appear more EU-friendly than the central states in which they are situated, they invoke the EU (when it suits them) as a political counterbalance to the central government to preserve or even extend their autonomy. In this way they appeal to the idea of a Europe of the regions. However, their position also contains the seeds of demise of a Europe of the regions, because that idea is in contrast to their nationalist endeavours to create traditional independent nation states. If such endeavours are successful, and the new state subsequently becomes a new member of the EU, it may well turn into a quite EU-critical member, because the EU will then be seen as interfering in the new nation state. It should not be forgotten that the principal objective of separatists and nationalists is obtaining unfettered power over the region they claim independence for. This could be seen in the Scottish independence referendum in 2014: the SNP planned to keep the British monarchy for an independent Scotland (Scottish Government 2013: 21, 45, 340), had no constitution in place for the possible new state, and all political parties in the Scottish Parliament except the SNP and the small Scottish Green Party were against independence. (How could a constitutional convention be formed for passing a Scottish constitution under these circumstances?) The result could have been a one-party state in form of an absolute monarchy, at least for an interim period. Political theorists should know that any assumptions about an innate benevolence in human nature are entirely out of place in politics, hence the absolute requirement for checks and balances in a constitutional system.

At the moment, the EU-friendliness of the Scottish nationalists is also a vehicle for distinguishing the Scots from the English (Ichijo 2004: 86). A central problem when nationalists are confronted with defining their nationalism in positive terms is: What does characterise Scottishness? The nationalists' positive attitude towards the EU is also a strategic tool for achieving Scottish independence, since separating from the UK but staying in, or rapidly joining, the EU is seen as a means of obtaining great political change, but risking little economic disruption (Ichijo 2004: 91-92). The experience of the position of the EU during the Scottish independence referendum in 2014 should have prompted Scottish nationalists to abandon this fantasy: in relation to existing members the EU may tend towards a diminution of the importance of the nation state, but in relation to aspiring members, it applies faithfully the classical rules of international law on the definition and secession of states, and on membership of international organisations.

Conclusion

It has been shown that the discourse in the Scottish independence referendum in 2014 shared many elements of irrationality with the Brexit referendum two years later. Both are symptoms of generally irrational, populist and romantic nationalisms, whether against the central state or the EU, but in each case in relation to something bigger against whom the little plucky underdog tries to assert his self-determination, without a clear notion as to what actually should be determined. A consensus can quickly be found in the form of hatred towards refugees, xenophobia and racism, which then become the wretched areas of agreement. In this context, a particular national character is also often established or unearthed. While this national character does not have the sublime cultural features Herder wanted to see, politics would be ill-advised to deny the existence of such national characters, which are there because too many people(s) believe they exist. Nationalism nevertheless remains an objectionable and dangerously destructive force. It does not become better if it is renamed 'civic nationalism' or 'patriotism', and Arthur Schopenhauer's snarky comments about nationalism (*Nationalstolz*) (Schopenhauer, 1976: 66)[36] are as valid today as they were in the nineteenth century. (One should also remember François Mitterrand's words in 1995: '*Le nationalisme, c'est la*

---

36   And also his important observation: 'Incidentally, individuality prevails by far over nationality, and with a given person the former deserves a thousand times more consideration than the latter.'

guerre!')³⁷ However, nationalism will not disappear if it is suppressed or disavowed in the constitutional framework of the EU and its policies on integration.

At the same time, cultural differences should not be deformed or destroyed by way of centralisation and unification. The major political challenge of the twenty-first century will be the reconciliation of cultural differences in a greater unity (and not only confined to Europe), based on mutual respect and appreciation. This paradox cannot, and should not, be resolved, but it may subdue nationalist forces. The idea of a European unity of cultures in their diversity did not emerge only with early German Romanticism. Gotthold Ephraim Lessing, the greatest writer of the late German Enlightenment, demonstrated it in a beautiful way in his play *Minna von Barnhelm* (Act 4, Scene 2, Lessing 1853: 221):

> 'Riccaut de la Marlinière: [...] – Mademoiselle parle français? Mais sans doute; telle que je la vois! – La demande était bien impolie; vous me pardonnerez, Mademoiselle. –Das Fräulein (Minna von Barnhelm): Mein Herr –Riccaut: Nit? Sie sprek nit Französisch, Ihro Gnad? - Das Fräulein: Mein Herr, in Frankreich würde ich es zu sprechen suchen. Aber warum hier? Ich höre ja, daß Sie mich verstehen, mein Herr. Und ich, mein Herr, werde Sie gewiß auch verstehen; sprechen Sie, wie es Ihnen beliebt.'

References

Althusius, Johannes (1965): The Politics of Johannes Althusius, Carney, Frederick Smith (ed.), London: Eyre & Spottiswoode.

BBC News (2016): "EU Referendum Results" (https://www.bbc.co.uk/news/politics/eu_referendum/results)

Berlin, Isaiah (1991): "Alleged Relativism in Eighteenth-Century European Thought." In: Hardy, Henry (eds.), The Crooked Timber of Humanity, London: Fontana Press, pp. 70–90.

Bloom, Peter (2016): "Authoritarian Capitalism in the Age of Globalization", Cheltenham: Edward Elgar.

Bodin, Jean (1955): "Six Books of the Commonwealth". Tooley, Michael. J. (ed.), Oxford: Basil Blackwell.

Bowd, Gavin (2013): Fascist Scotland. Caledonia and the Far Right, Edinburgh: Birlinn.

---

37 Mitterrand, 'Le nationalisme, c'est la guerre!' (INA, Institut François Mitterrand): https://fresques.ina.fr/mitterrand/fiche-media/Mitter00129/le-nationalisme-c-est-la-guerre.html (accessed 27 January 2019).

Carrall, Severin/Watt, Nicholas (2013): "Nigel Farage and Alex Salmond clash over protesters" In: The Guardian, 17 May 2013 (https://www.theguardian.com/politics/2013/may/17/nigel-farage-alex-salmond-clash-protesters).

Carrel, Severin (2014): "It's Scotland's pound and we're keeping it, says Alex Salmond: First minister indicates independent Scotland would use sterling even if formal sterling zone was rejected by UK government" In: The Guardian, 7 August 2014

Crawford, James R. (2007): The Creation of States in International Law, Oxford: Clarendon Press.

European Parliament (2012): Parliamentary Questions, Subject: Status of the United Kingdom if Scotland leaves, 08 March 2019, (http://www.europarl.europa.eu/sides/getDoc.do?type=WQ&reference=P-2012-009862&language=EN).

Foster, Peter (2019): "Theresa May leaves diplomats in "disbelief" after presenting EU leaders with unchanged Brexit demands" In: The Telegraph, 18 January 2019.

Ganshof, Francois (1964): Feudalism, 3rd. Ed., Grierson, Philip (ed.). London: Longman.

Gellner, Ernest (1998): Nationalism, London: Phoenix.

Hanham, Harold John (1969): Scottish Nationalism, London: Faber and Faber.

Herder, Johann Gottfried (1989): Ideen zur Philosophie der Geschichte der Menschheit, Bollacher, Martin (eds.), Frankfurt: Deutscher Klassiker Verlag.

Hinsliff, Gaby (2016): "A pyrrhic victory? Boris Johnson wakes up to the costs of Brexit" In: The Guardian, 24 June 2016.

Hobbes, Thomas (1985): Leviathan, Macpherson, Crawford (ed.), London: Penguin.

Ichijo, Atsuko (2004): Scottish Nationalism and the Idea of Europe: Concepts of Europe and the Nation, Abingdon (Oxon): Routledge.

Kiely, Richard/Bechhofer, Frank/McCrone, David (2005): "Birth, Blood and Belonging: Identity Claims in Post-Devolution Scotland." In: The Sociological Review 53/1, pp. 150–171.

Lessing, Gotthold Ephraim (1853): "G. E. Lessing's gesammelte Werke. Neue Rechtmäßige Ausgabe, Zweiter Band". Leipzig: G. J. Göschen'sche Verlagshandlung.

Loughlin, Martin (2003): "The State, the Crown and the Law" In: Sunkin, Maurice. (eds.), The Nature of the Crown : A Legal and Political Analysis, Oxford: Oxford University Press, pp. 33–76.

Maitland, Frederic W. (1909): "The Constitutional History of England". Cambridge: Cambridge University Press.

Maxwell, Stephen (2013): Arguing for Independence: Evidence, Risk and the Wicked Issues, Edinburgh: Luath Press.

Mitterrand, Francois (1995): "Le nationalisme, c'est la guerre!", INA, Institut François Mitterrand, January 27, 2019 (https://fresques.ina.fr/mitterrand/fiche-media/Mitter00129/le-nationalisme-c-est-la-guerre.html).

Montesquieu, Charles de Secondat (1995): De l'Esprit Des Lois, Versini, Laurent (ed.), Paris: Gallimard.

O'Toole, Fintan (2018): "The paranoid fantasy behind Brexit" In: The Guardian, 16 November 2018 (https://www.theguardian.com/politics/2018/nov/16/brexit-paranoid-fantasy-fintan-otoole).

Pfeffer, Anshel (2012): "Jews on Scottish independence: More faintheart than Braveheart" In: Haarez, 26 October 2012.

Pickard, Jim/Dickie, Mure (2014): "EU Commission president says Scotland membership not automatic" In: Financial Times, 16 February 2014.

Rahmatian, Andreas (2012): "The English Pound in an Independent Scotland'." In: Journal of International Banking Law and Regulation 27/9, pp. 336–339.

Rahmatian, Andreas (2014): "Schottland: Das hässliche Gesicht des Nationalismus" In: Die Zeit Online, 16 September 2014.

Rahmatian, Andreas (2016): "European Copyright Inside or Outside the European Union: Pluralism of Copyright Laws and the 'Herderian Paradox.'" In: IIC - International Review of Intellectual Property and Competition Law 47/8, pp. 912–940.

Rahmatian, Andreas (2017): "Brexit: Verhandeln um des Verhandelns Willen?" In: Der Standard (Austria), 24 August 2017.

Rahmatian, Andreas (2018): "Brexit and Scotland: Centralism, Federalism or Independence?" In: European Review 26/4, pp. 616–647.

Salmond, Alex (2014): "St. George's Day Speech: Full Text" In: New Statesman, 23 April 2014.

Schlesinger, Philip (1994): "Europeanness: A new cultural battlefield?" In: Hutchinson, John/Smith, Anthony D. (eds.), Nationalism, Oxford; New York: Oxford University Press, pp. 316–325.

Schopenhauer, Arthur (1976): Aphorismen zur Lebensweisheit, Frankfurt am Main: Insel Verlag.

Scottish Government (2013): "Scotland's Future: Your Guide to an Independent Scotland, Edinburgh". Edinburgh: The Scottish Government.

Scotland Act 1998, c. 46. (http://www.legislation.gov.uk/ukpga/1998/46/notes/contents)

Sparrow, Andrew (2019): "SNP Conference – Nicola Sturgeon's Speech: Politics Live Blog" In: The Guardian, 15 April 2019 (https://www.theguardian.com/politics/blog/live/2014/nov/15/snp-conference-nicola-sturgeons-speech-politics-live-blog).

Stenton, Doris Mary (1979): English Society in the Early Middle Ages, Harmondsworth: Penguin Books.

Supreme Court of the United Kingdom (2005): The Constitutional Reform Act 2005 (Commencement No. 11), Order 2009, SI 2009/1604.

Voce, Antonio, Antonia/Clarke, Seán (2018): "How did my MP vote on May's Brexit deal?" In: The Guardian, 15 January 2018.
Withe, Robin/Willock, Ian/McQueen, Hector (2013): The Scottish Legal System 5th Edition, Haywards Heath: Bloomsbury Professional.

True Bavarians
The Volatile Identity Politics of Born Regionalists

Roland Sturm

Introduction

Bavaria is a special case in German politics. The state has developed a strong regional identity. And this regional identity finds its political expression not only within the state of Bavaria, but also at the federal level. It would not be surprising if there was a strong political movement for Bavarian autonomy or independence. But the opposite is the case. Bavaria sees itself as a paragon of cultural, educational and economic success in a federal Germany. Bavaria lives the paradox of efficient regional identity politics in a non-secessionist environment. The EU is part of this environment and above all a forum for pursuing Bavarian economic preferences.

Contrary to the misunderstanding in the English language literature (Hepburn 2008; Hepburn 2010: 540; Padgett/Burkett 1986: 114), the present chapter argues that the Bavarian Christlich-Soziale Union (CSU) cannot be identified as 'separatist' or 'autonomist'. Rather, the CSU is a party with a regional base but national ambitions. This forces the party to give priority to the preferences of the Bavarian voter. Otherwise, the party would have no chance to win landslide election victories that are necessary to pass the national five-percent hurdle for elections to the German parliament.

The CSU has an agreement with its Conservative sister party, the Christlich Demokratische Union (CDU), that the latter does not contest general elections in Bavaria, leaving the field clear in favour of the CSU. After an election, the CDU and the CSU always join forces in one parliamentary party in the federal parliament. The CSU's absolute priority of winning regional elections and the Bavarian seats in a general election can lead to conflicts between the political preferences of Bavaria and Conservatives[1] at the national level. At first glance, this may look like a struggle

---

[1] Although Germany does not, as has been noted, have a single 'Conservative' party, the expression the Conservatives ('die Konservativen') is common as a shorthand for the federal CDU/CSU 'double party', which is, in most cases, considered a single force on the German political stage. Hence I will use the capitalised 'Conservatives' to refer to this political grouping.

for autonomy. It is, however, only part of the strategic necessity to put Bavaria first in order to stay involved in national politics. The CSU has to balance regional and national interests, and it has tried several models to organize this interest intermediation. It is beyond doubt, however, that among the strategies chosen, we do not find Bavarian autonomy being given priority over national integration.

There is a widespread myth that what the CSU wants is more autonomy for Bavaria or a greater decentralization of state powers in Germany (Hepburn/Hough 2011: 79). This misunderstanding is nurtured by the party itself and its self-styled role as a champion of federalism. The CSU is, indeed, a separate political entity, but the party's purpose is to perform a role in national and European politics. To secure this role, it uses its regional base. Here it needs to be successful. No matter what the CSU's allies in her conservative sister party want, the CSU will always have only one priority: an absolute majority of seats in the Bavarian parliament. This makes the CSU an awkward partner for Conservatives in the rest of Germany, at least as long as the Bavarian electorate has preferences that differ from those of Germany as a whole. Symbolic gestures directed against 'Berlin politics' may help to close the regional ranks, but should not be misunderstood as an expression of autonomist ambitions. The overarching aim of the CSU is not to strengthen the separate political existence of a Bavarian polity. On the contrary, over the years German federalism has become more centralized and unitary in character with the help and support of the Bavarian government (Sturm 2013a; Sturm 2015).

This chapter is structured as follows: The next section deals with the strategic choices the CSU has to make to balance its two hats as regional and national party without losing its grip on its Bavarian identity. This is followed by a discussion of what the core of Bavarian identity is. And finally, I ask whether Bavarian self-confidence is enough to even allow elements of a regional foreign policy.

The dominant role of the CSU as a multi-level party

The CSU has governed Bavaria for more than 50 years. Over this time, it had an absolute majority of seats in the regional parliament from 1946 to 1950, from 1962 to 2008 and from 2013 to 2018. Exceptions to single-party rule made possible by the parliamentary strength of the CSU were periods when the CSU needed coalition partners to stay in power and to support a CSU head of government. Only for a short period in the post-war years, from 1954 until 1958, was the CSU in opposition. The CSU's long period of undisputed rule in Bavaria made it possible for the party to merge – at least in the eyes of many observers inside and outside Bavaria – Bavarian politics with the party political image of the CSU. Success of the CSU in federal elections and European elections were also essential for the strength of the German Conservatives outside Bavaria. The CSU is therefore bound to have a tactical relationship to party political identity-building. This is evident in the range of positions the party has recently taken on Europe: from the strongly EU-critical position taken in the 2014 election campaign for the European parliament to fend off competitors on the right (Sturm 2018) to the pro-European turn of 2019, when the CSU hoped to make a CSU EU parliamentarian and chairman of the European People's Party, Manfred Weber, the next President of the EU Commission.

The volatility of CSU identity politics has its counterpoint in the stability of its commitment to Bavaria. The key question for the CSU is how to organize maximum political success in Bavaria. One precondition is that it has no conservative rival in Bavaria. As noted above, from the founding of the Federal Republic in 1949, the CDU and the CSU have agreed not to compete in Bavarian or federal elections. Though under the leadership of Franz Josef Strauss, a CSU politician with national popularity, there were initiatives from outside Bavaria for an all-German CSU, the party leadership hesitated to support this idea. German unification appeared to pose a problem for the CSU, because on paper, the increase in the electorate meant it could become more difficult to pass the five-per cent hurdle for membership in the German parliament at federal elections. The party leadership toyed with the idea of an East German partner, dubbed the DSU. The fear that the CDU would retaliate with a Bavarian branch stopped further efforts. Parties to the right of the CDU have also posed a threat to the dominance of the CSU: the Republikaner in the 1980s and the Alternative für Deutschland (AfD) today. As in the past, the CSU is now reacting to the challenge from the right by offering voters a manifesto that includes the major demands of such right-wing challenger parties. This may estrange the party from the CDU, as, for example, in recent years on the question of the maximum number of migrants Germany should welcome. However, more importantly for the party, such a strategy helped to solidify the CSU's approval rates. Today the Greens have become the main challenger to CSU dominance in Bavaria. The 'greening' of CSU policies is again following the pattern of stealing your opponent's clothes without consulting the CDU.

The second problem for the party is to find an optimal solution for the management of the party in the capital and in Bavaria. The key here is the best possible allocation of power centres at German and Bavarian level (Kießling 2004; Sturm 2013b). The party has to make two strategic decisions. One is whether the party chairman (no woman has yet held the position) should accept a ministerial post in Berlin (or previously in Bonn) or should the party chairman sit in Munich. A second decision to be made is whether the chairman of the party and the head of the Bavarian government (Ministerpräsident) should be the same person or different people should hold these two jobs. If the Bavarian Ministerpräsident is simultaneously party chairman, the CSU's man or woman in the capital heads the influential CSU Landesgruppe (the group of Bavarian MPs within the joint Conservatives parliamentary party). The Landesgruppe has a right to veto decisions of the CDU/CSU parliamentary party in the national parliament. The fact that strategic decisions at the federal level are so central to the party's strategic options demonstrates again that the CSU is not a party with an exclusive regional and autonomist focus. Its fabric always combines the national and the regional outlook. Given the choices detailed above, this leaves us with the options listed in table 1.

Table 1: *The strategic choices for the CSU in combining Bavarian and national politics*

Options	Power centres	Examples
1: The federal option: party led from a position in the national government	Split power centres: party chairman in federal capital (cabinet)/ CSU head of Bavarian government	1962–1978 Franz Josef Strauss/ Alfons Goppel; 1988-1993 Theo Waigel/ Max Streibl; 1994–1998 Theo Waigel/ Edmund Stoiber; 2018–2019 Horst Seehofer/ Markus Söder
2: The all-Bavarian option: party led from Bavaria	Regional power centres: party chairman in Munich/ CSU head of Bavarian government	1946–1949 Josef Müller/Hans Ehard; 2008 Erwin Huber/ Günter Beckstein;
3: The unified Bavarian option: party led by one person in Bavaria	Regional power centre: one person in Munich is both party chairman and Bavarian head of government	1949–1954 Hans Ehard; 1957–1960 Hanns Seidel; 1978–1988 Franz Josef Strauss; 1999–2007 Edmund Stoiber; 2008–2018 Horst Seehofer; 2019– Markus Söder

Source: Hanns-Seidel-Stiftung (1995) and my own data.

What is the best strategy for a regional party with national ambitions? History does not tell us. The CSU has tried all three options. Much of the effects of the option chosen depended on personalities, and all three options have advantages and disadvantages. It is, however, obvious that none of these options led to demands for greater autonomy for Bavaria. The challenge for the CSU remained how to continue to be an influential force in national politics while remaining authentically Bavarian and able to win absolute majorities in Bavarian elections. Option 1 seems to offer the most far-reaching degree of nationalization for a regional party. With the party heavyweights Franz-Josef Strauss (defence minister in the cabinet of Konrad Adenauer and finance minister in the cabinet of Kurt-Georg Kiesinger) and Theo Waigel (finance minister in the cabinet of Helmut Kohl) the CSU gained national prominence. This model could only work, however, with a father figure as the head of the regional government in Bavaria. An uncontroversial CSU politician as Bavarian Ministerpräsident, someone more interested in regional affairs than in the challenges of party politics and with an ability to act as a unifying force within Bavaria while avoiding conflict was able to rely on tradition and historical identities to legitimize CSU dominance in Bavaria. By contrast, the party chairman in the capital represented the party's policies and was willing to take a stand on policy matters. Only the combination of both characters guaranteed electoral success in Bavarian elections. During Alfons Goppel's time in office as Bavarian Ministerpräsident his regional popularity successfully mobilized support for the CSU even though the party chairman was restricted by cabinet discipline when he sought confrontation with the Bonn government. This successful model did not work well when Theo Waigel was chairman of the party. His first partner as Ministerpräsident in Bavaria, Max Streibl, did not succeed in developing a fatherly image as office holder. He eventually lost office because of a corruption scandal. His successor, Edmund Stoiber, tried to consolidate the CSU in Bavaria by provoking conflicts with the party chairman, among other things. As Minister of Finance, Theo Waigel was responsible for the introduction of the Euro. (He even invented its name.) As the Euro was unpopular in Bavaria, Edmund Stoiber attacked the introduction of the Euro and wanted Theo Waigel to resign from the party chair. This conflict illuminates the blame game that is possible if the jobs of party chairman and Ministerpräsident remain separated. The CSU can simultaneously be involved in national government decisions and opposed to these decisions. This blame game can, of course, also be played when options two or three are chosen.

Option 2 is the least attractive for the CSU, because it has no institutionalized role in national politics and is weakened by competing power centres. The party chairman can take part in coalition meetings in the capital if the Conservatives are part of the national government. But he lacks any kind of national electoral appeal that could be added to the influence on voters that comes from the Ministerpräsident.

Option 3, however, empowers the party leader, who is at the same time head of government in Munich. In this role, he can play the game of outsider to the national government and government critic in the name of Bavaria, and, at the same time, if the CSU is in the national coalition, he can intervene in national politics. Strong Ministerpräsidenten present their Bavaria as an example of good government for the whole of Germany. Two of them, Franz Josef Strauss in 1980 and Edmund Stoiber in 2002 even became the Conservative parties' candidate for the office of Federal Chancellor. Again, personality matters. No-one expects the present holder of the office of Ministerpräsident in Bavaria, Markus Söder, to take on a role of comparable significance. His wish to combine the offices of party chairman and Ministerpräsident shows, however, his strategic preferences.

The roots of Bavarian identity politics

Whereas most of the German states (Länder) were reshaped after the Second World War, Bavaria retained its traditional boundaries. Though it is internally divided by regional dialects and historic allegiances, a pan-Bavarian identity developed. At its core are above all certain symbols, traditions and customs, which outsiders, too, see as 'typically' Bavarian. This is a feature of a relatively passive regional culture that generally does not carry a political message, such as the option of separatism (Sturm 2016). Opinion polls show that non-political items are of central importance for Bavarian identity. The most commonly mentioned include: regional costumes and traditional dresses (traditional Bavarian dress such as the Dirndl and Lederhosen), beer and other traditions, followed by Oktoberfest, and the mountains (the Alps), lakes and forests. Of lesser importance, but still worth mentioning, are regional food and the Bayern Munich football club (Hanns-Seidel-Stiftung 2009: 59).

Tom Mannewitz's (2015: 351) comparative empirical research on regional cultures in Germany characterizes Bavaria as libertarian-constitutional. This is the framework in which the dominant cultural identity develops. Mannewitz finds that, for Bavarians, freedom is more important than equality. Social, political and economic competition is supported by 91 percent of the population. Only ten percent of Bavarians give priority to solidarity over competition. There is little or no support for socialist ideas, the welfare state is less popular than in other German Länder. Self-reliance is viewed more positively than a paternalistic state. The public role of the church still enjoys the respect of a much larger segment of regional society than elsewhere in Germany. Support for the constitution, legal procedures and the Federal Constitutional Court are also above average.

The Bavarian cultural identity embedded in this libertarian-constitutional political culture strengthens a feeling of social and cultural identity that is stronger than the proximity felt to Germany or Europe (see table 2). Research has shown (Sturm et al. 2010) that regional identities are based on the circumstances of day-to-day life and face-to-face communication. In Bavaria the difference between 'us' and 'them' originates from assumed emotional proximity, not, however, from political conflict. A dialect, for example, can draw emotional boundaries, yet in the Bavarian context it cannot be used as justification for separatism. Though cultural identity can justify regional self-confidence especially when – as is the case in Bavaria – this can be connected with regional economic success, this self-confidence is reined in by the constraints of Germany's system of interlocking federalism.

Table 2: Regional allegiance in Bavaria (in %)

	very strong	strong	not very strong	none	don't know
Town/village	63	26	7	3	1
Region	59	29	8	3	1
Bavaria	51	37	8	2	2
Germany	40	45	13	2	0
Europe	17	43	28	10	2

Source: Hanns-Seidel-Stiftung (2009): Heimatgefühl und Leben in Bayern. Generationenspezifische und regionale Unterschiede von Einstellungen zu Politik und Heimat, München: Hanns-Seidel-Stiftung: 33.

Federalism is less popular in Bavaria than one might expect. German interlocking federalism has managed to transform a system of shared rule and self-rule into a vehicle of constant bargaining behind the scenes. Bavarian citizens tend to see their regional government as an actor which rarely speaks for territorial interests. Unitary federalism implies that most important pieces of legislation originate at the national level. It is generally regional governments and, only occasionally regional parliaments that react to national government initiatives. Regional governments are better placed to register resistance if necessary, because they are represented in the quasi-second chamber of Germany's parliament, the Bundesrat, which has a role in national legislation. Empirical research has shown, however, that political conflict in the Bundesrat is rare, even though parties play a major role in its decision-making process. The Bundesrat is part of the German consensus culture, which easily overcomes party political competition (Finke et al. 2019). Still, on rare occasions territorial and/or financial interests lead to a confrontation with the federal government in the Bundesrat. At least symbolically, and certainly in its political communications, a Bavarian government is bound to defend a 'Bavaria first' logic. In the national context, this is not without problems, because the other Länder may see Bavaria as a wealthy and powerful neighbour with an inclination to dominate.

The International Dimension

The CSU's party political 'Bavaria first' logic finds its expression in the arena of foreign policy, too. Germany's cooperative federalism allows the Länder to pursue their own independent foreign policies. In the past, state governments have mainly concentrated on efforts to promote regional industries abroad. They see themselves as ambassadors for regional investment, supporting foreign direct investment in their states. In recent years, the Bavarian government has given its parallel foreign policy an explicitly political dimension. In its effort to increase party political support in Bavaria, the CSU has taken foreign policy initiatives that are in conflict with German foreign policy or at least tend to clash with the official position of the German government. For example, there are strong voices in the CSU's leadership that advocate a better relationship with Russia, not least for economic reasons. The then Bavarian Prime Minister Horst Seehofer, accompanied by the former Bavarian Prime Minister, Edmund Stoiber, visited Vladimir Putin several times. He supported the end of sanctions against Russia.[2] The Bavarian government shares a critical attitude towards Angela Merkel's refugee policies with Victor Orbán of Hungary. The Bavarian government has established a close relationship with the Visegrád countries and tends to play down democratic deficits in Poland and Hungary. In Bavaria, this disagreement with Berlin over foreign policy is not seen as a problem. It may not be a decisive vote-winning device to insist on these priorities visa-à-vis national politics, but it has the double advantage of securing regional interests (economic ones, and the interest of keeping refugees out) and of demonstrating to the Bavarian voter that the CSU defends Bavarian interests even if this means (low-level) conflict with the national government.

In this respect, the CSU is not immune to regional 'closure'. When this happens, it is usually the result of past experiences. Bavaria had hoped to become part of an institution with veto power within the EU. The Committee of the Regions (CoR) not only lacks this power, it became also increasingly self-centred. Successive Bavarian governments thus considered participation ineffective. As a result, Bavarian governments, though interested in multi-level politics, decided to do it 'their way' (Bocklet 2017). This, however, did not entail a turn towards Euroscepticism. It was more an effort to make the best out of a range of limited options. On the one hand, this meant Bavaria would use all points of access to influence European politics: the federal government, regional cooperation and lobbyism in Brussels. On the other hand, efforts were made to open up European channels for the regional parliament and to give regional parliamentary majorities the means to influence the national government in European affairs.

---

2   http://www.faz.net/aktuell/politik/bundestagswahl/parteien-und-kandidaten/die-csu-und-die-aussenpolitik-wie-horst-seehofer-die-provinzialitaet-abstreifen-will-14918807.html (Schäffer 2017)

Conclusions

Identity politics have a long tradition in Bavaria. For the governing CSU, they are a tool to secure power on the national *and* regional stages. Office-seeking and, as a precondition, vote-seeking, is more important than policy details. The CSU has always been flexible when it came to policy preferences. Policy choices obeyed the logic of power politics. A conflict with the national government and even with the Conservatives in power in the capital was (and is) quite frequent. However, conflict was not used to mobilise support for separatism. Bavaria is not a German Scotland or Catalonia. The CSU sees itself as a national party with regional roots but also has the ambition to play a role in the context of the German national government. The relationship to multi-level governance, including federalism, is tactical within the limits that interlocking federalism draws. True Bavarians never forget where they come from. They like their regional culture and traditions, but see their future in Germany and in the EU. For the CSU, the respect for cultural difference is, above all, a means to guarantee survival in national politics. The Bavarian cultural identity does not need protection; what is far more dangerous for the CSU is that Bavarian economic success, which attracts not only Germans from other regions but all the forces of globalization and migration, makes it harder for the party to claim that the CSU is the only party able to effectively represent Bavarian interests.

References

Bocklet, Reinhold (2017): "Vortrag." In: Rolle und Zukunft der Landesparlamente, München: Bayerischer Landtag, pp. 13–32.

Finke, Patrick/Müller, Markus M./Souris, Antonius/Sturm, Roland (2019): "Parteipolitik im Bundesrat. Neue Erkenntnisse aus der Analyse der Ländervoten in Seinen Ausschüssen." In: Europäisches Zentrum für Föderalismusforschung Tübingen (ed.), Jahrbuch des Föderalismus 2019, Baden-Baden: Nomos, pp. 145–60.

Hanns-Seidel-Stiftung (1995): Geschichte einer Volkspartei. 50 Jahre CSU, Hanns-Seidel-Stiftung (eds.), München: Hanns-Seidel-Stiftung.

Hanns-Seidel-Stiftung (2009): Heimatgefühl und Leben in Bayern. Generationenspezifische und regionale Unterschiede von Einstellungen zu Politik und Heimat, Hanns-Seidel-Stiftung (ed.), München: Hanns-Seidel-Stiftung.

Hepburn, Eve (2008): "The Neglected Nation: The CSU and the Territorial Cleavage in Bavarian Party Politics." In: German Politics 17/2, pp. 184–202.

Hepburn, Eve (2010): "Small Worlds in Canada and Europe: A Comparison of Regional Party Systems in Quebec, Bavaria and Scotland." In: Regional & Federal Studies 20/4–5, pp. 527–44.

Hepburn, Eve/Hough, Dan (2012): "Regionalist Parties and the Mobilization of Territorial Difference in Germany." In: Government and Opposition 47/1, pp. 74–96.

Kießling, Andreas (2004): Die CSU. Macherhalt und Machterneuerung, Wiesbaden: VS Verlag.

Mannewitz, Tom (2015): Politische Kultur und demokratischer Verfassungsstaat, Baden-Baden: Nomos.

Mintzel, Alf (1983): "Die Bayernpartei." In: Stöss, Richard (ed.), Parteienhandbuch. Band 1 AUDEFP, Wiesbaden: Westdeutscher Verlag, pp. 395–489.

Padgett, Stephen/Burkett, Tony (1986): Political Parties and Elections in West Germany, London: C. Hurst.

Schäffer, Albert (2017): "Wie Seehofer die Provinzialität abstreifen will", October 2, 2019 (https://www.faz.net/aktuell/politik/bundestagswahl/parteien-und-kandidaten/die-csu-und-die-aussenpolitik-wie-horst-seehofer-die-provinzialitaet-abstreifen-will-14918807.html)

Sturm, Roland (2013a): "Der deutsche Föderalismus – nur noch ein Ärgernis?" In: Gallus, Schubert/Alexander, Thomas/Thieme, Tom (ed.), Deutsche Kontroversen. Festschrift für Eckhard Jesse, Baden-Baden: Nomos, pp. 297–308.

Sturm, Roland (2013b): "Rolle und Gewicht Bayerns im Bund – Reflexionen zu den beiden letzten Jahrzehnten." In: Zur Debatte 6, pp. 40–42.

Sturm, Roland (2015): "Föderalismus in Deutschland heute." In: Kneuer, Marianne (ed.), Standortbestimmung Deutschlands: Innere Verfasstheit Und Internationale Verantwortung, Baden-Baden: Nomos, pp. 195–223.

Sturm, Roland (2016): "Regionale politische Kulturen im deutschen Föderalismus" In: Werz, Nikolaus/Koschkar, Martin (eds.), Regionale politische Kultur in Deutschland, Wiesbaden: VS Springer, pp. 75–92.

Sturm, Roland (2018): "Europäisierung Oder Europamüdigkeit vor und nach der Europawahl 2014? Das Thema 'Europa' und die europäische Integration im bayerischen Landtagswahlkampf 2013 und darüber hinaus" In: Bergbauer, Harald (ed.), Parteien und Landtagswahlen in Bayern, München: Landeszentrale für politische Bildungsarbeit, pp. 268–285.

List of Tables and Figures

Table 1: "The strategic choices for the CSU in combining Bavarian and national politics." Created by Sturm, Roland (2020) for this publication. Data partially taken from Hanns-Seidel-Stiftung (1995).

Table 2: "Regional allegiance in Bavaria (in %)." Created by Sturm, Roland (2020) for this publication. Data taken from Hanns-Seidel-Stiftung (1995).

III.
Unintended and Intended Consequences of EU Programs on Regional Developement

Can Money Buy Love?
The Impact of EU Cohesion Policy on European Identity

Fabian Landes

Introduction

The ambitious overall goal of the cohesion policy of the European Union (EU), often referred to as the regional policies of the EU, is to harmonise living standards in all European regions and to reduce economic, social and environmental inequalities (c.f. Maastricht TEU 1992: Title XIV, Article 130a). To fulfil these ambitions, the EU devotes almost one third of its entire budget to fostering regional development and creating economic and social cohesion between European regions (European Commission 2019). This represents a massive financial redistribution mechanism.

Both academics and policy makers have tended to focus on the impact and effects of cohesion policy investments, and studies have overwhelmingly focused on assessing the economic impact of the money that the EU has invested in Europe's regions. It is only in recent years that scholars have become interested in the question of whether cohesion policy also influences citizens' views on the European Union itself. This chapter investigates one of the effects of European programmes on regional development while also reducing the research gap by studying the interconnection of European identity and cohesion policy investments. The main theoretical argument of the analysis is that European identity formation in part follows rational economic-utilitarian considerations. When the European Union and its policies produce tangible added value for their citizens, it is more likely that they will start to identify as citizens of the Union. To account for the wide variety of regional circumstances in Europe, a second hypothesis assumes that this effect varies among European regions.

To test these two hypotheses, I developed a large data set that combines indicators of citizens' level of European identity from Eurobarometer Data with economic indicators of the EU's spending activities in the regions and of regional economic activity. The scope of the analysis stretches over the period from 2000 to 2014, and the data is analysed using a multi-level regression model.

The analysis presents evidence of a positive correlation between the level of cohesion policy investments in the region and the share of citizens reporting identification with both their nation state and the European Union. Likewise, the model shows a negative correlation between levels of EU investment and the share of citizens that identify solely with their country. This effect does not vary much *within* countries, but does so *between* countries, suggesting that national contexts play an important role and that economic considerations in EU identity formation are more important in some countries than in others.

The next section briefly introduces the literature on EU cohesion policy evaluation. I then discuss some theoretical aspects of EU identity and cohesion policy. A short introduction to the quantitative research design of the study is followed by a presentation of results, which are further discussed in light of the theoretical considerations. The last section of this chapter contains some concluding remarks.

Evaluating EU Cohesion Policy

In this chapter, cohesion policy refers to money allocated under the European Regional Development Fund (EFRE), the European Social Fund (ESF) or the Cohesion Fund (CF). The effects of these EU cohesion policy activities have been subject to substantial study. The literature can generally be divided into two categories: studies of regional context and the effect of various local government and economic structures on cohesion policy spending, and literature seeking to assess the net impact of money invested in European regions (Crescenzi/Giua 2017). Despite growing interest on the part of academics, no consensus has been reached on whether cohesion policy spending contributes to the economic and social cohesion of European regions (Bachtler et al. 2016). While some studies have shown that it increased territorial cohesion (Fiaschi et al. 2018; Rosik et al. 2017; Pontarollo 2017), others have stressed that, in specific contexts, cohesion policy might have no, or even negative effects on territorial cohesion (Bachtrögler et al. 2019; Kroll 2017; Medve-Bálint 2017). Only recently have studies added the dimension of European identity to cohesion policy evaluations (Aiello et al. 2018; Borz et al. 2018; Pegan et al. 2018), which is surprising considering that strengthening European solidarity is one of the main rationales behind the idea of a Europe-wide investment policy (European Commission 2019). The next section introduces the concept of European identity and discusses some arguments that have been made in the literature on the relationship between cohesion policy and European identity.

Cohesion Policy and European Identity

Social or collective identities refer to the phenomenon of an individual feeling solidarity with or belonging to a group and being able to identify certain common traits that are of defining nature for that group (Brubaker/Cooper 2000). These common traits can have either civic or cultural/ethnic characteristics (Reeskens/Hooghe 2010). In the case of European identity, most scholars have argued that civic traits (e.g. common values or shared historical experience) are most important (Smith 1992; Agirdag et al. 2016; Bail 2008), while ethnic and cultural traits (e.g. ethnicity, religion) play only a minor role in defining the group of 'Europeans' (Bruter 2003).

Concerning territorial identities, two main ideas that describe the relationship of different territorial entities as sources of identity have been put forward. The *nested model* describes the relationship of national and European identity as resembling concentric circles. It assumes that people have strong and narrow regional and national identities, on top of which is added the layer of European identity (Herrmann/Brewer 2004). The so-called *'marble-cake' model* assumes that national and European identity cannot be separated from each other but are an integral element of each other (Medrano/Gutiérrez 2001).

While the existing literature has uncovered a wide range of factors that influence individual and collective levels of European identity, the role of cohesion policy in the formation of European identity has only recently gained attention (Capello 2018; Chacha 2013; Chalmers/Dellmuth 2015; Medeiros 2017; Mendez/Bachtler 2017; Osterloh 2011; Pegan et al. 2018; Verhaegen et al. 2014). The discussion is structured around three principle arguments: the *awareness* argument, the *regional* argument and the *economic-utilitarian* argument.

The *awareness* argument considers the awareness of cohesion policy as a transition factor for a positive effect on European identity. Therefore, cohesion policy can only have an impact on European identity if people are aware of the existence and effects of such policy mechanisms (Borz et al. 2018; Mendez/Bachtler 2017). The perception of cohesion policy outcomes is thus more important than their actual effects. One criticism of the awareness argument is provided by Inglehart's (1970) model of cognitive mobilisation: awareness of EU policy and European identity cannot be considered to be independent from each other, as higher European identity is also likely to raise the awareness of EU policies (ibid.). There is thus a danger of circularity.

The *regional* argument highlights the importance of regional context for strengthening European identity though cohesion policies. When citizens have strong regional attachments, they perceive policies that empower local or regional authorities as something very positive. Inhabitants of regions with a strong longing for regional autonomy are particular likely to perceive the EU as an institution that provides regional authorities with the means to pursue their own policies (Chacha 2013; Capello 2018). The effect of cohesion policy on EU identity depends on regional identity structures and local institutional capacities.

Economic-utilitarian approaches to European identity describe the identity process as a calculation of the costs and benefits of EU membership and an evaluation of the performance of the EU (Eichenberg/Dalton 1993). The economic situation of individuals should thus be an important factor in explaining their European identity (Clements 2011). In this view, a positive European identity is therefore rather a function of economic advantages that the individual had in the past or imagines experiencing in the future. As such, cohesion policy can be considered as one factor in these cost-benefit calculations. People who live in regions with high levels of cohesion policy spending tend to consider the EU as a source of identity because the EU contributes to their everyday wellbeing (Osterloh 2011; Verhaegen et al. 2014).

The (admittedly very bold) aim of this study is to investigate the success of cohesion policy in contributing to increasing European identity. In doing so, this study will follow the *economic-utilitarian* argument, as developed by Osterloh (2011) and Verhaegen et al. (2014). This study's ambition to produce comparable results among all European regions makes the *regional* argument problematic as a theoretical foundation. That argument's highlighting of the importance of regional context makes it difficult to use as a framework for a comparative research question. The *awareness* argument, on the other hand, seeks to explain how citizens perceive regional investments by the EU, and not how those investments influence their identification with the EU. Therefore, the next section will develop a quantitative research design in order to test the following hypotheses, which postulate an economic-utilitarian approach:

> H1: Cohesion policy spending has a positive impact on regional collective identification with the EU.

Since it seems oversimplified to assume a general effect for all regions, a second hypothesis takes into account the great heterogeneity of European regions and acknowledges regional differences:

> H2: The effect of cohesion policy on European identity varies among regions.

Research Design

To test the hypotheses, I developed a large data set with European identity as the dependent variable and two independent variables: the amount of cohesion policy spending and regional gross domestic product (GDP) per capita. The level of analysis is level 2 of the *nomenclature des unités territoriales statistiques* (NUTS2), a set of regional entities that was standardised by the European Commission for the purpose of survey statistics and policy planning. Inconsistent regional units among the various data sources and changes over time required deviation from the NUTS2 level in some circumstances and aggregation of some of the data.

European identity was measured using the so-called 'Moreno question' from Eurobarometer (EB) surveys. The question asks the respondents for their feeling of belonging to their nation state in comparison to the EU.[1]

Using the Moreno question, and Eurobarometer data generally, is problematic. Many scholars have criticised the validity of this specific survey item (Bruter 2008; Mendez/Bachtler 2017), accused the European Commission of political bias in collecting the data (Nissen 2014), and called into question the use of quantitative surveys for oversimplification (Armbruster et al. 2003; Maier/Rittberger, 2008).

Even though the literature is divided on the application of the Moreno question, it was still used in a variety of recent studies on European identity (Fligstein et al. 2012; Mendez/Bachtler 2017; Roose 2013). Considering the broad comparability of EB data (Hobolt/Vries 2016), it seems justifiable to use this item in the following analysis. Since the level of analysis is the region, the variable was aggregated into three dependent variables:

1. Share of respondents with national identity only
2. Share of respondents with a mixed identity (both national and European)
3. Share of respondents with European identity only

The first independent variable is the level of cohesion policy spending. The Commission provides extensive data on modelled annual expenditure for regional cohesion policy. This model is based on simulations of expenditure patterns in the member states and regions, and seems to be more accurate than just considering monetary transfers from the Commission to the member states (Lo Piano et al. 2017). As the control variable, the regional gross domestic product per capita is included in the data set, to control for differences in purchasing power and thus differing impacts of the same amount of money across European regions.

Since the effect can be expected to be very gradual, each variable was recorded yearly for the period 2000–2014. This timeframe marks some important developments of EU cohesion policy, such as the RIS3 reforms and the eastern enlargement of the EU, and thus seems appropriate for the analysis. However, restrictions in data availability also influenced this decision.

The data is analysed using a multi-level regression model. Normal multiple regression models cannot account for hierarchical data structures, but the present hierarchical data require a more sophisticated analysis. The models include three levels:

---

1   Original wording of the question: *'In the near future, do you see yourself as…? 1 NATIONALITY only 2 NATIONALITY and European 3 European and NATIONALITY 4 European only 5 Don't know'*

- Single observation in one region
- Regions (consists of 14 years per region)
- Countries (consists of 196 regions in total)

The outputs of the analysis allow for an interpretation of both fixed effects at the general level and random effects at the lower two levels. Those models are also called random slope-random intercept models. This enables comparison of the variability of regression slopes between regions within countries and between countries, thus allowing assessment of whether the effect of cohesion policy spending varies between regions or between countries. At the same time, it will make it possible to compare regions and countries in terms of the size and direction of the effect, so that the role of regions and countries in the effect of cohesion policy on identity can be explored.[2]

As there are three dependent variables, I discuss three statistical models in the next chapter.

Empirical Findings

The empirical findings consist of two parts: the fixed-effects and random-effects regression parameters. A multilevel random slope-random intercept model provides a single regression line for the whole model (fixed effects) and different regression lines for each country and region (random effects). Thus, for all three models, both dimensions have to be considered. For the fixed effects, the outputs are similar to conventional regression outputs. The random effects are more difficult to interpret, since there are different slopes and intercepts both for all countries and for all regions. The first step in interpreting this large number of parameters is to regard the distribution of both intercepts and slopes, which follows below.

---

2   For a more elaborate discussion of multi-level regression model analysis, see Steenbergen & Jones (2002) or Luke (2004).

Table 1: fixed effects regression parameters

Model	(I)***	(II)***	(III)**
	national	mixed	European
Expenditure/cap in			
EUR	-0.00009**	0.00014***	-0.00003**
	(0.00003)	(0.00003)	(0.00001)
GDP/cap in	-0.0035***	0.0034***	0.00001
1 000 EUR	(0.0004)	(0.0004)	(0.00001)
_cons	0.523***	0.421***	0.0259***
	(0.0203)	(0.019)	(0.005)
N	1963	1963	1961

t statistics in parentheses * $p < 0.05$, ** $p < 0.01$, *** $p < 0.001$

Table 1 reports the fixed-effects parameters for the three models for each of the three dependent variables. The first observation is that the three models and cohesion policy expenditure fulfil the significance criteria; regional GDP is also significant except for model III. The second important insight is that, in general, cohesion policy spending has a stronger effect on identity formation than GDP, as indicated by higher constants.[3] Although it is difficult and unrealistic to interpret the coefficients literally, their comparison allows for such an observation.

Furthermore, models I and II provide evidence for accepting the first hypothesis. These models predict that increasing cohesion policy spending per capita will negatively influence the share of citizens that have only national identity and positively influence the share of citizens that have mixed EU/national identity.

Model III contradicts this conclusion, as it predicts a negative impact of cohesion policy expenditure on those with only European identity. There are however some problems with model III in general. The dependent variable has very homogeneous and very small values, all of which are not optimal preconditions for a multiple regression analysis. The share of citizens that have only European identity is very small in all countries and shows almost no variance over time. Together with the relatively low level of significance, this provides an argument for not considering the model as a whole.

---

3   Note that the scale of the variable expenditure per capita is 1 EUR/capita. Introducing the variable with the more convenient scale of 1 000 EUR/capita would have exceeded the computing efficiency of the software due to the very small numbers involved.

The distribution of the random parameters is indicated in graph 1 for model I and in graph 2 for model II. This gives an insight into how the effect varies between countries and regions. For both models, the negative relationship between slopes and intercepts suggests a sort of saturation point. Once the share of citizens with only national or mixed identity reaches a certain point, cohesion policy expenditure or GDP has no further impact in reducing or increasing that share, respectively. This is not surprising, since national and European identity are very multicausal phenomena.

Figure 1: Model I

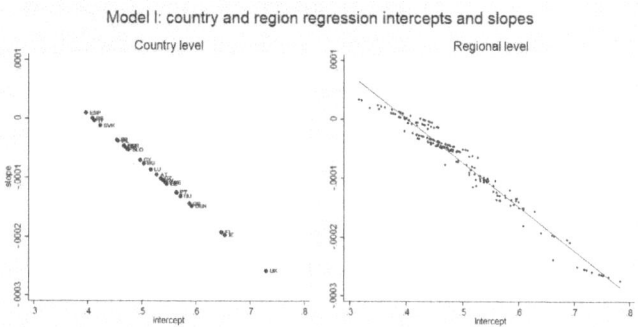

Source: own depiction

The country level of model I shows that the effect is stronger in some countries than in others. In the UK, for example, the effect of cohesion policy spending and GDP is very strong in reducing the share of citizens that identify only with their nation. At the same time, the intercept is very high. The intercept represents the share of citizens that have a national identity in a hypothetical world with zero GDP and zero cohesion policy investments. This of course does not make much sense, but it gives an idea of what influences the formation of a purely national identity in the UK. On the other side of the spectrum are countries such as Spain, Belgium and Italy, in which national identity is not much influenced by cohesion policy expenditure or GDP.

The regional level shows that regions within countries don't vary much, since the regions are scattered around lines by country. This indicates that the effect of cohesion policy is strongly dependent on the country, and that this effect is rather homogeneous between regions of one country. This contradicts H2, since it is not the *regional* context that is the most important factor, but the *national* context.

Figure 2: Model II

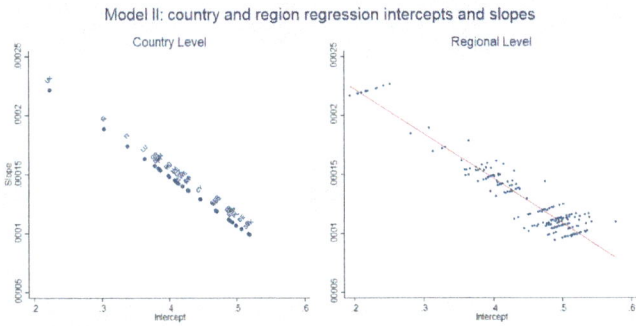

Source: own depiction

Model II shows very similar characteristics but the other way around. All observations have a positive slope, which supports the conclusion from the fixed-effects parameters that cohesion policy spending increases the share of citizens with a mixed identity. The UK now shows the highest effect, meaning that, in the UK, cohesion policy spending influences the formation of a mixed identity more than in countries such as Slovakia, Italy and Belgium. Because of the statistical problems with model III, the random effects of Model III will not be discussed in detail. While the model itself seems to be biased, the outputs don't reveal any evidence for accepting or rejecting the hypotheses.

After this short attempt to describe the outputs of the multi-level regression model, the discussion considers these results from the perspective of the considerations made above.

Discussion

Overall, the analysis provides evidence that supports hypothesis I: that cohesion policy spending has a positive impact on European identity. Leaving model III aside due to the problems with the dependent variable, model I shows a significant negative effect of cohesion policy on the share of citizens with only national identity, and model II shows a significant positive effect of cohesion policy on the share of citizens that identify with both their nation state and the EU. This and the fact that both models and the independent variables meet the criteria of significance allows to accept hypothesis I: that cohesion policy spending positively influences the level of identification with the EU.

However, European identity does not replace identification with the member state, as the strongest effect was measured with regard to mixed identity in model II. Cohesion policy spending rather contributes to acceptance of the EU as a source of identity alongside the nation state, it does not seem to replace it.

Hypothesis II must be rejected. The distribution of the effects suggests that there is strong variability among countries, while regions within countries follow more or less similar patterns. This speaks for a very strong impact of country-level factors and gives a rather pessimistic picture of European regions breaking out of their 'national containers'. This has some consequences for our understanding of the regional argument on the influence of cohesion policy. The regional context does not seem to be as important as the national context. There is a danger of a tautological argument here, since European identity was measured versus national identity, but the strong similarities between countries suggest making a *national argument* instead: that the impact of cohesion policy on European identity depends strongly on national contexts.

The results also provide a basis for considerations regarding the characterisation of European identity. As the regression parameters hint at a positive influence of cohesion policy and GDP on European identity, this in turn provides evidence for the economic-utilitarian argument. Cohesion policy and GDP can only influence European identity if European identity is (at least partly) underpinned by economic cost-benefit considerations. The difference between countries also shows that these cost-benefit considerations play a greater role in forming a mixed identity on the part of British, Irish and Finnish citizens, while citizens from countries such as Belgium, Italy or Spain are not as exposed to economic-utilitarian considerations when thinking of their relationship towards the EU. In other words, the EU must provide concrete and economic added value to British citizens in order to be accepted as a source of identity, while Spanish citizens do not care as much about the direct economic benefits of the EU but about other factors, which are outside the scope of this study. While this conclusion seems more obvious in the case of the UK, it is neither the aim nor the claim of this study to explain these differences among EU member states.

At this point, some of the shortcomings of the study should be mentioned, as there is room for some legitimate criticism of the results presented. In the end, the research object of any social sciences research is the human being, and reducing the complexities of human social interactions to numbers carries the danger of oversimplification. An obvious point of criticism is the validity of the measurement of the dependent variable. The problems with the Moreno question have already been mentioned, but, besides that, every single-item measurement can and has been criticised for falling short in capturing the immense complexities associated with an individual's identification with a supranational entity (Armbruster et al. 2003; Maier/Rittberger, 2008).

Furthermore, the multi-causal nature of European identity makes it necessary to include more independent variables than those considered in this study. It is possible that the measured effect is transmitted via undetected third variables, to which the previous analysis remains blind. One important factor is education, as discussed above. Not only do different member states have different levels of education, but cohesion policy investments are also sometimes targeted at increasing the educational level of a region. Assuming the cognitive-mobilisation hypothesis, cohesion policy would only have an indirect effect on European identity by increasing the educational level of a given population.

Finally, a regression analysis as applied in this study measures only correlation between variables, and, as the correlation measured in this contribution is backed by theoretical arguments, it seems adequate to derive some conclusions on the phenomena. While the models have implications for the real world, namely that it is likely that cohesion policy does have a positive effect on the formation of a European identity, it would be wrong to interpret the values of the models literally. In the end it is just a model, which, when translated into real life, might have very different consequences.

Conclusion

The analysis provides some evidence that economic-utilitarian considerations have an influence on European identity formation. The positive regression coefficient in model II and the negative regression coefficient in model I show that increasing cohesion policy expenditure is positively correlated with the regional share of citizens that identify with both the EU and their home country. At the same time, increasing cohesion policy expenditure is negatively correlated with the share of citizens that only identify with their nation.

The regional distribution of the effect is more complex. While the effect varies between countries, it is more or less homogeneous between regions of the same country. One factor seems to be the existing level of identification: countries that have a smaller share of citizens with a mixed identity are also countries in which cohesion policy can have a greater influence, and vice versa.

However, the results can be criticised from many viewpoints, and there is much more work to be done before we can make such statements with greater confidence and precision. There are many conceptual and methodological issues that can be legitimately subject to criticism. They range from the argument that the Moreno question is an inadequate measurement of European identity, via statistical problems concerning the low variety and low values of the independent variable, to the uncertainty over other confounding variables.

Academics have only just started to recognise the relationship between cohesion policy and European identity as a field of research, and this study has attempted to contribute to this discussion. While other studies have already acknowledged a positive relationship between cohesion policy and European identity (Aiello et al. 2018; Osterloh 2011; Verhaegen et al. 2014), this study is the first to undertake a Europe-wide analysis of the effect. As a result of this pan-European perspective, it allowed comparison of the effect between regions and countries. The results show substantial differences in the effect of cohesion policy on European identity, which calls for further investigation by means of qualitative or comparative research designs that can find causes or explanations for these differences.

Besides academics, the results of this study should also encourage practitioners, policy makers and European, national and regional civil servants to continue working on and improving the European cohesion policy. While many unsolved problems remain, ranging from corruption, inefficiency and unfair procedures, this contribution enhanced our understanding of the cohesion policy's influence on a very important common good – European identity.

Acknowledgements

I wish to warmly thank Nurudeen Alimi, Elias Pekkola, Lisa Henckel, Annalena Rehkämper, Elisabeth Donat and Graeme Currie for their helpful comments to this contribution.

References

Aiello, Valentina/Brasili, Cristina/Calia, Pinuccia/Monasterolo, Irene (2018): "Report on the Probabilistic Model of Estimation of Citizens' Identification with the EU Projects and Reanking of the Case Stury Regions." In: Perception and Evaluation of Regional and Cohesion Policies by Europeans and Identification with the Values of Europe Delliverable 2.4.

Armbruster, Heidi/Rollo, Craig/Meinhof, Ulrike H. (2003): "Imagining Europe: Everyday Narratives in European Border Communities." In: Journal of Ethnic and Migration Studies 29/5, pp. 885–899.

Bachtler, John/Begg, Iain/Charles, David/Polverari, Laura (2016): EU Cohesion Policy in Practice What Does It Achieve?, Lanham: Rowman & Littlefield.

Bachtrögler, Julia/Fratesi, Ugo/Perucca, Giovanni (2019): "The Influence of the Local Context on The Implementation and Impact of EU Cohesion Policy." In: Regional Studies, pp. 1–14.

Borz, Gabriela/Brandenburg, Heinz/Mendez, Carlos (2018): "The Impact of EU Cohesion Policy on European Identity." In: COHESIFY Research Paper 14.

Bruter, Michael (2003): "Winning Hearts and Minds for Europe: The Impact of News and Symbols on Civic and Cultural European Identity." In: Comparative Political Studies 36/10, pp. 1148–1179.

Bruter, Michael (2008): "Legitimacy, Euroscepticism & Identity in the European Union – Problems of Measurement, Modelling & Paradoxical Patterns of Influence." In: Journal of Contemporary European Research 4/4, pp. 273–285.

Capello, Roberta (2018): "Cohesion Policies and the Creation of a European Identity: The Role of Territorial Identity." In: JCMS: Journal of Common Market Studies 56/3, pp. 489–503.

Chacha, Mwita (2013): "Regional Attachment and Support for European Integration." In: European Union Politics 14/2, pp. 206–227.

Chalmers, Adam William/Dellmuth, Lisa Maria (2015): "Fiscal Redistribution and Public Support for European Integration." In: European Union Politics 16/3, pp. 386–407.

Clements, B. (2011): "Understanding 'Utilitarian' Support for European Integration in Scotland and Wales: The Role of Economic Interests, National Identity and Party Support." In: Regional and Federal Studies 21/1, pp. 1–21.

Crescenzi, Ricardo/Giua, Mara (2017): "Different Approaches to the Analysis of EU Cohesion Policy" In: Bachtler, John/Berkowitz, Peter/Hardy, Sally (eds.), EU Cohesion Policy: Reassessing Performance and Direction, London: Routledge, pp. 21–32.

Eichenberg, Richard C./Dalton, Russell J. (1993): "Europeans and the European Community: The Dynamics of Public Support for European Integration." In: International Organization 47/4, pp. 507–534.

European Commission (2018): "The EU's Main Investment Policy", November 20, 2019 (http://ec.europa.eu/regional_policy/en/policy/what/investment-policy/)

Fiaschi, Davide/Lavezzi, Andrea Mario/Parenti, Angela (2018): "Does EU Cohesion Policy Work? Theory and Evidence." In: Journal of Regional Science 58/2, pp. 386–423.

Fligstein, Neil/Polykova, Alina/Sandholtz, Wayne (2012): "European Integration, Nationalism and European Identity." In: JCMS: Journal of Common Market Studies 50/1, pp. 106–122.

Herrmann, Richard K./Brewer, Marilynn B. (2004): "Identities and Institutions: Becoming European in the EU" In: Herrmann, Richard K./Risse-Kappen, Thomas/Brewer, Marilynn B. (eds.), Transnational Identities: Becoming European in the EU, Lanham: Rowman & Littlefield, pp. 1–24.

Hobolt, Sara/Vries, Michiel (2016): "Public Support for European Integration." In: Annual Review of Political Science 19/1, pp. 413–432.

Kroll, Henning (2017): "The Policy Challenge in Smart Specialisation: A Common Approach Meets European Diversity" In: Bachtler, John/Berkowitz, Peter/Hardy, Sally (eds.), EU Cohesion Policy: Reassessing Performance and Direction, London: Routledge, pp. 115–126.

Lo Piano, Samuele/Chifari, Rosaria/Saltelli, Andrea (2017): "Regionalisation of ESIF Payments 1989-2015", November 20, 2019 (https://op.europa.eu/en/publication-detail/-/publication/cd2133d5-1d04-11e8-ac73-01aa75ed71a1/language-en/format-PDF/source-68135162).

Medeiros, Eduardo (2017): "From Smart Growth to European Spatial Planning: A New Paradigm for EU Cohesion Policy Post-2020." In: European Planning Studies 25/10, pp. 1856–1875.

Medrano, Juan Díez/Gutiérrez, Paula (2001): "Nested Identities: National and European Identity in Spain." In: Ethnic and Racial Studies 24/5, pp. 753–778.

Medve-Blaint, Gergo (2017): "Funds for the Walthy and Plotocally Loyal? How EU Funds May Contribute to Increasing Regional Disparities in East Central Europe" In: Bachtler, John/Berkowitz, Peter/Hardy, Sally (eds.), EU Cohesion Policy: Reassessing Performance and Direction,London: Routledge, pp. 220–240.

Mendez, Carlos/Bachtler, John (2017): "European Identity and Citizen Attitudes to Cohesion Policy: What Do We Know?" In: COHESIFY Research Paper 1.

Nissen, Sylke (2014): "The Eurobarometer and the Process of Europan Integration." In: Quality and Quanitity 48, pp. 713–727.

Osterloh, Steffen (2011): "Can Regional Transfer Buy Public Support?" In: ZEW Discussion Papers no. 11-011.

Pegan, Andreja/Mendez, Carlos/Triga, Vasiliki (2018): "What do citizens think of Cohesion Policy and does it matter for European Identity?" In: COHESIFY Research Paper no. 13.

Peter/Hardy, Sally (eds.), EU Cohesion Policy: Reassessing Performance and Direction, London: Routledge, pp. 220–240.

Pontarollo, Nicola (2017): "Does Cohesion Policy affect regional growth? New Evidence from a Semi-Parametric Approach" In: Bachtler, John/Berkowitz, Peter/Hardy, Sally (eds.), EU Cohesion Policy: Reassessing Performance and Direction, London: Routledge, pp. 69–84.

Roose, Jochen (2013): "How European is European Identification? Comparing Continental Identification in Europe and Beyond." In: JCMS: Journal of Common Market Studies 51/2, pp. 281–297.

Rosik, Piotr/Stepaniak, Marcin/Komornicki, Tomasz (2017): "An Evaluation of the Impact of the Construction of Motorways and Expressways in Poland during the Period 2004-13 on Accessibility and Cohesion" In: Bachtler, John/Berkowitz,

Peter/Hardy, Sally (eds.), EU Cohesion Policy: Reassessing Performance and Direction, London: Routledge, pp. 87–100.

Verhaegen, Soetkin/Hooghe, Marc/Quintelier, Ellen (2014): "European Identity and Support for European Integration." In: Kyklos: International Review for Social Sciences 67/2, pp. 295–314.

List of Tables and Figures

Figure 1: "Model I." Created by Landes, Fabian (2020) for this publication.
Figure 2: "Model II." Created by Landes, Fabian (2020) for this publication.
Table 1: "fixed effects regression parameters." Created by Landes, Fabian (2020) for this publication.

The EU's Regional Investments After the Financial Crisis
Paradigm Change or Business as Usual?

Moritz Neujeffski

Introduction

The President of the European Investment Bank (EIB), Werner Hoyer, made a bold statement in 2016. In the preface of an EIB report, Hoyer praised the novelty of European Commission President Juncker's flagship project aimed at rebooting investments in Europe after the global financial crisis (GFC):

> Today, the paradigm shift in the use of public funds – away from grants and subsidies, in favour of loans and guarantees –[...] namely the Investment Plan for Europe and its pillars European Fund for Strategic Investments (EFSI) and European Investment Advisory Hub (EIAH), offer us an historical opportunity to go the extra mile and mobilise more private and public sector funding [...] (EIB 2016)

The €500bn Investment Plan for Europe (IPE) was the EU's supra-national answer to the severe credit crunch in the European real economy induced by the GFC. Launched in 2014 by the European Commission (EC), the IPE gave leeway to riskier investment policies and relied on less prominent actors such as the EIB to carry out the investment recovery.

The influential political scientist Peter A. Hall would, however, probably raise an eyebrow at Hoyer's claim. According to Hall, true paradigm shifts go beyond the introduction of new policy instruments. Rather, they alter 'the hierarchy of goals behind a policy' altogether (Hall 1993: 282). To determine how far the introduction of the IPE in 2014 marks a paradigmatic shift, this chapter compares the introduction of the IPE with the evolution of the 'EU's main investment policy tool' (European Commission, n.d. a), namely the European Structural and Investment Funds (ESI Funds). In doing this, it highlights the role of strategic discourses put forth by the advocates of competing policies in stipulating policy change.

According to Walter Deffaa the former Directorate-General for Regional and Urban Policy (DG REGIO), the two funds represent 'different intervention philosophies' (Deffaa 2016: 162). The IPE is a leveraged fund, using small public contributions to crowd-in private capital. Based on loans and guarantees, it can be considered a market-enforcing policy. ESI Funds, on the other hand, are predominantly transfer based, rely on grants and can be considered a market-correction tool for taming regional inequalities in Europe.

This chapter argues that the resistance of the economically strong member states (MS) towards addressing the EU's 'fiscal capacity gap' (Braun/Hübner 2018: 131) in order to promote macro-economic stability amplified the pressure to rely on market-based instruments (such as the IPE) to cope with the credit crunch. Even though the two funds are formally unrelated, the opposition of economically strong MS to a 'Marshall Plan for Europe' or to transforming the Cohesion Policy into a 'major tool for investment, growth and job creation' (Friends of Cohesion 2012), as demanded by the economically weaker MS, created the space for the EC to strengthen innovative financial policies. Thus, contrary to Hoyer, the very absence of a disruptive third-order change after the GFC – away from austerity-based policy frameworks towards expansionary fiscal policies – led to a stronger reliance on 'private funds which look for profits' (Deffaa 2016: 162). The argument is akin to Wolfgang Streeck's insight that the expansion of market principles is the logical consequence of a consolidation state in which government debt reduction takes primacy (2015).

The chapter starts by discussing Hall's theory of policy change (1993) and Streeck's political-economic approach to the EU mode of governance. It highlights the importance of discourse coalitions (Hajer 1993) in stipulating whether policies are changed or maintained. In subsequent sections, the theoretical framework is then applied to examine the development of the ESI Funds and the EFSI and the accompanying discursive struggles. After introducing the functioning and rationale of the ESI Funds, this chapter identifies a redefinition of goals towards fostering competitiveness prior to the crisis. The third section then analyses the intergovernmental negotiations over the 2014–2020 Multiannual Financial Framework (MFF) within the European Council and singles out the discourse of 'better spending' introduced by the net contributors. Fourth, the introduction of the EFSI and the increasing use of financial instruments within the ESI Funds are also examined. These measures were promoted by the EC and the EIB in terms of 'doing more with less', and this chapter identifies a similar efficiency-enhancing discourse in this regard.

Policy Change and Paradigm Maintenance

Peter Hall's influential theory of policy change and social learning (Hall 1993) distinguishes between three different orders of policy change, where each indicates a different magnitude of alteration. Whereas first-order changes represent incremental, 'routinized decision making' (ibid.: 280), the implementation of new measures constitutes a second-order change and is identified with more 'strategic action' (ibid.). Hall regards both these orders of changes as 'normal policymaking' (ibid.: 279) or adaptations of instruments to attain unchanged policy objectives. He exemplifies this with the occasional adjustment of macro-economic policies under the Keynesian British governments of the 1970s.

Third-order changes, on the other hand, alter 'the hierarchy of goals behind a policy' (ibid.: 282), are more political in nature and 'are often preceded by significant shifts in the locus of authority over policy' (ibid.: 280). Third-order changes often follow societal changes and economic crises as the 'accumulation of anomalies' (ibid.) can no longer be explained by the current paradigm.

However, this raises the question of why a third-order change did not occur after the GFC. As Mark Blyth put it 'Indeed, if there was ever a perfect case for a paradigm shift in a Bayesian term surely this was it?' (Blyth 2013: 206). Furthermore, although many governments across the globe implemented stimulus packages (e.g. Germany's car-scrapping premium) and performed massive bank bailouts, the return to fiscal consolidation strategies to deal with the growing debt-to-GDP ratios followed shortly afterwards.

In addition, Blyth highlights the constructivist nature of paradigms in invoking or resisting change, and points to the role of ideas and the shift of authority needed for a policy change to occur. Rather than the anomalies itself, the struggle over their interpretation by competing actors (ibid.: 211) is crucial for third-order changes to come about. Hajer's concept of discourse coalitions can be fruitfully applied to examine how different actors offer interpretations strategically to induce or prevent policy changes. A discourse coalition is an 'ensemble of a set of story lines, the actors that utters these story lines, and the practices that conform to these story lines, all organized around a discourse' (Hajer 1993: 47). Dieter Plehwe adds that discourse coalitions need to be understood as 'social forces acting jointly, though not necessarily in direct interaction in pursuit of a common goal' (2011: 130).

In the context of the GFC, gaps in the institutional architecture of European Monetary Union (EMU), i.e. the inability to revert to currency devaluation coupled with the absence of some form of transfer system or joint liabilities, posed severe obstacles for struggling MS. With external devaluation unavailable for less competitive MS, Streeck sees 'only a financial transfer between rich and poor Member States' (Streek 2013: 325) as a viable alternative to an internal devaluation (cutting wages and social benefits), possibly 'in form of an active regional-policy [...] in favour of the latter' (ibid.). In the absence of a paradigm shift in economic governance towards a Keynesian, expansionary fiscal framework (Blyth 2013a), Streeck predicts that public investment gaps (e.g. in infrastructure or social housing) must be replaced '[...] with private investment backed by the public' (Streek 2015: 22). This process of financialisation comprises two distinct developments initiated by the pressure of growing macro-economic imbalances: The contraction of public, redistributive transfer programs between MS (and hence also of market-correction tools) and the initiation and expansion of market-based alternatives. The conceptual framework of discourse coalitions provides us with fruitful insight into how a struggle over a two-stage process proceeds. It helps us to understand how the discourse formation of EMU, in which MS, market actors, practices and ideas enable and facilitate the expansion of market-based alternatives as the 'viable solution', becomes dominant, opposed to solutions based on joint liabilities or transfer systems.

In order to understand how these discursive strategies are practised, the following section starts by describing the main rationale of the ESI Funds and then traces how the notion of competitiveness led to a reorientation of these funds' policy goals.

The Structural Funds: From Redistribution to Increasing Competitiveness

Since the foundation of the European Economic Community (EEC), the creation and expansion of a single market has been prioritised, strengthening market forces in Europe. At the same time, the EU is committed to social inclusion and cohesion objectives, which provided the reasons for public transfers (agricultural policy, regional and structural funds) According to David Harvey (1982), capitalist production brings about uneven geographical developments due to agglomeration effects and economies of scale, among other factors. This is also true for the EU, and the four rounds of enlargement since the 1980s increased socio-economic differences within the EU, as Greece (1981), Spain and Portugal (1986) and the eleven Central and Eastern European Countries (CEE) entered with much lower levels of GDP than the northern MS. Policy conflicts between the completion of the single market, on the one hand, and social inclusion and cohesion between and within the member states, on the other, have increased as a result.

Social and economic inequalities are acknowledged to have manifold negative effects for societies and are associated with reduced overall life expectancies (Rasella et al. 2013), decreasing social mobility (Kearney/Levine 2014) and higher levels of dissatisfaction with the democratic system (Schäfer 2010). Recently, regional inequalities have been interpreted as a cause of intensified political polarisation and increasing vote shares for Eurosceptic parties (Dijkstra et al. 2018; Manow 2018). Borin, Macchi & Mancini (2018) suggest that adequate compensation within economically disadvantageous regions in the EU has positive effects on approval rates towards the European project.

The good news: Income inequality in the EU has decreased slightly in recent years, at least when GDP levels between MS are compared (Dauderstädt 2019: 3).

This results mostly from the strong catch-up processes of the CEEs. Yet, average income levels between MS such as Bulgaria and Luxembourg remain very high, and inter-regional inequalities within member states have been rising since the 1980s (Hadjimichalis 2011: 257; Rosés/Wolf, 2018; Dauderstädt 2019: 3).

To counteract unequal regional living standards, the European Community saw early on the need for a regional transfer policy and introduced the Cohesion Policy with the Single European Act in 1985. This is reflected in the Act's goal to 'promote its overall harmonious development', (Article 174, TFEU) especially by 'reducing disparities between the levels of development of the various regions and the backwardness of the least favoured regions' (ibid.).

Until the European financial crisis, the budget share allocated to the ESI Funds had grown steadily and is currently equal to one-third of the total EU budget. The funds are invested locally and can be described as an 'active form of EU solidarity' (Europa.eu n.d.) Jointly administered by the EU and the MS, the ESI Funds are usually based on a co-financing system in which contributions by the EU are matched by the receiving regions. Table 1 displays the main ESI Funds for the current funding period (2014–2020). The funds themselves consist of programmes that are intended to achieve the ESI Funds' overall goals and policy objectives. Table 2 shows the funds' growth between 1989 and 2020. Organised along core-periphery logics, funding is secured through MS allocating around one percent of their Gross National Income (GNI), which is often interpreted as a rather modest contribution. The budget is redistributed along certain eligibility criteria for regions, which automatically creates net contributors and net beneficiaries. This funding is vital for certain less developed regions, as it can make up for four percent of their GDP (Krieger-Boden 2018: 10), especially through the Cohesion Fund, which targets regions with a GNI per capita average below 90 percent of the EU average.

Table 1: The European Structural and Investment Funds

Funds (2014-2020 MFF period)	Rationale
European Regional Development Fund (**ERDF**)	corrects imbalances between regions and fosters cohesion in social and economic terms
European Social Fund (**ESF**)	Investments in human-capita, promotes employment
Cohesion Fund (**CF**)	Environment & infrastructure projects in countries where GNI per capita is below 90% of EU average
European Agricultural Fund for Rural Development (**EAFRD**)	targets the challenges for rural areas
European Maritime and Fisheries Fund (**EMFF**)	focuses on EU coastal regions and fishery-industry

Table 2: ESIF Funding in Million Euros from 1989 to 2020 (five funding periods)

Funding period	1989-1993	1994-1999	2000-2006	2007-2013	2014-2020
ERDF	28 640		122 012	180 547	199 237
ESF	Not available	Not available	66 003	71 000	83 924
CF	-	18 078	30 619	66 186	63 297
YEI	-	-	-	-	8 847
EAGGF / EAFRD	923	17 905	22 200	86 107	100 079
Total	**29 564**	**113 719**	**240 834**	**403 841**	**461 117**

Sources: The amounts for the different funds can be found on the Commission's website: https://cohesiondata.ec.europa.eu

The budget size, the overall goals and the regional eligibility criteria for funding are shaped by recurring negotiations between the MS and the supra-national institutions (especially the EC). The most encompassing policy change can be observed with the introduction of the Lisbon Strategy in 2000. The strategy's intention to turn the EU into 'the most competitive and dynamic knowledge-based economy in the world' (European Council 2000) altered the Cohesion Policy towards targeting competitiveness and growth as additional policy objectives. Thus, next to market-correction objectives, it also introduced market-enhancing ones.

However, achieving cohesion by increasing regional competitiveness and growth is contested. Trade-offs exist between enhancing regional equality and economic productivity, as economic growth generally does not spread out equally within a country. Rather it is based on cluster effects. These entail geographical investment concentrations (Krieger-Boden 2018: 11), as productive regions possess advantages, e.g. more developed infrastructures, skilled labour, and specialised service providers, which create economies of scale (Pauli 2019). In this context, Giordano and Dubois (2018) speak of 'territorial tensions' (ibid.: 2) that have emerged (especially within the ERDF) since the 2007 funding period.

Besides the reorientation of goals, the 2007-2013 period also broadened the eligibility criteria for regions to receive funding. Whereas Objective 2 of the Cohesion Policy was previously only available to former industrial areas, it is now accessible to all regions to promote competitiveness and innovation (Bodirsky 2015). This was the second change in the ESI Funds to decrease the redistributive nature of the policy, since regions that are already productive can now gain funding.

These policy restructuring measures were accompanied by changes in discourse, too, as competitiveness became the catchphrase of the day. These discursive shifts have been embedded within the general rise of 'new regionalism' since the 1990s, which confers the notion of corporate competitiveness onto regions. According to this concept of interlocational competition between regions at a global level, governments should compete in attempting to provide the most business-friendly environments in a competition over the location of businesses themselves. Greater regional competitiveness is expected to bring about jobs and economic growth. It seems uncertain how far this approach can decrease regional disparities if unevenly developed regions are competing more directly over resources. Bradanini (2009) places the increasing focus on competitiveness and efficiency gains in the broader context of the development of EU institutions and policies to show how market logics were given more and more precedence over social concerns. Introducing competitiveness, innovation and growth as a remedy for decreasing regional disparities can be interpreted as a third-order policy change, as overall objectives have changed fundamentally. These policy changes, however, need to be analysed in the context of political struggles between different coalitions and actors within the EU's multilevel governance system to enhance our understanding of how policy changes are pushed through. Thus, the following section examines the negotiations over the reinterpretation of the Cohesion Policy in more detail, focusing especially on the notion of 'better spending' by net-contributing countries within the EU.

Political Conflict Lines After the Financial Crisis: The 2014-2020 Budget Negotiations

The GFC pushed the European banking system and the real economy to the brink of collapse. For about twelve months, stimulus packages (Blyth 2013) and massive bank bailouts were introduced by governments worldwide to counteract the deteriorating economic situation. Anxious that the consequence of growing government debt-to-GDP ratios would destabilise the Eurozone as a whole, the (relatively) unshaken Northern MS soon started to demand that the Eastern and Southern MS impose strong fiscal consolidation measures. Thus, the negotiations held in 2012 over the ESI Funds in the 2014–2020 MFF were ill-fated from the start. In this respect, the negotiations over the Cohesion Policy in 2011 provide an important entry point. The Commission's legislative proposal to restructure the Cohesion Policy in 2011 was soon taken over by the net contributors, who acted as the drivers of policy change. Comparing the economic developments of the net-contributor countries and the net beneficiaries shows that the latter were affected more severely. At the time of negotiation in 2012, loan defaults by (non-financial) companies had increased to over ten percent (median) within the beneficiary countries and remained relatively stable in the net-contributor countries (see Figure 1). Figure 2 below shows the growing spread between France, Germany, Spain and Italy in terms of the ability of their banking sectors to contract loans with non-financial companies. Especially for the beneficiaries, this caused additional political pressure to stabilise the economy through governmental investments.

Figure 1: Bank non-performing loans (npl) to total gross loans (%) in the EU, Figure 2: loans to non-financial companies by banks (stock) (%) in the EU (in billions)

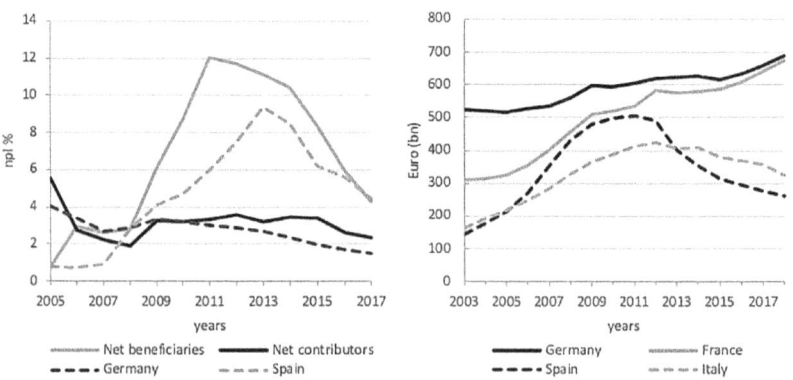

Source: data.worldbank.org The chart displays the median for the net-beneficiaries and the net-contributors, *Source: European Central Bank (Statistical Data Warehouse)

Politically, the 'tortuous battles' (Kölling/Serrano Leal 2012) over the 2014–2020 MFF intensified against the background of the Eurozone crisis. The hardened fronts were represented by two groups of member states in the European Council: The net beneficiaries (Friends of Cohesion) and the net contributors (Friends of Better Spending) to the ESI Funds (see table three below). They represented opposing discourse coalitions. Whereas the Friends of Better Spending demanded strong contribution cuts and stronger conditionalities, the Friends of Cohesion stressed the necessity of redistributive policies and aimed at expanding the Cohesion Policy.

Table 3: "Friends of Better Spending" and "Friends of Cohesion"

Friends of Better Spending	Friends of Cohesion
Germany, France, Finland, Austria, Sweden and the Netherlands	Bulgaria, the Czech Republic, Estonia, Greece, Latvia, Lithuania, Malta, Portugal, Slovakia, Slovenia and Spain

The Friends of Cohesion were not the only actors that argued for an expansion of grant-based transfers. To revive economic activity and stabilise the EMU, social-democratic and progressive actors such as the German Federation of Trade Unions (DGB) called for a 'Marshall Plan for Europe' (DGB 2012), demanding much higher transfers between core and periphery countries, with a base calculation of €260bn annually. For the same purpose, the Friends of Cohesion saw the need to improve the 'conditions for sustainable growth and jobs' (Friends of Cohesion 2012). They argued that 'the European budget, and the Cohesion Policy in particular, should play a strong role in this regard' (ibid.) and conceived the ESI Funds as the toolkit for an anti-cyclical approach 'to invest out of the crisis' (ibid.) as well as to utilize the Cohesion Policy for this as it 'remains a key investment tool for our countries' (ibid.).

The Friends of Better Spending constituted the discourse coalition at the other end of the spectrum. Germany's resistance to setting up shared liabilities (e.g. Eurobonds) and its demand for growth-friendly consolidation has been widely studied (Blyth 2013a; 2013b; Moravcsik 2012; Plehwe 2018). In terms of overall funding, the Friends of Better Spending called for a €100bn cut in the Cohesion Policy (of €1 trillion in planned spending) within the period 2014-2020 (Sweden demanded even stronger cuts). Spearheaded by Merkel and Sarkozy, the Friends of Better Spending stuck to the discourse of enhancing growth and competition discussed in the previous section: 'Structural and cohesion funds should be used to support essential reforms to enhance economic growth and competitiveness in the Euro Area' (Merkel/Sarkozy, 2011). In addition, they suggested placing the ESI Funds under the fiscal consolidation rules so that 'In the future, payments from structural and cohesion funds should be suspended in Euro Area countries not complying with recommendations under the excessive deficit procedure' (ibid.). Additional proposals were put forward to revise the eligibility criteria so that certain amounts would safely go to transitioning regions of the more developed MS. The notion of 'better spending' was thereby utilised to frame the Cohesion Policy as inefficient, to legitimise a restructuring of funding and to reduce overall funding. Through this efficiency-enhancing 'storyline', the better spenders achieved a reduction in overall spending within the Cohesion Policy and the introduction of conditionalities via the linkage to the European Semester.

Yet, this could not do away with the credit crunch. Streeck's insight that the logical consequence of budget consolidation is to engender a stronger reliance on private capital is observable in European regional investment as well. In their joint declaration, the Friends of Better Spending also called for stronger involvement of the European Investment Bank (Friends of Better Spending 2012: 2), which previously had a role in advocating public-private partnerships (Liebe/Howarth 2019). The following section analyses how the EIB became involved in two market-enhancing developments. By first carrying out the Juncker Plan and second promoting the usage of financial instruments within the ESI Funds, the EIB played a crucial part in buttressing a new understanding of regional development policy. Both the Commission and the EIB relied on a similar efficiency-enhancing discursive frame as deployed by the better spenders to gain support for their ambitions.

The Return of Keynes or 'Juncker-Voodoo'?

To undo the Gordian Knot of investing in the real economy while being prevented from investing in the real economy, the newly elected Commissioner Jean-Claude Juncker proposed an Investment Plan for Europe in 2014. Based on three pillars, the Commission set up the European Fund for Strategic Investments (EFSI), initiated the European Investment Advisory Hub to support investment and sought to remove regulatory investment barriers. The EFSI's initial size of €315bn to invest in innovation, infrastructure and SMEs was extended to €500bn in 2016. But what seems like a strong response to the credit crunch and exceeds the Structural Funds' volume (€450bn in 2014–2020) needs to be put in perspective.

The EFSI does not comprise fresh public money but uses an initial sum of €21bn partly drawn from the existing EU budget[1] to provide guarantees for private investments. It aims to mobilise private capital by securing against potential investment

---

1　€8bn was taken from the Horizon 2020 budget, €8bn was provided in forms of EU guarantees and another €5bn was provided by the EIB.

defaults and thereby to leverage the limited pubic resources at a ratio of 1:15. Mertens and Thiemann have termed this initiative, which is connected to the Capital Markets Union (CMU), an extension of market-based finance (Mertens/Thiemann 2018), yet it is state led, and has revived the 'securitization markets' (ibid.: 3). Against the backdrop of the GFC, in which asset-backed securities (especially on mortgages [MBS]) in combination with high leverage ratios caused a financial meltdown, it seems surprising that the Commission relied on such instruments to regain macro-economic stability (Braun/Hübner 2018: 118).

Through the EFSI, the Commission created the supranational institutional structures for an active state-led investment policy that could potentially be equipped with higher levels of public funds in the future, while current state-aid rules and market-failure provisions could be relaxed (Mertens 2019). However, although the Commission has already declared the Juncker Plan a success story, critics have pointed to various problems. First, progressive proponents of a real Marshall Plan for Europe regarded the Commission's initiative as insignificant (0.4 percent of EU-wide GDP) to turn the tide in the real economy. Second, the EFSI entails large-scale investment in public-private partnerships (PPP)[2] and fosters the blending of public and private funds (Counter Balance 2017). PPPs turn public goods into commodities and are often more expensive for the public in the long run due to higher interest rates, among other factors (Whiteside 2011; 2017). By means of guarantees from the MFF and by installing investment platforms, the EIB shares investment risks with investors and covers the riskier tranches. 'In this way, EFSI works as a guarantee facility and a giant PPP for a variety of projects ranging from transport, R&D and housing to the energy sector' (Mertens/Thiemann 2018: 194). Third, the EIB did not earmark investments for regions that were particularly exposed to the crisis. Pauli has argued that a 'strategic' plan, should especially address the growing disparities between EU regions that have been 'left behind' and the more prosperous ones (Pauli 2019). In this regard, the European Court of Auditors criticised the fact that investments 'went to a few larger EU 15 Member States with well-established national promotional banks' (European Court of Auditors 2019: 62).

It would be misleading to describe the Juncker Plan as a replacement for the grant-based system of ESI Funds. Both fulfil different purposes and represent 'different intervention philosophies', according to Walter Deffaa (2016: 162), the former head of DG REGIO. Yet, financial instruments, which the EFSI is based on, have been gradually introduced within the ESI Funds, too. Mertens and Thiemann have traced the growing relevance of the EIB in promoting financial instruments within

---

2   This is managed by the European PPP Expertise Centre (EPEC) which 'support[s] the public sector across Europe in delivering better public-private partnerships (PPPs)'.

the ESI Funds since the end of the 1980s (Mertens/Thiemann 2019).[3] Faced with limited public spending, the Commission argued that 'grants [...] can be efficiently complemented by financial instruments, which have a leverage effect and are closer to the market' (European Commission n.d.b). The Commission encouraged MS to double the amount of FIs within the ESI Funds funded projects (European Commission 2015). By the end of 2018, the amount invested via financial instruments had already exceeded the total amount invested in the previous funding period (European Commission 2018).

Most importantly, links have been established to utilise ESI Funds within the realm of the EFSI. Both the Commission and the EIB have advocated this on different occasions. In 2016, Walter Deffaa stated that 'ESIF are expected to play a key role in helping to ensure the delivery of the IPE under all three pillars' (Deffaa 2016: 162). The advisory centre for PPP projects within the EIB established guidelines on how to better combine financial instruments and ESI grants by relying Public-Private-Partnership structure.

To convince member states, the EC and the EIB utilised a similar efficiency-enhancing 'storyline' (Hajer 1993: 47) as the Friends of Better Spending, promoting financial instruments to 'do more with less'. Whereas the Friends of Better Spending aimed at decreasing redistribution and grant payments, the EIB sought to expand market-based finance. 'Doing more with less' even amplifies the notion of better spending, as it more directly advocates efficiency gains. In 2018, the EIB organised the 'doing more with less' conference (EIB 2018), with high-ranking EU officials and a special panel on 'Financial Instruments in Cohesion Policy' (ibid.). The connection to the notion of 'better spending' was acknowledged by the German Ministry of Finance, too, which regards the EFSI as 'a continuation of the "Better-Spending"-concept for the EU budget' (German Ministry of Finance 2015). In an Interview, EIB President Hoyer offered the same interpretation, stating that the EFSI 'is logical and is consistent with the commission's policy of "better spending"' (Berschens 2016).

Choosing a market-based approach to tackle the credit crunch and explicitly referring to the better-spending notion can be interpreted as a conscious decision against traditional anti-cyclical solutions. By relying on a similar efficiency- and competitiveness-enhancing discursive strategy and by sticking to austerity, the two actor coalitions have enforced the usage of 'private investment backed by the public' (Streeck 2015: 22): the Friends of Better Spending by lessening the redistributive

---

3   Introduced for the first time in 1994, they were extended between 2007 and 2013 within programs such as JESSICA. Anguelov et al. (2018) describe how through JESSICA the potential return of investments became an important selection criterion for choosing fundable urban infrastructure projects.

component of the ESI Funds and the EIB and the EC through enforcing the EFSI and the greater usage of financial instruments.

Conclusion and Outlook

This chapter has examined how far a third-order paradigm shift from redistributive regional investments to market-based financial instruments can be identified with regard to regional investments in Europe. To accomplish this, it has analysed major reforms within the ESI Funds prior to and after the GFC and has compared this instrument to the Investment Plan for Europe. By employing the concept of discourse coalitions it has been possible to identify which competing actors have pushed for or prevented reforms. As has been shown, a major shift to attain greater cohesion by promoting regional competitiveness was already introduced prior to the GFC by coupling the ESI Funds to the Lisbon Strategy. While this did not alter 'the hierarchy of goals' (Hall 1993: 282) altogether, it did constitute a substantive alteration of policy objectives, which was deepened by the 2014–2020 MFF reforms. Against this backdrop, Hoyer's claim of a 'paradigm shift [...] away from grants and subsidies, in favour of loans and guarantees' (EIB 2016) must be interpreted as a result of the very absence of a third-order policy change. Rather than a clear-cut shift, it represents a continuous strengthening of market-based instruments and the endorsement of more competitiveness. In other words: Business as usual. The introduction of the EFSI and the expansion of financial instruments that rely on market-based tools are the logical consequence of what Streeck (2015) calls the consolidation state.

Both the ESI Fund reforms and the introduction of the EFSI were advocated based on efficiency-enhancing discourse strategies. First, in terms of the notion of 'better spending' to counter the demands of the Friends of Cohesion that the ESI Funds be transformed into an anti-cyclical investment tool. Second, by the Commission and the EIB to frame the EFSI and the expansion of financial instruments as 'doing more with less'. Connections between the two concepts were explicated by both the German Financial Ministry and EIB President Werner Hoyer. The continuous expansion of market-based finance is thus paralleled by a stable discourse coalition to push things through.

In the current negotiations, Brexit and the phasing out of rebates for net-contributor MS place additional pressure on the ESI Funds. The Friends of Better Spending have already called for the further reduction of Cohesion Funds by ten percent. Since investments to foster the single market are likely to increase (Bachtler/Mendez 2019: iii), the transformation of the originally transfer-based and market-compensating character of the ESI Funds is likely to continue.

The post-2020 'InvestEU' fund will act as a continuation of the EFSI and bring 'a multitude of financial instruments under one umbrella' (Kelly 2018). Expanded to €650bn, InvestEU objectives will also include social investments (especially in social housing). Because this attracts fewer profits, the expected leverage ratio has already been reduced to 1:13.7. In this institutionalised form, EFSI 2.0/InvestEU could function as a bargaining option for opponents of the ESI Funds. For instance, the neoliberal thinktank EPICENTER has already suggested that in order to avoid 'a mere public hand-out [EFSI] [...] should play a more prominent role in future regional development projects' (Burleigh 2017). The Friends of Cohesion seem to have accepted the new role private capital will play in the future of the ESI Funds. In their 2018 declaration, they highlighted the need for EU resources 'to promote public and private investments' (Friends of Cohesion 2018: 2).

References

Anguelov, Dimitar/Leitner, Helga/Sheppard, Eric (2018): "Engineering the Financialization of Urban Entrpreneurialism: The JESSICA Urban Development Initiative in the European Union." In: International Journal of Urban and Regional Research 42/4, pp. 573–593.

Bachtler, John/Mendez, Carlos (2019): "Reforming the MFF and Cohesion Policy 2021-27: pragmatic drift or paradigmatic shift?" In: European Policy Research Paper 107.

Berschens, Ruth (2016). "How to Invest in Europe." In: Handelsblatt 10/04/2016. November 28, 2019 (https://www.handelsblatt.com/today/finance/handelsblatt-exclusive-how-to-invest-in-europe/23541332.html?ticket=ST-9498776-KzqUJbLkmavo41XNweXs-ap5).

Blyth, Mark (2013a). "Paradigms and paradox: The politics of economic ideas in two moments of crisis." In: Governance 26/2, pp. 197–215.

Blyth, Mark (2013b). "The Austerity Delusion." In: Foreign Affairs May/June 2013, pp. 41–56.

Bodirsky, Katharina (2015): "Nach der Krise wie vor der Krise?" In: Emanzipation - Zeitschrift Für Sozialistische Theorie Und Praxis 5/9, pp. 54–68.

Borin, Alessandro/Macchi, Elisa/Mancini, Michele (2018): "EU Transfers and Euroscepticism: Can't Buy Me Love?" In: SSRN Electronic Journal 704/289, pp. 1–42.

Bradanini, Davide (2009): "The Rise of the Competitiveness Discourse – A Neo-Gramscian Analysis." Bruges Political Research Paper 10, pp. 1–40.

Braun, Benjamin/Hübner, Marina (2018): "Fiscal fault, financial fix? Capital Markets Union and the quest for macroeconomic stabilization in the Euro Area." In: Competition and Change 22/2, pp. 117–138.

Burleigh, Caroline (2017): "The Future of EU Cohesion Policy – Boosting Innovation Instead of Handouts." In: EPICENTER, November 28, 2019 (http://www.epicenternetwork.eu/blog/the-futureof-eu-cohesion-policy-boosting-innovation-instead-of-handouts/).

Counter Balance (2017): "Doing the same thing and expecting different results?", November 28, 2019 (https://quoteinvestigator.com/2017/03/23/same/).

Dauderstädt, Michael (2019): "Europas Kohäsion: Fortschritt im Schneckentempo." In: WISO Direkt 2019/09, pp. 1-4.

Deffaa, Walter (2016): "The new generation of structural and investment funds – More than financial transfers?" In: Intereconomics, 51/3, pp. 155–163.

DGB (2012): A Marshall plan for Europe, November 28, 2019 (https://www.dgb.de/themen/++co++985b632e-407e-11e2-b652-00188b4dc422).

Dijkstra, Lewi/Poelman, Hugo/Rodríguez-Pose, Andrés (2018): "The Geography of EU Discontent." In: European Commission Working Papers 2018/12, pp. 1–33.

EIB (2016): "Access-to-finance conditions for KETs companies". November 28, 2019 (https://www.eib.org/attachments/pj/access_to_finance_study_for_kets_en.pdf).

EIB (2018): "'Doing More with Less': The case for Financial Instruments in the next multiannual
EU budget", November 28, 2019 (https://ecdpm.org/events/doing-more-with-less-multiannual-eubudget/).

Europa.eu (n.d.): "Regional investment and solidarity". November 28, 2019, (https://europa.eu/european-union/topics/regional-policy_en).

European Commission (n.d. a): "Contribution of the European Structural and Investment Funds to jobs and growth, the Investment Plan and the Commission's priorities", November 28, 2019 (https://ec.europa.eu/regional_policy/en/policy/what/investment-policy/esif-contribution/).

European Commission (n.d. b): "New Cohesion Policy", November 28, 2019 (https://ec.europa.eu/regional_policy/en/2021_2027/#2).

European Commission (2015). "The European Fund for Strategic Investment: Questions and Answers" November 28, 2019 (http://europa.eu/rapid/press-release_MEMO-15-3223_en.htm).

European Court of Auditors (2019): "European Fund for Strategic Investments: Action needed to make EFSI a full success", November 28, 2019 (https://www.eca.europa.eu/Lists/ECADocuments/SR19_03/SR_EFSI_EN.pdf).

European Council (2000): "Lisbon Strategy", November 28, 2019 (http://www.europarl.europa.eu/summits/lis1_en.htm).

European PPP Expertise Center (2016): "Blending EU Structural and Investment Funds and PPPs in the 2014-2020 Programming Period Guidance Note", November 28, 2019 (https://www.eib.org/attachments/epec/epec_blending_ue_structural_investment_funds_ppps_en.pdf).

Friends of Better Spending (2012): "Non-paper submitted by AT, DE, FI, FR, IT, NL, SE."

Friends of Cohesion (2012): "Joint Declaration on the Multiannual Financial Framework 2014 –2020", November 28, 2019 (https://www.vlada.gov.sk//friends-of-cohesion-joint-declaration-onthe- multiannual-inancial-framework-2014-2020/)

Friends of Cohesion (2018): "Joint Declaration on the Multi Financial Framework 2021–2027", November 28, 2019 (https://www.vlada.cz/en/media-centrum/aktualne/friends-of-cohesion-jointdeclaration-on-the-multiannual-financial-framework-2021-2027-177497/)

German Ministry of Finance (2015): "Investitionen für Europa", November 28, 2019 (https://www.bundesfinanzministerium.de/Content/DE/Monatsberichte/2015/07/Inhalte/Kapitel-3-Analysen/3-4-investieren-in-europas-zukunft-investitionsoffensive.html)

Giordano, Benito/Dubois, Alexandre (2018): "Combining territory and competitiveness in EU Regional Policy? Analyzing ERDF investment profiles in regions with specific geographical features." In: Regional Studies 53/8, pp. 1221-1230.

Hadjimichalis, Costis (2011): "Uneven geographical development and socio-spatial justice and solidarity: European regions after the 2009 financial crisis." In: European Urban and Regional Studies 18/3, pp. 254–274.

Hajer, Maarten A. (1993): "Discourse Coalitions and the Institutionalization of Practice: The Case of Acid Rain in Britain." In: Fischer, Frank (ed.), The Argumentative Turn in Policy Analysis and Planning, London: Routledge, pp. 43-76

Hall, Peter (1993): "Policy Paradigms, Social Learning, and the State: The Case of Economic Policymaking in Britain." In: Comparative Politics 25/3, pp. 275–296.

Harvey, David (1982): The Limits to Capital, Oxford: Blackwell.

Kearney, Melissa S/Levine, Phillip B. (2014): "Income Inequality, Social Mobility and the Decision to Drop out of High School", November 28, 2019 (http://www.nber.org/papers/w20195)

Kölling, Mario/Serrano Leal, Cristina (2012): "The Negotiation of the Multiannual Financial Framework: Budgeting Europe 2020 or Business as Usual?" November 28, 2019 (https://papers.ssrn.com/sol3/papers.cfm?abstract_id=2167194)

Krieger-Boden, Christiane (2018): "What Direction Should EU Cohesion Policy Take?" In: CESifo Forum 19/1, pp. 10–15.

Liebe, Moritz/Howarth, David (2019): "The European Investment Bank as Policy Entrepreneur and the Promotion of Public-Private Partnerships." In: New Political Economy.

Manow, Philip (2018): Die Politische Ökonomie des Populismus. Berlin: Suhrkamp.

Mawdsley, Emma (2018a): "Development geography II." In: Progress in Human Geography 42/2, pp. 264–274.

Mawdsley, Emma (2018b): "'From billions to trillions.'" In: Dialogues in Human Geography 8/2, pp. 191–195.

Merkel, Angela/Sarkozy, Nicolas (2011): "Joint letter from Nicolas Sarkozy, President of the Republic, and Angela Merkel, Chancellor of Germany, to Herman Van Rompuy, President of the European Council (2011)", November 28, 2019 (https://uk.ambafrance.org/French-and-Germanleaders-defend)

Mertens, Daniel (2019): "Das Comeback der Staatsbanken?" In: Die Zukunft Des Euro 2, November 28, 2019 (https://www.boeckler.de/wsi_blog_119097.htm)

Mertens, Danial/Thiemann, Matthias (2018): "Market-based but state-led: The role of public development banks in shaping market-based finance in the European Union." In: Competition and Change 22/2: pp. 184–204.

Mertens, Danial/Thiemann, Matthias (2019): "Building a hidden investment state? The European Investment Bank, national development banks and European economic governance." In: Journal of European Public Policy 26/1, pp. 23–43.

Moravcsik, Andrew (2012): "Europe After the Crisis How to Sustain a Common Currency." In: Foreign Affairs 91/3, pp. 54–68.

Pauli, Roland (2017): "Juncker-Plan: Marktkonformes Schaumschlagen." In: Makroskop, November 28, 2019 (https://makroskop.eu/2017/03/juncker-plan-marktkonformesschaumschlagen/)

Plehwe, Dieter (2011): "Transnational discourse coalitions and monetary policy: Argentina and the limited powers of the 'Washington Consensus.'" In: Critical Policy Studies 5/2, pp. 127–148.

Plehwe, Dieter (2018): "Fighting the Financial Crisis or Consolidating Austerity? The Eurobond Battle Reconsidered." In: McBride, Stephen/Evans, Bryan M. (eds.): The Austerity State, Toronto/Buffalo/London: Toronto University Press, pp. 189–218.

Rasella, Davide/Aquino, Rosana/Barreto, Mauricio L. (2013): "Impact of income inequality on life expectancy in a highly unequal developing country: The case of Brazil." In: Journal of Epidemiology and Community Health 67/8. pp. 661–666.

Rosés, Joan/Wolf, Nikolaus (2018): "The return of regional inequality: Europe from 1900 to today." In: VoxEU.Org, November 28, 2019 (https://voxeu.org/article/return-regional-inequality-europe-1900-today#.WwUy_kIeIyw.twitter)

Schäfer, Armin (2010): "Die Folgen sozialer Ungleicheit für die Demokratie in Westeuropa." In: Zeitschrift Fur Vergleichende Politikwissenschaft, 4/1, PP. 131–156.

Streeck, Wolfgang (2013): "Nach der Krise ist in der Krise." In: Leviathan, 41/2, pp. 324–342.

Streeck, Wolfgang (2015): "The Rise of the European Consolidation State." In: MPIfG Discussion Paper 15/1.

Whiteside, Heather (2011): "Unhealthy policy: The political economy of Canadian public-private partnership hospitals." In: Health Sociology Review 20/3, pp. 258-268.

Whiteside, Heather (2017): "The Canada Infrastructure Bank: Private finance as poor alternative." In: Studies in Political Economy 98/2, pp. 223-237.

List of Tables and Figures

Figure 1: "Bank non-performing loans (npl) to total gross loans (%) in the EU." Taken from http://data.worldbank.org.

Figure 2: "loans to non-financial companies by banks (stock) (%) in the EU (in millions)." Taken from European Central Bank (Statistical Data Warehouse).

Table 1: "The European Structural and Investment Funds." Created by Neujeffski, Moritz (2020) for this publication. Data taken from https://cohesiondata.ec.europa.eu (July 30, 2019).

Table 2: "ESIF Funding in Million Euros from 1989 to 2020 (five funding periods)" Created by Neujeffski, Moritz (2020) for this publication. Data taken from https://cohesiondata.ec.europa.eu.

Table 3: ""Friends of Better Spending" and "Friends of Cohesion"" Created by Neujeffski, Moritz (2020) for this publication.

Cross-border Cooperation in Central Europe
A Comparison of Culture and Policy Effectiveness in the Polish-German and Polish-Slovak Border Regions

Urszula Roman-Kamphaus

Introduction

Cross-border cooperation is widely recognised as playing an important role in regional development concepts. Cooperation is useful in coordinating policy and jointly exploiting common development potential. Some border regions are seen as handicapped by their peripheral location and because national borders tend to hinder flows of trade, information and people (Anderson et al. 2003; Bufon 2003). In such a context, competent cross-border cooperation can help to create synergies, provide networking opportunities and stimulate development. It is for these reasons that cooperation is increasingly important in EU cohesion policy (Mirwaldt et al. 2009); since the start of the 2007–2013 funding period, cross-border cooperation has been funded by the EU as one of the fundamental objectives of cohesion policy: European Territorial Cooperation. Because territorial cooperation, and especially cross-border cooperation, is likely to play an increasingly important role in the future, it is worth examining the determinants of effective cooperation.

Cross-border cooperation is conditioned by the distinctive context of each border region. European borders differ considerably in their physical, political and economic circumstances (Arbeitsgemeinschaft Europäischer Grenzregionen 2008). Comparisons between early West European cross-border initiatives and certain more recent efforts in Central and Eastern Europe (CEE), in particular, have shown that effective cooperation is often more difficult to achieve in CEE (Kepka & Murphy 2002; Yoder 2003). This is because conditions such as cross-border linkages or financial resources tend to be less favourable in CEE than in many Western European border regions. For cooperation to have a positive effect, it must be tailored to build on regional strengths while simultaneously addressing local problems.

Previous studies (Perkmann 2003; Yoder 2003) have identified a range of background conditions that shape cooperation in specific regions. However, these studies have relied almost entirely on in-depth case study research that does not permit generalisation. Systematic comparative analysis to determine what factors promote policy effectiveness has so far been conspicuously absent. This suggests that comparing carefully selected cases could help to determine the impact on the ground of different contextual factors. Consequently, this chapter compares cooperation experiences in the Polish-German and Polish-Slovak border regions. These two regions face similar political, economic and legal problems. However, in terms of cultural interlinkages across the border, the Polish-Slovak border benefits from a far more favourable context than does the Polish-German border region. Thus, comparing these two cases makes it possible to identify the impact of different cultural and social backgrounds on the effectiveness of cooperation.

The analysis relies on documentary evidence such as the programmes themselves, implementation documents and annual reports from the two regions. In order to interpret this basic information, the analysis also relies on 36 semi-structured interviews with policymakers conducted between March 2009 and September 2011. The next section, which traces the development of cross-border cooperation in Europe, is followed by a review of previous enquiries into contextual factors. The fourth section compares the Polish-German and Polish-Slovak cross-border programmes in the 2000–2006 and 2007–2013 funding periods with regard to three dimensions of policy effectiveness: policy definition, policy implementation and policy innovation. The comparative conclusions reveal that close cultural links facilitate policy definition and, above all, implementation in the Polish-Slovak border region but that the absence of such links in the Polish-German border region has inspired policymakers to innovate.

Cross-Border Cooperation in the European Context

Cross-border cooperation is defined here as institutionalised collaboration between subnational authorities such as regions or municipalities that adjoin each other across international borders. There are many different forms of cooperation across borders, but EU-funded cross-border cooperation is particularly intensive and has become widespread since 1990.

Cross-border cooperation began in the 1950s and 1960s in West European regions such as the Dutch-German borderlands, the Upper Rhine valley and the Lake Constance region (Scott 1996; Blatter 2004). The Dutch-German 'Euregio', where subnational authorities agreed to mutually beneficial cooperation across the border, was launched in 1958 as the first initiative of this sort. There was a perception that the borderlands suffered from their peripheral position – both geographically and politically – in the Netherlands and Germany. Cooperation was seen as a means of addressing these negative effects. In institutionalising cooperation, Dutch and German border municipalities first engaged in relationship-building across the border and then lobbied jointly for concrete goals such as improvements in cross-border infrastructure. The Euregio has subsequently been described as a model for cross-border cooperation and was the inspiration for several similar initiatives in the 1970s (Scott 1996; Perkmann 2003).

In the 1980s and 1990s, European institutions began to provide legal and financial support for cross-border cooperation (Perkmann 1999). First, a number of multilateral agreements were concluded through the Council of Europe, such as the European Outline Convention on Transfrontier Cooperation, which was signed in 1980 and committed the member states to facilitating and fostering cross-border cooperation. Second, the EU started supporting cross-border cooperation financially in 1990, when the INTERREG Community Initiative was first introduced as the main funding instrument for territorial cooperation (Ferry & Gross 2005).

Following the introduction of legal and financial support instruments, cross-border initiatives mushroomed all over Western Europe. According to one estimate, there were 15 cross-border regions by the end of the 1970s, 30 by the end of the 1980s and 73 by the end of the 1990s (Perkmann 2003). Today, there is hardly any European border that is not covered by a cross-border agreement. Cross-border cooperation takes place on the territory of what are known as 'Euroregions', voluntary associations of municipalities that lie adjacent to state borders. Examples include the original Dutch-German Euregio, the Transmanche region that stretches across the English Channel and the Pyrenees-Mediterranean Euroregion, which links French and Spanish regional authorities.

Partly due to the proliferation of cross-border initiatives, INTERREG has become ever more important since its introduction in 1990, both in terms of funding and the scope of its activities, which have been expanded over time to cover diverse forms of territorial cooperation. Cooperation has also acquired a high profile in EU cohesion policy. Thus, since the adoption in 1999 of the European Spatial Development Perspective, an attempt to harmonise spatial planning at the European level, and with the gradual embracing of the 'territorial cohesion' objective in the 2000s, cross-border cooperation has been seen as good way of promoting more even spatial development (Mirwaldt et al. 2009). With the start of the 2007–2013 funding period, territorial cooperation was upgraded further, as INTERREG became the third core objective of EU cohesion policy (Objective 3), after convergence and competitiveness and employment. In the same period, the budget for the implementation of all 52 cross-border programmes was €5.6 billion from the European Regional Development Fund (ERDF), the main financial instrument of EU cohesion policy.

In Objective 3 programmes, just as in INTERREG previously, a formal agreement between regional authorities is followed by the definition of multi-annual programmes that lay down the medium-term priorities of a particular cross-border region. These programmes are implemented through projects in such areas as planning, tourism and services infrastructure. Like all Structural Funds programmes, they are notoriously difficult to implement because institutional structures are complex and because the European Commission has established strict regulations for managing and implementing its funds (Bachtler et al. 2005). For example, while a managing authority has overall responsibility, substantive managerial and supervisory competences lie with a monitoring committee. Various other committees, authorities and working groups are responsible for processing applications and for ensuring compliance with the EU's demanding financial rules.

While the first cross-border ventures were bottom-up initiatives that arose out of local needs, the creation of a European opportunity structure was crucial in bringing about the proliferation of cooperation initiatives in the 1980s and 1990s (Church & Reid 1999; Perkmann 1999, 2002, 2003). The influence of European support in stimulating new cross-border ventures is particularly apparent in Central and Eastern Europe.

Until 1989, the communist states were cut off by the Iron Curtain. There was very little cross-border cooperation within the communist bloc and certainly no intensive, multi-dimensional cooperation of the sort described above in certain Western European regions (Kepka & Murphy 2002; Halás 2007). After the end of the Cold War, with preparations underway to extend the European integration process eastward, Hungary, Poland and Czechoslovakia almost immediately instigated cooperation with Western Europe and subsequently with each other. The trilateral Neisse-Nisa-Nysa Euroregion between Germany, Poland and Czechoslovakia (the Czech Republic after 1993) was founded in 1991 as the first such venture. Others soon followed.

Many CEE cross-border initiatives suffered from historical disadvantages that made it difficult to apply the Western model. There was only a weak tradition of regionalism in CEE states (Batt & Wolczuk 2002; Kepka & Murphy 2002), and local and especially regional authorities either did not exist or lacked the powers to conclude and implement cross-border agreements. National administrations commonly sought to control cross-border ventures, often because they viewed regional autonomy as a challenge to the integrity of the state (Keating & Hughes 2003). Slovakia's Prime Minister Vladimír Mečiar, for example, attempted to centralise power and obstructed cross-border cooperation until the end of his period in power in 1998. Mečiar may have been an extreme example, but scepticism about subnational empowerment and cross-border cooperation could also be detected in other CEE states, including the Czech Republic (Bazin 2003). As a result of the top-down nature of cross-border cooperation in CEE, this cooperation was sometimes accused of being insensitive to local peculiarities (Popescu 2006).

Borders were much harsher barriers in CEE than anywhere in Western Europe. In the communist bloc, they had been largely closed to citizen traffic (Batt & Wolczuk 2002; Kepka & Murphy 2002). Moreover, many of these borders were historically associated with deep-seated conflict. For example, the Hungarian-Romanian border was linked with territorial losses after the World Wars, the Czechoslovak-German border had seen forced population transfers, and Poland's border with the Soviet Union was associated with both. As a result, cross-border flows were extremely limited after 1989, and CEE had no tradition of cross-border interaction comparable to most border regions in Western Europe (Yoder 2003).

How does the CEE context affect the governance of cross-border cooperation and, by implication, the success of the programmes? In order to answer this question, the next section considers a number of crucial background conditions, introduces the Polish-German and Polish-Slovak case studies, and develops three criteria to evaluate cooperation.

Explaining the Governance of Cross-Border Cooperation

Conditions on the ground have a decisive influence over the effectiveness of cooperation. Informed by policymakers' assessments, previous analyses have identified a range of crucial background conditions. These overlap and cannot always be told apart easily but, broadly speaking, there are five types of factors: regional and local self-government; legal background; socio-economic factors; funding; and culture

First, it has been shown that strong local authorities are better able to ensure successful territorial cooperation than weak ones (Bachtler et al. 2005: 135). In cooperation between regions belonging to different states, problems often result from differences in administrative structures and subnational competences that hinder formal institution-building or coordination (Assembly of European Regions 1992).

Second, cross-border cooperation typically takes place on an uncertain or vaguely defined legal basis. As most cooperation initiatives have no legal personality and no public law status, they sometimes lack the legal basis to implement decisions (Assembly of European Regions 1992). New legal instruments, such as the European Grouping for Territorial Cooperation (EGTC) introduced in 2007, are not yet used widely.

Third, socio-economic factors include the level of development, welfare gaps that coincide with a border and weakly developed cross-border infrastructure. Development gaps can make programmes more dynamic (Bachtler et al. 2005) but they can also give rise to competition and mutual suspicion. An absence of links between socio-economic actors, as well as compartmentalised markets, tends to inhibit cooperation (Krätke 1999).

Fourth, insufficient financial resources pose a major obstacle to territorial cooperation. There are often no genuinely common funds, making it difficult and time-consuming to take budgetary decisions (Assembly of European Regions 1992).

EU-funded territorial cooperation suffers from the bureaucratic effort involved in implementing these programmes (Bachtler et al. 2005).

Fifth, culture refers, on the one hand, to a region's cross-border networks, a sense of regional identity or widespread language skills – all factors that facilitate day-to-day transactions. On the other hand, it also refers to administrative culture, as cooperation is more likely to be successful between partners that share similar organisational and management styles (Ratti 1993; Hofstede 2001).

While previous studies have been able to identify influential factors, most have so far largely ignored the tools of social science to determine how these factors influence cooperation on the ground. To this end, comparative analysis is necessary. It is sometimes argued that different countries' idiosyncrasies come together and interact to produce a complex combination of explanatory factors, making inference difficult (Przeworski & Teune 1970; Macintyre 1971). However, a thorough review of existing research and corresponding case selection make it possible to identify the impact on the ground of diverging independent variables, even if they may not fully explain all aspects of cross-border cooperation.

Comparing a small number of cases makes it possible to combine the rigour of comparative enquiry with the thoroughness of in-depth analysis. There are two main ways of comparing a small number of cases. In what are known as 'most-similar systems designs', very similar cases that differ in terms of outcome are contrasted, so as to identify the influence of the divergent independent variables. Conversely, 'most-different systems designs' compare different cases with a similar outcome, pinpointing the influence of the common features (Landman 2003). This chapter employs a most-similar design in comparing the Polish-German and Polish-Slovak border regions. As Table 1 shows, these two borders face similar political, economic and legal problems. However, in terms of cultural interlinkages across the border, the Polish-Slovak border region benefits from a far more favourable context than the Polish-German border region.

Table 1 shows that the two border regions resemble each other in many respects. As in many CEE border regions, the environment is less than favourable. First, subnational competences are mismatched in an organisational sense at both borders insofar as German *Länder* have more competences than Polish *województwa*, while Slovak *kraje* are still less influential. In terms of the legal basis, a number of EGTCs are in the process of being established at both borders. Until they are finalised, the uncertain legal footing represents a problem. Third, both regions are characterised by a relatively low level of development in comparison to the national average, including infrastructure development. There are also considerable socio-economic disparities at both borders. Finally, since 2007, both regions have benefited from funding through Objective 3 (European Territorial Cooperation) of the ERDF.

In terms of cross-border culture, however, the Polish-German and Slovak-German border regions could not be more different. In the Polish-German border region, whatever cross-border networks had existed prior to World War II were destroyed as a result of the war, boundary shifts and population transfers (Urban 2004). The border was closed to citizen exchanges for most of the communist period. Thus, when the border was opened in 1991, Polish and German citizens were almost completely estranged (Matthiesen & Bürkner 2001; Rada 2004). By contrast, cross-border networks largely survived the communist period in the Polish-Slovak border region, even though cross-border contact and cooperation were limited during this period. The border was gradually opened after 1989, and the two sides were able to benefit from linguistic, cultural and social similarities (Halás 2007).

Table 1 shows that both regions grapple with several fairly difficult background conditions. These are broadly similar in both regions. Only in terms of culture is there a major difference between the unpromising environment of the Polish-German border region and the dense interconnections across the Polish-Slovak border. This suggests that the two border regions are suitable cases for comparative analysis of a 'most-similar' type (King et al. 1994; Landman 2003).

The question remains of how to operationalise the rather abstract dependent variable *effectiveness of cooperation*. On the one hand, past evaluations have used procedural indicators such as data on financial and physical progress, though these need to be complemented by rich information in order to make sense of the raw numbers (Bachtler et al. 2005). There is some merit in using these indicators: they are readily available and easy to compare across different contexts. Moreover, slow progress is usually indicative of deep-seated problems in a programme. On the other hand, these measures say very little about the governance of EU funds or how well cooperation is suited to the local context. Another measure is needed to take account of this factor. In what follows, it is suggested that cooperation experiences can be conceptualised along different dimensions and that these dimensions can be used to assess the governance of cooperation. Here, the focus is on three key aspects, namely policy definition, policy implementation and policy innovation.

The first dimension is the policy definition stage. For territorial cooperation programmes, this refers to the steps after programmes are approved by the European Commission. After approval, details such as the type and amount of available support, eligibility and selection criteria as well as committees and other rules governing the allocation of funds must be defined. The question of how long it takes to agree these implementation procedures is important because it determines when the first projects can begin. For the 2000–2006 funding period, there was enormous variation across Europe. A two-year transition period, in which projects from the previous funding period are concluded and the parameters for the new period are established, is nothing unusual (Bachtler et al. 2005). Even so, in the 2007–2013 funding period, certain West European programmes, such as the Scottish-Irish cross-border programme or the Danish-German Syddanmark-Schleswig-K.E.R.N initiative, were able to start funding projects as early as 2008. A programme start after 1 January 2009 indicated a serious delay.

The second step is to review the implementation of the programmes. Reviewing financial and physical progress is generally accepted as a cornerstone of evaluating EU cohesion policy, including cross-border cooperation (Bachtler et al. 2005: 52). In other words, in the 2007–2013 period, what are the most up-to-date commitment and payment rates at the time of writing? How many projects are already being implemented and how many have been concluded? This is important as a general indicator of implementation progress. At the same time, delays in spending money can lead to automatic loss of funds. According to the EU's 'n+2/n+3 rule' funds are automatically lost if they are not spent within two or three years of being committed. New member states, as well as Greece and Portugal, have three years to make payments ('n+3'), while West European member states mostly comply with the 'n+2 rule'. Thus, swift progress in committing and paying out funds is crucial, and delays are usually a symptom of deep-seated problems associated with the programme. Analysing progress by type of priority is also helpful in gauging the substantive progress of the programme.

The final aspect of cooperation being considered here is policy innovation. Cross-border cooperation is not normally evaluated according to how well it copes with a given context, and conventional measures of policy effectiveness do not capture this aspect. Nevertheless, it is one of the central claims of this chapter that adaptation to the local environment is a precondition of successful cross-border cooperation. Because differences in background condition each programme, it is important to address local weaknesses and to resolve swiftly any possible problems in the programme. In order to assess the effectiveness of cooperation, therefore, this chapter considers the ways in which programmes were modified to address local problems.

In what follows, the Polish-German and Polish-Slovak cross-border cooperation programmes will be compared along these three dimensions. Particular attention will be paid to cultural factors that distinguish the two regions.

Comparing Polish-German and Polish-Slovak Cross-Border Cooperation

Figure 1 and Table 2 display some basic information about the Polish-German and Polish-Slovak border regions. The Polish-Slovak border is slightly longer than the Polish-German border, however; the two border regions have a comparable population of just over six million inhabitants.

There are four Euroregions with Polish-German participation that were created in the early 1990s. The Polish-Slovak border region consists of three Euroregions that are slightly younger than those at the Polish-German border.

The EU began funding Polish-German cross-border cooperation in 1994 through INTERREG IIA and PHARE CBC. Poland joined the EU in 2004 and thus became eligible for INTERREG, later Objective 3, funding. In the Polish-Slovak border region, the experience gained in this period contributed to the 2004–2006 INTERREG IIIA programme and the 2007–2013 Objective 3 programme.

Table 2 shows that there are three programmes in the Polish-German border region, corresponding to the three German *Länder* bordering Poland, while there is only one programme at the Polish-Slovak border, reflecting the more centralised character of Polish-Slovak cooperation. As a result, the available ERDF funds for Polish-Slovak cross-border cooperation are less than half of those the three Polish-German programmes have at their disposal. The implications of this will be analysed below.

Policy Definition

The three Polish-German programmes started very late, in the course of 2009. New legal standards made it necessary to re-conceptualise the Mecklenburg-Vorpommern-Zachodniopomorskie programme, for example, and the ensuing preparation of key documents took so long that the first funding decisions could only be taken in the autumn of 2009. Similarly, the implementation document for the Polish-Saxon programme was adopted in April 2009, and the monitoring committee decided on the first project applications only in September of that year. The Brandenburg-Lubuskie programme began slightly earlier, in March 2009. Overall, therefore, all three programmes were seriously delayed.

Policymakers in the region were unanimous in condemning these delays. For example, one Euroregional representative marvelled: 'Incredible, it's already 2009. No projects were supported in 2007 and 2008. [...] Money was supposed to be available as early as 2007 but it is still not available.'[1] Another explained: 'When we made the transition from Phare CBC to INTERREG, there was a similar delay, until 2005. Now we have the same problem: it's already 2009 but still nothing.'[2]

Germans and Poles offered different explanations for the delays: German policymakers criticised the high staff turnover in the Polish administration, which impeded coordination on a personal basis and the development of trust. Conversely, Polish officials blamed their German counterparts for their inflexibility and lack of

---

1 Author's interview with policymaker, Frankfurt (Oder), 2 March 2009.
2 Author's interview with policymaker, Jelenia Góra, 1 April 2009.

creativity. According to one interviewee, different administrative cultures had led to infighting over the 'rules of the game':

> In the Dutch-German border region, where they had a seamless transition [between the programmes], cooperation is a matter of course. Here, we still don't have a common administrative culture and common culture of communication.[3]

In other words, policymakers claimed that cultural differences and dissimilar administrative cultures gave rise to internal disagreements that, in turn, led to delays in the start of the programme.

Conversely, work on the implementation document for the 2007–2013 Polish-Slovak cross-border cooperation programme began in December 2006, a year before the launch of the new programme. In the course of 2006, 13 meetings were held of the working group responsible for drawing up the programme. Even though the working group had prepared the key documents at the start of 2007, it took a whole year to distribute them among potential beneficiaries to enable them to apply for funding. Only thanks to the high interest among potential beneficiaries did the first call for projects start in August 2008. A first list of accepted projects was published by the monitoring committee in April 2009.

In other words, although project applications were accepted within the acceptable two-year window after the programme start, almost two years were lost in the allocation of funds. Regional and local policymakers responsible for the implementation of the programme blamed indolence and a lack of organisation in the managing institutions, notably the Polish Ministry of Regional Development. As a representative of the contact point at the marshal's office in Małopolska complained: 'All documents for applicants were prepared in 2007; I do not understand why it took them so long to print them out and distribute them among beneficiaries.'[4] It has been suggested that, prior to 2004, cross-border cooperation was seen by the ministry as an excellent source of funding. However, this became a much lower priority once Poland joined the EU and thus became eligible for the much more lucrative Structural Funds. This would explain why the Ministry did not make a stronger effort to get the new programme underway.[5] Dissatisfaction with the managing authority was also pronounced on the Slovak side:

> Recruitment of new employees to the [Joint Technical Secretariat] in Kraków started only after the first project call in August 2008. Everything took longer than it should [...] that is why there was a delay in assessing the projects.[6]

---

3   Author's interview with policymaker, Dresden, 2 April 2009.
4   Author's interview with policymaker, Kraków, 1 June 2010.
5   The author is grateful to Maciej Smętkowski for raising this point.
6   Author's interview with policymaker, Žilina, 1 July 2010.

The second reason identified by policymakers was the transition from INTERREG IIIA to European Territorial Cooperation. New rules adopted by the EU for the 2007–2013 period caused some confusion:

> I have been working on the Slovak-Polish border for almost ten years, and each programme is a bit different. On PHARE CBC, we have all been learning, then INTERREG came and now it is different again. Much more emphasis is now put on the trans-border effect [...][7]

Representatives of the Joint Technical Secretariat who are responsible for conducting project calls pointed to the extremely high level of interest in the programme among Slovak and Polish beneficiaries as a reason for the delay: 'Already in the first competition, €20 million have been available for allocation. The level of interest was overwhelming.'[8] High demand may have caused some delays but it also permitted the Polish-Slovak programme to advance quicker than the Polish-German programme by 2009, as the next section will show.

Policy Implementation

To give an overview of the 2000–2006 period, Table 3 presents the programme results for the Mecklenburg-Vorpommern-Zachodniopomorskie programme, which one of the three Polish-German programmes.

The programme had seven priorities, but technical and tourist infrastructure development (Priority B: 144 projects) as well as culture and cooperation (Priority F: 107 projects) together made up over 75 percent of the programme. These two priorities tended to have the most generous allocations in all three programmes; infrastructure because projects such as road or bridge construction are extremely expensive, and culture because there is a lot of demand for projects in this area, even though these are often inexpensive (see subsection 4.3 on the fund for microprojects). Table 3 also shows that the final outcome of the programme was very similar to what was initially envisaged. Overall, €111 million of ERDF money were spent on 430 projects. The Polish partners were only eligible for INTERREG money after Poland's EU accession in 2004, but these figures suggest that approximately 60 projects were carried out each year on average.

As Table 4 shows, during the three years of the Polish-Slovak INTERREG IIIA programme, 312 projects worth some €26 million (around €20 million from the ERDF fund) were carried out, averaging over 100 projects a year. This means that

---

7   Author's interview with policymaker, Bielsko–Biała, 2 June, 2010.
8   Author's interview with policymaker, Kraków, 1 June 2010.

all the money allocated for this programme was spent, making it one of the most successful programmes in CEE.

Table 4 also indicates that the programme was divided into two substantive priorities: infrastructural development and socio-economic development. These priorities were subdivided into seven measures. The most popular measures included Measure 2.1 for human resources development and promotion of entrepreneurship (31 projects), Measure 2.2 for the protection of the natural and cultural heritage (42 projects), and Measure 2.3, which supported microprojects (189 projects). This means that the Polish-Slovak programme was somewhat more balanced than the Mecklenburg-Vorpommern-Zachodniopomorskie programme, which focused heavily on infrastructure and cultural cooperation.

In the Polish-German border region during the 2000–2006 programming period, it emerged that it is difficult to meet targets when there is a large number of many precisely defined funding categories. As a result, all three Polish-German programmes reduced their funding categories to two or three in the 2007–2013 period. These broader priorities cover a variety of themes. For example, the Polish-Saxon priority of cross-border development encompasses sub-priorities such as economics and science, tourism, traffic, the environment and spatial and regional planning.

Table 5 illustrates progress in the 2007–2013 Saxony-Dolnośląskie programme. It shows that, by December 2010, only eleven projects had been accepted in Priority 1, equivalent to a 25 percent commitment rate. According to the 2010 annual report, this is partly because the programme overestimated the need for cross-border funds among local enterprises, who have access to several different sources of financial support (Sächsische Aufbaubank 2011). Demand for Priority 1 increased in 2010 compared to earlier years. Nonetheless, with 75 percent of the funds allocated to Priority 1 still available at the end of 2010, slow progress in this priority raised concerns, and the monitoring committee introduced the possibility of shifting funds from Priority 1 to Priority 2 if necessary (Sächsische Aufbaubank 2011). Conversely, with 35 projects in Priority 2, projects in the area of social integration were well underway. Most were in the sub-areas of education and culture. Examples include the establishment of a cultural centre and a network of teachers from the region. The commitment rate in Priority 2 amounted to over 57 percent. By December 2010, the payment rate was 0.08 percent for Priority 1 and 5.2 percent for Priority 2, reflecting the differential progress in the two areas.

Slow progress is not surprising given the delayed start of all German-Polish programmes. However, there is some variation between programmes, as Table 6 indicates. The table shows progress in the Brandenburg-Lubuskie and the Mecklenburg-Vorpommern-Zachodniopomorskie programmes that share the same priorities. As the table also indicates, progress has varied between priorities. With 49 projects, the Brandenburg-Lubuskie programme had achieved a 53 percent commitment rate and a 4.8 percent payment rate at the end of 2010. This was much higher in Priority 1, concerning infrastructure, than in Priority 2, which is designed to stimulate cross-border economic links and economic and scientific cooperation. Here, the commitment rate amounted to only 37 percent, something that the programme authorities blamed on a lack of potential beneficiaries in the region (Ministerstwo Rozwoju Regionalnego 2011a). In 2010, two projects were completed in Priority 1, namely the modernisation of a leisure and sports facility and the fitting out of a Polish-German meeting centre.

In the Mecklenburg-Vorpommern-Zachodniopomorskie programme, which had committed more than 62 percent of the €125 million of available ERDF funds, 39 projects were accepted. This high overall percentage is due largely to the 74 percent commitment rate in the category of human resources and cooperation. Slow progress in payments raised concern about the n+3 rule: ways of preventing decommitment were debated in the monitoring committee for the Mecklenburg-Vorpommern-Zachodniopomorskie programme though, in the end, n+3 targets were met at the end of 2010 (Ministerium für Wirtschaft, Arbeit und Tourismus Mecklenburg-Vorpommern 2011).

Table 7 illustrates progress in the Polish-Slovak cross-border cooperation programme for 2007–2013 up to 31 December 2010. Ninety-one projects within priority axes 1 and 2 were accepted, but one applicant dropped out before signing the financial agreement. By December 2010, 90 projects had been contracted for financial support, as well as 369 microprojects (234 in the first call and 135 in the second call), which are covered under one umbrella programme.

The first call was very successful and received overwhelming interest from potential beneficiaries. The value of applications amounted to €178 million, exceeding the total ERDF budget of €157 million. Most applications were submitted in priority axis 2 on social and economic development, notably in the sub-priorities of protecting the cultural and natural heritage, developing cross-border cooperation in tourism and networking. At the start of 2010, a second call was publicised, and 42 new projects worth over €53 million were accepted. The second call met with great interest from applicants. This time, there were 203 applications, and their value totalled €254 million. Second time applicants had more time to acquaint themselves with the programme's rules, find a partner and prepare projects and the required documentation. Many projects submitted for the second call were projects that had been rejected during the first call due to technical shortcomings. Most applications were again submitted in priority axis 2.

After two calls, costs in priority axes 1 and 2 amounted to more than €117 million from the ERDF, equivalent to 97 percent of available funds for the first and second priorities of the entire programme. By December 2010, €132 million had been assigned to projects, equivalent to more than 89 percent of the total ERDF budget for the programme, and far more than in the Polish-German programmes.

The high commitment rate is due to the very great interest among potential beneficiaries in the Polish-Slovak programme as well as enduring basic infrastructural and development needs in the region. However, it is likely that cultural similarities constitute one of the most important reasons for the success of the programme. After a short stay on the Polish-Slovak border, even an untrained observer will notice a multiplicity of similarities in material and folk culture on both sides of the borderline as reflected in such things as architectural styles, national dress, and methods of land cultivation and animal husbandry in the mountainous territories. Another bond that connects many along much of the Polish-Slovak border is the identity of the ethnic groups inhabiting them. *Górale* (Highlanders) on both sides of the border tend to identify with each other more than with other Poles or Slovaks they share citizenship with, as they have a common dialect, traditions and origin. This is also connected to the specificity of borderlands as peripheries:

> This is due to discrepancies between the sense of identity of the centre and that of the periphery. Related observations have also been made by Ewa Orlof [6], who examined the Polish-Slovak borderland and ties between the Polish and Slovak Highlanders. Her research shows that in both the Tatras and Podhale, the Highlanders, regardless of nationality, have more in common with each other as a social group living in the border area than with respect to the centre of Poland or Slovakia. (Masłoń 2014:69 [author's translation])

Communication between people from each side of the border is easy because, unlike in the Polish-German border region, there is no major language barrier. Information exchange is straightforward as a result. In informal settings such as joint training, professional interpreters are not needed. Moreover, previous experiences such as local festivals or school exchanges helped to establish linkages between local authorities, rendering them more likely to cooperate formally and jointly apply for EU funds.[9] Interviewees at the European level actively stressed the meaning and significance of the 'local culture':

> Definitely the long tradition of CBC helps. The best projects come from these border regions that share long tradition of CBC. Also, the cultural similarity helps to achieve the successful cooperation. [...][10]

Apart from payments towards priority axis 4 of the Polish-Slovak programme (Technical Assistance, which is not a substantive priority and thus not shown in

---

9   Around 80 percent of projects are conducted by partners who already cooperated with each other either in INTERREG projects or earlier during spontaneous events (Author's interview with policymaker, Krakow, 2 July 2010; author's interview with beneficiaries in Žilina, 1 September 2011).

10 Author's interview with a senior officer at the European Commission DG Regio CBC Unit conducted in Brussels, June 2013.

Table 6), there had been 137 payments amounting to €13.5 million by December 2010. This represents a nine percent payment rate, far higher than in any of the Polish-German programmes (Ministerstwo Rozwoju Regionalnego 2011b).

Policy Innovation

The Polish-German border region faced a special challenge from the outset, owing to the fact that the region differs in cultural and historical terms from many West European border regions. The citizens who live in those other border regions have, over time, developed dense cross-border networks. A multitude of exchanges take place across these borders every day, facilitated by widespread language skills (Eder & Sandtner 2002; Kepka & Murphy 2002; Strüver 2005). By contrast, few linkages across the Polish-German border survived World War II and the Cold War. In the early 1990s, there were no shared cultural traditions, no widespread language skills, and only extremely limited cross-border social networks (Jajeśniak-Quast & Stokłosa 2000). In many cases, citizens showed outright hostility: on the day the visa agreement came into force, the first Polish coaches arriving in Frankfurt on Oder on were greeted by stone-throwing neo-Nazis (Rada 2004).

This lack of cross-border networks is important not only as a shortcoming in its own right but also because it tends to undermine regional cross-border development proposals (Krätke 1999; Guz-Vetter 2002). Thus, in the early 1990s, policymakers realised there was a need to bring people from the two sides of the border together in informal settings. This would enable them to get to know each other, and the hope was that such encounters would counter negative stereotypes and contribute towards trust-building in the border region. However, at the time there were no funds available to support the kinds of initiatives policymakers had in mind, including sporting events, exhibitions or local fairs. The Phare CBC regulations on the Polish side were a particular hindrance because projects had to be worth at least €2 million to qualify, which was far too much for the purposes of small-scale encounters.

As a result, a 'fund for microprojects' was set up in 1995. Funds of around €2 million were reserved for small projects on both sides of the border (Jałowiecki & Smętkowski 2004). The implementation was simplified in comparison to regular projects and left to the Polish-German Euroregions (Mirwaldt 2012). Although it is too early to tell whether microprojects can bring about a sense of mutual trust among Poles and Germans in the border region, the fund has been deemed a great success. In the 2000–2006 funding period, for example, over 2,700 microprojects were carried out in the region, bringing together thousands of Poles and Germans. Examples included a Polish-German children's' party in Euroregion Pro Europa Viadrina and a photo exhibition in Euroregion Neisse–Nisa–Nysa. There is a general consensus that such encounters have a positive effect. As one policymaker put it:

> Such organised encounters in a majority of cases really [do] trigger further encounters, where people [from different sides of the border] meet at a fair, connect, decide to hold their own fair, get together in the meantime. [...] And the effect is long-term because one meeting leads to another.[11]

So popular is the idea of a microprojects facility that the European Commission now recommends the setting-up of such a facility in its guidance documents. Nearly all CEE cross-border programmes feature a fund for microprojects, even where cultural cross-border connections between citizens and administrations are already strong, as in the Polish-Slovak border region. In other words, one of the major problems holding back the Polish-German border region – its lack of socio-cultural linkages across the border – also brought about major policy innovation.

Few innovations were introduced to the 2000–2006 and 2007–2013 Polish-Slovak programmes. Unlike the Polish-German border region, where a lack of linkages across the border initially defined most other cross-border ventures, the Polish-Slovak border region had to grapple with several minor hurdles, and the only major problem resulted from insufficient available funds. As a result, no major innovation comparable to the Polish-German invention of the fund for microprojects was introduced.

However, certain rules and conventions have been adapted slightly to local needs. First, experiences from the implementation of INTERREG IIIA at the Polish-Slovak border indicated that more emphasis should be placed on the training of future beneficiaries. Most applicants had already been beneficiaries in the earlier INTERREG IIIA programme, and some projects in the 2007–2013 period were a continuation of previous successful INTERREG projects. However, under Phare CBC and only three years of INTERREG, beneficiaries had few opportunities to learn how to put together high quality applications. In particular, they had trouble defining the transborder effect of their project correctly, a crucial condition for projects to be funded. In order to respond to this problem, special emphasis was placed on training the applicants during the 2007–2013 programme. Training was offered by the Joint Technical Secretariat in Kracow and by regional authorities on both sides of the border, particularly before new calls were publicised and in specially organised conferences. Additionally, regional contact points in each region support future applicants.

A second decision that shaped implementation procedures was to limit the eligible territory under INTERREG IIIA. Earlier, it had been possible, for example, to submit applications for infrastructural projects that would be undertaken quite far

---

11 Author's interview with policymaker, Gorzów Wielkopolski, 4 May 2009.

from the border. However, these projects had no realistic chance of being funded because their distance from the border made it impossible to argue that they would have a genuine transborder effect. With the start of the INTERREG IIIA programme, the eligible territory was therefore limited to certain areas closely adjoining the Polish-Slovak border: the Bielski, Nowosądecki and Krośnieńsko-Przemyski subregions (*podregiony*), on the Polish side, and the Žilina and Prešov regions (*kraje*) in Slovakia. Policymakers claimed that excluding projects which had no chance of being selected saved time during the assessment of applications.

Finally, following proposals from beneficiaries, a new procedure to implement changes within projects was approved in 2010. This introduced a high-speed IT-based notification system to systematise and speed up the process of altering projects during their realisation. Additionally, the process of reimbursement underwent a reform, which simplified the formal requirements of financial reports (Ministerstwo Rozwoju Regionalnego 2011b).

In sum, the Polish-Slovak programme was able to build on its regional strengths, notably the close cultural connections across the border. Policymakers were also able to deal with certain problems connected specifically with the programme. However, the region has not witnessed any momentous policy innovations, and one of the main problems in the Polish-Slovak programme – the insufficient amount of funding – remains unsolved.

Conclusions

The main aim of this chapter has been to analyse the effect of different contextual factors affecting the governance of cross-border cooperation. This was done by comparing the Polish-German and Polish-Slovak cross-border cooperation programmes for 2000–2006 and 2007–2013. These two regions are very different in terms of the cultural connections that span the border, and comparison made it possible to identify the effect of this difference on three dimensions of policy effectiveness: definition, implementation and innovation.

In terms of policy definition, the Polish-German and Polish-Slovak programmes were delayed far beyond the 2007 start date. Only in early 2009 did the first projects begin in the Polish-Slovak and in the Brandenburg-Lubuskie programmes. In the Mecklenburg-Vorpommern-Zachodniopomorskie and Saxony-Dolnośląskie programmes, it took until autumn 2009 for the first projects to be accepted. Policymakers presented various reasons for the delays. In the Polish-Slovak case, preparations began with plenty of time to spare. The programme could have started much earlier but for the delay in sending the relevant documentation out to beneficiaries. High demand among potential beneficiaries was another reason for the delay in the Polish-Slovak programme: the competent authorities were so overwhelmed by the interest from applicants that they took longer than usual to make project decisions. Usually, though, high demand on the part of potential beneficiaries is seen as a very good sign. At the Polish-German border, delays were blamed on a lack of successful communication and divergent administrative cultures between authorities on both sides of the border.

As for policy implementation, progress has been variable in the three Polish-German programmes. With 46 projects and a 41 percent commitment rate, Saxony-Dolnośląskie has been the slowest to develop. Here, the late start no doubt had a negative impact on progress. Conversely, the Brandenburg-Lubuskie and Mecklenburg-Vorpommern-Zachodniopomorskie programmes were broadly up to date by the end of 2010 and boasted overall commitment rates of 53 percent and 62 percent, respectively. However, demand has been highly uneven among different priorities. In the Saxony-Dolnośląskie and Mecklenburg-Vorpommern-Zachodniopomorskie programmes, for example, progress was much better in the area of culture than in the areas of infrastructure or development, and policymakers had to take special measures to stimulate demand in the neglected priorities.

In contrast, progress has been swift in the Polish-Slovak border region. After just two years of accepting project applications, the programme had already achieved an overall commitment rate of 89 percent. One reason was the exceptionally high demand, as applicants submitted many high-quality project applications. Longstanding cross-border networks, easy communication and cultural connections between potential beneficiaries on both sides go a long way towards explaining the high number of sound applications. Moreover, with its low level of development, lack of cross-border infrastructure and high demand for social initiatives, the border region's needs are immense. As a result, it is hardly surprising that available funds are exhausted quickly. At the same time, it is necessary to point out that the swift progress in the Polish-Slovak programme is due partly to the significantly smaller budget involved compared with the Polish-German border region. Local authorities have been very vocal in criticising this lack of funds.

Thus, the Polish-Slovak programme has so far been more successful in terms of policy definition and implementation than the Polish-German programmes. As regards policy innovation, however, the roles are reversed. It was at the Polish-German border that a major policy innovation in European cross-border cooperation was conceived. The lack of historical cross-border networks and a common culture of communication that has held the region back in other regards inspired local policymakers to create the fund for microprojects. Conversely, the rather more favourable cultural background in the Polish-Slovak border region has not made any major innovations necessary. Few innovations were introduced in the 2000–2006 and 2007–2013 programmes. Policy innovation has been more incremental than in the Polish-German border region and has involved some minor adjustments in the areas of training, area delineation and project administration. In other words, in this one sense at least, it seems as though a difficult background can sometimes also inspire policymakers to find genuine solutions to local problems.

The analysis has confirmed that it is not enough simply to list the background conditions that might have a positive or negative impact on cross-border governance. Rather, comparison of different programmes is crucial in determining exactly what impact these different conditions have on the way cooperation functions on the ground. This chapter has done this for culture as a contextual factor, and it has shown that different cross-border cultures have a very important impact on different aspects of policy. For policymakers, the important lesson is that even the most daunting regional weaknesses can be turned into strengths and give innovative impulses to otherwise struggling programmes.

References

Anderson, James/O'Dowd, Liam/Wilson, Thomas M. (2003): "Why Study Borders Now?." In: Anderson, James/O'Dowd, Liam/Wilson, Thomas M. (eds.), New Borders for a Changing Europe: Cross-Border Cooperation and Governance, London: Frank Cass.

Arbeitsgemeinschaft Europäischer Grenzregionen (2008): Zusammenarbeit Europäischer Grenzregionen: Bilanz und Perspektiven, Baden-Baden: Nomos.

Assembly of European Regions (1992): Les Régions Frontalières et L'Intégration Européenne, Livre Blanc de l'Assemblée des Régions d'Europe, Strasbourg: Assembly of European Regions.

Bachtler, John/Taylor, Sandra/Olejniczak, Karol (2005): A Study of the Mid Term Evaluations of INTERREG programmes for the programming period 2000 until 2006, Vienna: INTERACT Programme Secretariat.

Batt, Judy/Wolczuk, Kataryna (2002): Region, State and Identity in Central and Eastern Europe, London: Frank Cass.

Bazin, Anne (2003): "Germany and the enlargement of the European Union to the Czech Republic." In: Rupnik, Jan/Zielonka, Jacques (eds.), The road to the European Union, Volume 1: The Czech and Slovak Republics, Manchester: Manchester University Press.

Blatter, Joachim. (2004): "From 'Spaces of Place' to 'Spaces of Flows'? Territorial and Functional Governance in Cross-border Regions in Europe and North America." In: Journal of Borderlands Studies 28/3.

Bufon, Milan (2003): "Cross-Border Cooperation in the Upper Adriatic." In: O'Dowd, Liam/Anderson, James/Wilson, Thomas M. (eds.), New Borders for a Changing Europe: Cross-Border Cooperation and Governance, London: Frank Cass.

Church, Andrew/Reid, Peter (1999): "Cross-border Co-operation, Institutionalization and Political Space Across the English Channel." In: Regional Studies 33/7, pp. 643–655.

Eder, Susanne/Sandtner, Martin (2002): "Common Spirit in the Upper Rhine Valley?" In: Kaplan, David H./Häkli, Jouni (eds.), Boundaries and Place: European Borderlands in Geographical Context, Lanham, MD: Rowman & Littlefield.

Ferry, Martin/Gross, Frederike (2005): The future of territorial cooperation in an enlarged EU, Benchmarking Regional Policy in Europe Conference, 24–26 April 2005, Riga.

Guz-Vetter, Marzenna (2002): Polsko-niemieckie pogranicze: Szanse i zagrożenia w perspektywie przystąpienia Polski do Unii Europejskiej, Warsaw: Instytut Spraw Publicznych.

Halás, Marian (2007): "Development of Cross-Border Cooperation and Creation of Euroregions in the Slovak Republic." In: Moravian Geographical Reports 15/1, pp. 21–31.

Hofstede, Geert (2001): Culture's consequences: Comparing values, behaviors, institutions, and organizations across nations, Thousands Oaks, CA: Sage.

Jajeśniak-Quast, Dagmara/Stokłosa. Katarzyna (2000): Geteilte Städte an Oder und Neiße, Berlin: Arno Spitz.

Jałowiecki, Bohdan/Smętkowski, Maciej (2004): "Małe projekty Euroregionalne," In: Gorzelak, Grzegorz/Bachtler, John/Kasprzyk Mariusz (eds.), Współpraca Transgraniczna Unii Europejskiej: Doświadczenia Polsko-Niemieckie, Warsaw: Wydawnictwo Naukowe 'Scholar'.

Keating, Michael/Hughes, James (eds.) (2003): The Regional Challenge in Central and Eastern Europe: Territorial Restructuring and European Integration, Brussels: Peter Lang.

Kepka, Joanna M. M./Murphy, Alexander (2002): "Euroregions in Comparative Perspective." In: Kaplan, David H./ Häkli, Jouni (eds.), Boundaries and Place: European Borderlands in Geographical Context, Lanham, MD: Rowman & Littlefield.

King, Gary/Keohane, Robert O./Verba, Sidney (1994): Designing Social Enquiry: Scientific Inference in Qualitative Research, Princeton, NJ: Princeton University Press.

Krätke, Stefan (1999): "Regional Integration or Fragmentation? The German-Polish Border Region in a New Europe." In: Regional Studies 33/7, pp. 631–641.

Landman, Todd (2003): Issues and Methods in Comparative Politics: An Introduction, London: Routledge.

Macintyre, Alasdair (1971): "Is a Science of Comparative Politics Possible?" In: Alasdair Macintyre (ed.), Against the Self-Images of the Age: Essays on Ideology and Philosophy, Notre Dame, IN: University of Notre Dame Press.

Masłoń, Kinga (2014): Zjawisko kształtowania się tożsamości na terenach pogranicza, pp. 66–71.

Matthiesen, Ulf/Bürkner, Hans-Joachim (2001): "Antagonistic Structures in Border Areas: Local Milieux and Local Politics in the Polish-German Twin City Gubin/Guben." In: GeoJournal 54/1, pp. 43–50.

Ministerium für Wirtschaft Arbeit und Tourismus Mecklenburg-Vorpommern (2011): "Durchführungsbericht 2010." Schwerin, Ministerium für Wirtschaft, Arbeit und Tourismus Mecklenburg-Vorpommern.

Ministerium für Wirtschaft, Arbeit und Tourismus Mecklenburg-Vorpommern (n.d.): "Ergebnisse der grenzübergreifenden Zusam-menarbeit im Regionalen Programm Mecklenburg–Vorpommern/Brandenburg–Polen (Wojewodschaft Zachodniopomorskie) im Zeitraum 2000–2006", February 1, 2011 (http://www.interreg4a.info/index.php?id=29&L=fyxomzehqhpckpda) .

Ministerstwo Rozwoju Regionalnego (2011a): Raport Roczny 2010, Program Operacyjny Współpracy Transgranicznej Polska (Wojedództwo Lubuskie)–Brandenburgia 2007–2013 w Ramach "Europejskiej Współpracy Terytorialnej", Warsaw: Ministerstwo Rozwoju Regionalnego.

Ministerstwo Rozwoju Regionalnego (2011b): Raport Roczny 2010, Program Wspólpracy Transgranicznej Republika Polska–Republika Slowacka 2007–2013, Warsaw: Ministerstwo Rozwoju Regionalnego.

Ministerstwo Rozwoju Regionalnego (n.d.): "Współpraca polsko-słowacka. Przeszłość, Teraźniejszość, Przyszłość", February 1, 2011 (http://pl.plsk.eu/files/?id_plik=2103).

Mirwaldt, Katja (2012): "The Small Projects Fund and Social Capital Formation in the Polish-German Border Region: An Initial Appraisal." In: Regional Studies 46/2, pp. 259–272.

Mirwaldt, Katja/McMaster, Irene/Bachtler, John (2009): Reconsidering Cohesion Policy: The Contested Debate on Territorial Cohesion, European Policies Research Centre: University of Strathclyde.

Perkmann, Markus (1999): "Building governance institutions across European Borders." In: Regional Studies 33/7, pp. 657–667.

Perkmann, Markus (2002): "Euroregions: Institutional Entrepreneurship in the European Union." In: Perkmann, Markus/Sung, Ngai-Ling (eds.), Globalization, Regionalization and Cross-Border Regions, Houndmills: Palgrave Macmillan.

Perkmann, Markus (2003): "Cross-border regions in Europe: Significance and Drivers of Regional Cross-border co-operation." In: European Urban and Regional Studies 10/2, pp. 153–171.

Popescu, Gabriel (2006): "Geopolitics of Scale and Cross-Border Cooperation in Eastern Europe: The Case of the Romanian-Ukrainian-Moldovan Borderlands." In: Scott, James Wesley (ed.), EU Enlargement, Region Building and Shifting Borders of Inclusion and Exclusion, Aldershot: Ashgate.

Przeworski, Adam/Teune, Henry J. (1970): The Logic of Comparative Social Inquiry, New York: Wiley.

Rada, Uwe (2004): Zwischenland: Europäische Geschichten aus dem deutsch-polnischen Grenzgebiet, Berlin: be.bra verlag.

Ratti, Remigio (1993): "How can Existing Barriers and Border Effects be Overcome? A Theoretical Approach." In: Cappellin, Riccardo/Batey, Peter W.J. (eds), Regional Networks, Border Regions and European Integration, London: Pion.

Sächsische Aufbaubank (2011) "Jahresdurchführungsbericht 2010" Dresden: Sächsisches Staatsministerium für Wirtschaft, Arbeit und Verkehr.

Scott, James W. (1996): "Dutch-German Euroregions: A Model for Transboundary Cooperation?" In: IRS Regio 9, pp. 83–103.

Strüver, Anke (2005): "Spheres of Transnationalism Within the European Union: On Open Doors, Thresholds and Drawbridges Along the Dutch-German Border." In: Journal of Ethnic and Migration Studies 31/2, pp. 323–343.

Urban, Thomas (2004): Der Verlust: Die Vertreibung der Deutschen und Polen im 20. Jahrhundert, Munich: C. H. Beck.

Yoder, Jennifer A. (2003): "Bridging the European Union and Eastern Europe: Cross-border Cooperation and the Euroregions." In: Regional & Federal Studies 13/3, pp. 90-106.

List of Tables and Figures

Figure 1: "MAP OF THE POLISH-GERMAN AND POLISH-SLOVAK EURORE-GIONS." Created by Roman-Kamphaus, Urszula (2020) for this publication.

Table 1: "Contextual factors in the Polish-German and Polish-Slovak border regions." Created by ibid. for this publication.

Table 2: "KEY DATA ON THE POLISH-GERMAN AND POLISH-SLOVAK BORDER REGIONS" Created by ibid. for this publication.

Table 3: "2000–2006 OP MECKLENBURG-VORPOMMERN/BRANDENBURG-ZACHODNIOPOMORSKIE." Created by ibid. for this publication. Data taken from Ministerium für Wirtschaft, Arbeit und Tourismus Mecklenburg-Vorpommern (n.d.).

Table 4: "2004–2006 OP POLAND-SLOVAK REPUBLIC."Created by Kamphaus, Urszula (2020) for this publication. Data taken from Ministerstwo Rozwoju Regionalnego (n.d.).

Table 5: "2007–2013 OP SAXONY-DOLNOŚLĄSKIE: BUDGET AND COMMITMENTS." Created by Kamphaus, Urszula (2020) for this publication. Data taken from Sächsische Aufbaubank (2011).

Table 6: "2007–2013 OPS MECKLENBURG-VORPOMMERN-ZACHODNIOPOMORSKIE AND BRANDENBURG-LUBUSKIE." Created by Kamphaus, Urszula

(2020) for this publication. Data taken from Ministerium für Wirtschaft, Arbeit und Tourismus Mecklenburg–Vorpommern (2011) and Ministerstwo Rozwoju Regionalnego (2011a).

Table 7: "2007–2013 OP POLAND-SLOVAK REPUBLIC: BUDGET, COMMITMENTS AND NUMBER OF ACCEPTED PROJECTS ON 31 DECEMBER 2010." Created by Kamphaus, Urszula (2020) for this publication. Data taken from Ministerstwo Rozwoju Regionalnego (2011b).

Appendix

Table 1: Contextual factors in the Polish-German and Polish-Slovak border regions

		Polish-German border	Polish-Slovak border
Regionalisation		Dissimilar competences: German *Länder* are somewhat more powerful than Polish *województwa*. Cross-border cooperation is more centralised on the Polish side, whereas it is a *Land* competence in Germany. Local authorities are strong in both countries.	Dissimilar competences: Polish *województwa* have more competences than Slovak *kraje*. Cross-border cooperation is more centralised in Slovakia, where financial audits are carried out in Bratislava. Polish local authorities have more authority than Slovak *obce*.
Laws		Legal basis of cross-border programmes unclear until the creation of new EGTC. Neisse-Nysa-Nisa EGTC is in preparation. Eurodistrict Oderland Nadodrze EGTC between Brandenburg and Poland is in preparation.	Legal basis of the cross-border cooperation programme unclear. Tritia EGTC prepared in the summer of 2010. Agreement between Slovakia's Žilina region, the Czech Moravia-Silesia region and Poland's Silesia and Opole provinces.
Economy		Welfare gap: Germany's eastern *Länder* are wealthier than Poland's western *województwa*. However, the development prospects are better on the Polish side, while much of East Germany has been in socio-economic and demographic decline since the 1990s. Cross-border infrastructure is deficient.	Welfare gap: Slovak border regions are developing more dynamically than the Polish border regions. Both sides are underdeveloped by national standards. The regions compete in the area of tourism. Transport infrastructure is better developed on the Polish side, though in need of modernisation.
Funding		Three Objective 3 programmes totalling an ERDF budget of some €343 million for 2007–2013. No genuinely common funds but regulations ensure that projects have a genuine cross-border effect.	One Objective 3 programme with an ERDF budget of roughly €148 million for 2007–2013. Insufficient funding tends to be a problem. No genuinely common fund but regulations ensure that projects have a genuine cross-border effect.
Culture	Very different: prejudices, distrust and stereotypes among border region residents. Lack of language skills, especially in Germany. Divergent administrative cultures, but cordial personal relations are developing among policymakers.	Quite similar: the Slovak and Polish sides of the border share a similar language, history and folk culture. Stable contacts between local authorities pre-date the programme, usually school exchanges or small cultural events.	

Figure 1: MAP OF THE POLISH-GERMAN AND POLISH-SLOVAK EUROREGIONS

Table 2: Key data on the Polish-German and Polish-Slovak border regions

	Polish-German border	Polish-Slovak border
Population	6.17 million	6.01 million
Length of border	467km	541km
Euroregions (year founded)	Neisse-Nisa-Nysa (1991) Spree-Neisse/Nysa-Bóbr (1993) Pro Europa Viadrina (1993) Pomerania (1995)	Karpacki (1993) Tatry (1994) Beskidy (1999)
Objective3 Operational Programmes	Mecklenburg-Vorpommern-Zachodniopomorskie, Brandenburg-Lubuskie, Saxony-Dolnośląskie	Poland-Slovak Republic
ERDF-Funds 2007–2013 (€, without Technical Assistance)	342,928,640	147,963,297

Table 3: 2000– 2006 OP Mecklenburg-Vorpommern/Brandenburg-Zachodniopomorskie

	Initial ERDF budget (€)	ERDF money spent (€)	No. of projects
Priority A– Economic development and cooperation	6,658,512	6,353,819	89
Priority B – Improving technical and tourist infrastructure	67,591,565	66,509,620	144
Priority C – Environment	6,978,988	6,842,924	40
Priority D – Rural development	6,108,023	6,092,843	21
Priority E – Qualification and measures to create jobs	4,738,379	4,578,639	23
Priority F – Inner-regional cooperation, investments in culture and encounters, small projects fund	18,568,272	18,329,007	107
Priority G – Special support for border areas in the accession states	2,610,440	2,610,440	6
Total	113,254,179	111,317,292	430

Note: Technical Assistance is excluded. Source: Ministerium für Wirtschaft, Arbeit und Tourismus Mecklenburg-Vorpommern (n.d.): "Ergebnisse der grenzüber-greifenden Zusammenarbeit im Regionalen Programm Mecklenburg–Vorpommern/Brandenburg–Polen (Wojewodschaft Zachodniopomorskie) im Zeitraum 2000–2006", February 1, 2011 (http://www.interreg4a.info/index.php?id=29&L=fyxomzehqhpckpda).

Table 4: 2004–2006 OP Poland-Slovak Republic

	ERDF contribution (€)	Total money spent (€)	No. of projects
Priority 1: Infrastructure development	11,515,546	15,677,180	50
Measure 1.1: Technical and communication infrastructure	6,347,132	8,594,453	26
Measure 1.2: Infrastructure for environmental protection	5,168,414	7,082,728	24
Priority 2: Socio-economic development	7,775,725	10,501,449	262
Measure 2.1: Human resources development and promotion of entrepreneurship	2,065,907	2,760,344	31
Measure 2.2: Protection of natural and cultural heritage	3,728,687	5,082,767	42
Measure 2.3: Support for local initiatives (Micro-projects)	1,981,131	2,658,339	189
Total	19,291,271	26,178,629	312

Note: Technical Assistance is excluded. Source: Ministerstwo Rozwoju Regionalnego (n.d.): "Współpraca polsko-słowacka. Przeszłość, Teraźniejszość, Przyszłość", February 1, 2011 (http://pl.plsk.eu/files/?id_plik=2103).

Table 5: 2007–2013 OP Saxony-Dolnośląskie: Budget and Commitments

	ERDF budget (€)	Commitments (€)	Commitment rate (%)	No. of projects
Priority axis 1 – Cross-border development	49,754,945	12,478,491	25.1	11
Priority axis 2 – Cross-border social integration	49,049,395	28,024,040	57.1	35
Total	98,804,340	40,502,531	41.0	46

Note: Technical Assistance is excluded. Source: Sächsische Aufbaubank (2011) "Jahresdurchführungsbericht 2010" Dresden: Sächsisches Staatsministerium für Wirtschaft, Arbeit und Verkehr.

Table 6: 2007–2013 OPs Mecklenburg-Vorpommern-Zachodniopomorskie and Brandenburg-Lubuskie

	MVP-Zachodniopomorskie			Brandenburg-Lubuskie		
	ERDF budget (€)	Commitment rate (%)	No. of projects	ERDF budget (€)	Commitment rate (%)	No. of projects
Priority 1 – Infrastructure for cross-border cooperation and environmental situation	55,381,094	60.7	14	71,739,587	59.7	29
Priority 2 – Cross-border economic links and economy-sciences cooperation	29,951,364	49.97	7	12,150,033	37.0	8
Priority 3 – Cross-border HR and cooperation in health, culture and education	39,511,452	74.6	18	35,390,770	47.3	11
Total	124,843,910	62.6	39	119,280,390	53.7	49

Note: Technical Assistance is excluded. Sources: Ministerium für Wirtschaft Arbeit und Tourismus Mecklenburg-Vorpommern (2011): "Durchführungsbericht 2010." Schwerin, Ministerium für Wirtschaft, Arbeit und Tourismus Mecklenburg-Vorpommern. Ministerstwo Rozwoju Regionalnego (2011a): Raport Roczny 2010, Program Operacyjny Współpracy Transgranicznej Polska (Wojedództwo Lubuskie)–Brandenburgia 2007–2013 w Ramach "Europejskiej Współpracy Terytorialnej", Warsaw: Ministerstwo Rozwoju Regionalnego.

Table 7: 2007–2013 OP Poland-Slovak Republic: Budget, Commitments and Number of Accepted Projects on 31 December 2010

	ERDF Budget (€)	Commitments (€)	Commitment rate (%)	No. of projects
Priority axis 1 – Development of cross-border infrastructure	67,685,338	67,685,338	100.0	26
Priority axis 2 – Socio-economic development	53,518,639	50,090,473	93.6	64
Priority axis 3 – Supporting local initiatives (microprojects)	26,759,320	14,823,006	55.4	1 umbrella project (369 microprojects)
Total	147,963,297	132,598,817	89.6	91

Note: Technical Assistance is excluded. Source: Ministerstwo Rozwoju Regionalnego (2011b): Raport Roczny 2010, Program Współpracy Transgranicznej Republika Polska–Republika Slowacka 2007–2013, Warsaw: Ministerstwo Rozwoju Regionalnego.

IV.
Still Dreaming of a "Europe of Regions"? On the Interplay of Regions in the EU

New Multi-Level Governance in the EU?
The European Committee of the Regions and Regional Diversity

Justus Schönlau

Disclaimer: The views expressed in this article are those of the author and do not represent the institution for which he works

Introduction

The European Committee of the Regions (CoR), which celebrated the 25th anniversary of its first plenary meeting in 2019, has been described as the 'institutionalisation' of multi-level governance in the European Union (Warleigh 1999). Despite not being recognised as an 'EU institution' as such, the CoR is indeed the key institutional element within the EU Treaties (Art 300; 305-307 TFEU) that formally brings representatives of 'regional and local bodies who either hold a regional or local authority electoral mandate or are politically accountable to an elected assembly' (Art 300.3 TFEU) into the EU decision-making process. In this regard, the Committee therefore embodies the general principle, enshrined in Art 4.2 TEU, that the EU shall respect the member states' identities 'inherent in their fundamental structures, political and constitutional, *inclusive of regional and local self-government*' (emphasis added). The pairing of 'regional and local' in both treaty references is, of course, one of the constitutive elements of the Committee of the Regions and contributes to its internal heterogeneity – to the extent that it has been an issue for debate from the early days of the CoR whether this is a source of strength or of weakness (Christiansen 1996, Piattoni/Schönlau 2015).

While it will be shown in this chapter that, in fact, the dichotomy between 'local' and 'regional' seems to be less significant for the institutional development and daily work of the CoR than some may have thought, the Committee has also had to grapple with the even more fundamental question of the extent to which a purely consultative body can contribute in a significant manner at all to building genuine multi-level governance (Domorenok 2009). Against the background of the recent

EU crises, which have raised both longstanding and new questions of identity and legitimacy regarding the European integration project, the present chapter will address some of the CoR's activities beyond its consultative role in the Treaties. These activities are to be understood both as the attempt of the Committee to expand its own remit and influence (Schönlau 2017), but also as a catalyst and channel for the assertion of sub-national interests in the integration process. Obviously, the degree to which individual territorial entities or their representatives are active in trying to influence EU policy-making, whether via the CoR or using other means, is determined to a large extent by external factors such as their constitutional position within the national context, the interplay and potential conflicts between historical or cultural identities at the national and regional or local levels, and other key socio-economic and political factors.

In this situation, as I will argue, an internally diverse body such as the Committee of the Regions with its nominally weak consultative role has been able to show, through concrete action in various policy fields, how unity can be built out of diversity. In fact, as will be shown, the CoR has been able to use the notion of 'multi-level governance' (MLG) to foster not only more sensitivity to the needs and concerns of sub-national levels of governance among other institutional players at EU level, but also to promote the role of local and regional authorities in shaping EU policy, and by this action also to advance its own role in the institutional framework (Schönlau 2017, Piattoni/Schönlau 2015). These trends have, in fact, been reinforced by the growing recognition that current policy challenges require joint efforts *by and at* all levels of governance. This is particularly true for the issue of climate change, where the central role of cities and regions in understanding, developing, promoting and implementing the profound transitions which are necessary to meet the challenge is increasingly being acknowledged not only at EU level, but also nationally and on the global stage. At the same time, the EU as a level of governance, despite being recognised as a central element of the necessary solutions in a complex and inter-connected world, faces serious concerns in terms of the effectiveness of its regulatory action and thus finally about the very legitimacy of its existence.

In this context, the sub-national levels of governance have been identified as crucial *subjects* and *arenas* of policy communication and consensus building, and the Committee of the Regions is developing various tools to try to contribute to rebuilding citizens' trust in the notion and instruments of European integration. The Committee's action in this respect focusses on the two opposite ends of the EU policy process: democratic input to the debates about the general direction of integration and the development of new legislation, on the one hand, and the implementation of existing EU legislation at the local and regional levels, on the other. In the former case, the CoR has been active in the run up to the 2019 European elections in organising 'citizens' dialogues' in the context of the other institutions' debate on the future of Europe, and is now seeking to develop a concept for a more 'permanent and structured' form of involving citizens at local or regional level (CoR 2018). With regard to the latter, the CoR has launched a pilot-project entitled 'RegHubs', a network of regional and local contact points to gather feedback from practitioners on the ground regarding the difficulties they face when implementing EU legislation: This is intended as a contribution to the European Commission's 'better law-making' agenda.[1]

The present chapter will thus, after a brief overview of the CoR's role and history, present two examples of how the Committee translates the concerns and ambitions of sub-national actors into concrete policy action. The first example is taken from the area of climate change, specifically the CoR's role in the 'Covenant of Mayors', and the second concerns the RegHubs initiative. In this context the Committee, representing all levels of sub-national governance, needs to constantly balance a wide variety of interests and perspectives, and overcome its internal geographical, structural, political and cultural cleavages. In seeking to achieve this, the position of the CoR as a player with a consultative role in the EU's institutional system enables it to experiment with new forms of cooperation, thereby also promoting direct contacts between its members and their territorial units, and fostering an understanding of shared interests and endeavours. In this regard, it is argued, practical multi-level governance beyond the structures formally foreseen by the Treaties helps to find common solutions and make the European project more resilient to internal and external crises.

The European Committee of the Regions as Institutionalised Multi-Level Governance

When the Committee of the Regions was created during the inter-governmental conference that led eventually to the Treaty of Maastricht in 1993, the concept of multi-level governance had not yet been 'codified' in the academic literature, let alone in the political discourse – in fact, when coining the term, Gary Marks and Lisbet Hooghe referred to 'the Maastricht debates' (Marks 1993; Piattoni 2009) as its origin. In trying to determine how a committee to represent sub-national levels of governance should be structured in terms of membership, it became clear early on that the CoR itself would have to contain more than just one level of governance – whether or not this took the form of two separate chambers (Wassenberg 2020; Warleigh 1999). Yet some thought the diversity of members' institutional roles, representing local, provincial or regional authorities at either legislative or executive levels according to each EU member state's preferences, would be a potentially debilitating weakness rather than a strength (Christiansen 1996). Based

---

1 https://cor.europa.eu/en/our-work/Pages/network-of-regional-hubs.aspx (CoR 2019c)

on the initially narrow set of policy areas for which the CoR was given the right of 'mandatory consultation', and the widely diverging degrees of competence in these policy fields between different sub-national levels in different member states, it was presumed that the CoR could only ever provide lowest-common denominator suggestions that it would be all too easy for the other EU institutions to ignore (Hönnige/Kaiser 2003). Moreover, in view of the duality of its organisation into national delegations and political groups (Pazos-Vidal 2019), the CoR's weak institutional basis as an offshoot of the European Economic and Social Committee, and the EU's absorption with larger issues, notably enlargement and subsequent treaty changes, it seemed unlikely that the Committee would be able to exert significant influence.

With the benefit of hindsight, however, the CoR's institutional development appears quite different: In fact, each change to the EU Treaties (the 1996 Amsterdam reforms, Nice 2000 and, most importantly, the Convention on the Future of Europe that eventually led to the Treaty of Lisbon in 2009) has brought a gradual growth in the CoR's areas of competence and institutional standing. In particular, the recognition of the CoR's right to defend its own prerogatives before the European Court of Justice and its role in defending the principle of subsidiarity not just politically, but also legally (see below) following the Lisbon Treaty, mark significant steps (Schönlau 2017). Moreover, the Committee has managed to increase its institutional capacity significantly over that period in terms of internal organisation, administrative structures, staff and budget (Piattoni/Schönlau 2015). While certain goals formulated by the CoR early on in this regard (such as the formal recognition as an 'EU institution', for example) have not yet been achieved, some recent observers do agree that the body's ability to aggregate the views and experiences of sub-national levels, and to feed them into the EU policy process through both formal and less formal means, has seen noticeable improvements (Decoster et al. 2019; Pazos-Vidal 2019).

These advances in the CoR's capacity and standing have been achieved, not least, because of the 'institutional activism' of the Committee's members and administration (Schönlau 2017), and are a result, in several instances of the development and testing of new forms of activity aimed at increasing the CoR's expertise and credibility on specific subject matters. Combining this with the conscious construction of political connections, the CoR's networking opportunities in the EU's institutional system and the CoR members' claim to legitimacy as democratically elected representatives of sub-national governments, it has gradually been possible to increase the visibility of the CoR and its recognition by the other EU institutions. While it remains a challenge for the CoR to adequately respond to the dual and sometimes conflicting expectations of providing both technical information (for instance on the impact of EU legislation on the ground) and a distinct form of additional democratic legitimacy (Christiansen/Lintner 2005; Piattoni/Schönlau), a balanced combination of the two seems to be increasingly appreciated by the European Commission and the European Parliament.

These trends have indeed been increasingly visible in recent years, as a result of the multiple crises and political challenges that the EU is facing. Given the complexities of regulatory and policy-making tasks in various areas, where political contestation, diverging national interests and limited problem-solving capacities at several levels require ever more sophisticated coordination and interaction, the other EU institutions are increasingly aware of the need to involve sub-national authorities with their distinct experiences, capabilities and legitimacy, and the CoR is seen as one of the useful conduits for that. This is why we are now turning to two separate and quite distinct examples of CoR activism, which each in their turn show how concerted and institutionally aggregated input from the diversity of sub-national structures in the EU member states can be used to reinforce multi-level governance in the service of European integration.

The CoR and Multi-Level Climate Action[2]

The range of activities aimed at addressing climate change is a good example of how the CoR has tried to put the rather abstract concept of multi-level governance into practice in a specific policy area. This applies in particular to its role in supporting and promoting the Covenant of Mayors. The idea that sub-national actors and networks play a crucial role in developing and implementing action to mitigate climate change was on the agenda long before the Lisbon Treaty added climate change to the areas of 'mandatory consultation' for the CoR (Betsill/Bulkeley 2007). Since its first opinions on the Kyoto protocol (CoR 1997), the Committee has moved from general assertions of the role that local and regional authorities should play in climate policy, to more concrete demands and proposals on being directly involved in policy shaping and implementation. Already in the 1997 opinion, the CoR called for support for the *coordination* of local and regional climate initiatives at EU level and coordinated surveys of local energy consumption and greenhouse gas emissions as a basis for setting local targets (CoR 1997: 4.8).

Initially, however, it seems to have been difficult to get the European Commission to follow these suggestions: in its 2001–02 opinion on the proposed Council Decision on EU ratification of the Kyoto-Protocol, the CoR complained that its 'proposals for initiating a dialogue with local and regional authorities […] have largely been ignored by the Commission' (CoR 2001: 2.1), and in the following years the

---

2   The following section builds in large parts on Schönlau, J. (2017). 'Beyond mere "consultation": Expanding the European Committee of the Regions' role', Journal of Contemporary European Research 13/2, pp. 1166-1184, in particular pp. 1177-79.

enthusiasm for concrete steps to involve cities and regions directly in EU climate governance via the CoR seems to have diminished, even within the CoR itself. Interestingly, the impetus for the next steps in this direction came from the European Commission, rather than the CoR: in the EC's 2006 Action Plan on Energy Efficiency, the idea of a Covenant of Mayors was launched, to bring 'together in a permanent network the mayors of 20-30 of Europe's largest and most pioneering cities'. (European Commission 2006 545: 18). Di Martino notes in this context that the Committee of the Regions was subsequently even 'invited by DG-TREN to implement the Covenant, running its central office and through it the Covenant relations with regions and cities', but declined this invitation (Di Martino 2012: 3).

The European Commission's idea of involving just '20-30 mayors of Europe's largest and most pioneering cities' did, of course, create certain problems for the Committee of the Regions, which represents not only large cities, but also smaller ones, as well as regions and intermediate authorities of various sizes and competencies. Moreover, there were probably also some general reservations in the CoR regarding the available administrative, financial and human resources within its own structures, which may explain why the CoR did not accept the Commission's offer to run the Covenant. The Covenant of Mayors thus was launched in 2008 officially in partnership between the Commission and the CoR, but administered, under a contract granted by the European Commission, by a consortium of EU-level NGOs.[3]

Soon after the Covenant was established, the CoR, in this position of not being directly involved, but rather supporting the Covenant in institutional terms, adopted an opinion entitled 'How Regions Contribute to Achieving European Climate Change and Energy Goals, with a Special Focus on the Covenant of Mayors'. In it, the CoR expresses its political support, but also raises some of its key concerns: specifically, it insists on the need 'to make explicit the opportunity for *all* sub-national authorities, including regions, to be members' (CoR 2008: cover page; emphasis added) and calls for local action plans to be embedded in 'regional and national plans' (ibid), thus highlighting the challenge of ensuring coordination and synergies across the multiple levels of governance that need to be involved.

Since the launch of the Covenant in the run-up to the Copenhagen COP15 UN Conference of Parties in 2009, the Committee of the Regions has consistently sought close contact with, and provided political support for, the Covenant. Yet it has also tried in parallel to assert its institutional role by demanding a stronger role for cities and regions in all aspects of EU climate policy (including adaptation to climate change, as well as source-based measures in areas such as energy, agriculture

---

3   The "Covenant Office" is run jointly by Energy Cities, CEMR, Climate Alliance, EUROCITIES, FEDARENE and ICLEI Europe (Covenant of Mayors 2019a).

and biodiversity), and by sending CoR delegations to every year's COP negotiations (CoR brochure 2009b). The CoR has also adopted resolutions every year, which form the basis for the political activities of the CoR-COP delegations. At the same time, it has enhanced its institutional cooperation with the European Commission, the EP and other EU institutions and network partners. The Committee is also active in trying to promote the very idea of Covenant-like structures, not just in opinions dealing directly with climate change and energy policy, but also in other policy areas, such as resource efficiency, noise and water management (CoR 2015a; CoR 2012; CoR 2011).

The COP 21 agreement made at Paris in 2015 and the ensuing debate about the implementation of the Paris commitments within the EU has triggered a new phase of activity around the Covenant. In its opinion on the future of the Covenant (CoR 2015a), the CoR not only committed to become more active in spreading the idea of the Covenant beyond the EU's borders, but also to create a network of CoR 'ambassadors' for the Covenant (CoR 2015a: points 14, 19). By means of this structure, which was formally launched by the Committee of the Regions together with EU Commissioner on Energy, Miguel Arias Cañete, in June 2016, CoR members representing territorial units that have signed up to the Covenant have agreed to explain and promote the initiative to their peers at local and regional level, aided by information material provided by the Committee of the Regions.[4]

In preparing the launch of the Covenant Ambassadors, the CoR had also carried out a consultation of its own networks of local and regional authorities to identify their needs and expectations of a future Covenant. It also commissioned a substantial study on technical issues of 'Multi-level governance and partnership practices in development and implementation of Sustainable Energy Action Plans (SEAPs)', which are the central element of Covenant signatories' commitments.[5] In parallel, the Committee of the Regions has also pushed, through its own opinions and a series of events and activities, to have the central issue of energy poverty recognised at European level and included formally in the Covenant of Mayors. This, in fact, did happen in 2016, acknowledging the crucial impact that climate action may have at all levels of society.[6]

In the more general context of promoting genuine multi-level governance in climate policy in the European Union, not exclusively linked with the Covenant of Mayors, but closely related, the Committee of the Regions has argued since 2017

---

4   [84] http://cor.europa.eu/en/news/Pages/Local-and-regional-leaders-become-new-EU-climate-action-ambassadors.aspx (CoR 2019d; accessed July 2, 2019)
5   The CoR report is available at http://cor.europa.eu/en/events/Documents/SEAP.pdf (accessed 2 July 2016)
6   See the Covenant website at https://www.covenantofmayors.eu/support/energy-poverty.html (Covenant of Mayors 2019b)

for the idea of a system of 'locally determined contributions' (LDCs) to complement, and to be recognised as part of, the 'nationally determined contributions' to CO_2 reduction which form one of the central pillars of the Paris Agreement (CoR 2017). This call, which has also been taken to the various COPs, was most recently reiterated in the context of the debate about the EU member states' Integrated National Energy and Climate Plans (INECPs), which constitute the building blocks of the EU's collective contribution under the Paris Agreement rulebook. Once again, the CoR is demanding consistent and early involvement of local and regional authorities in the elaboration of these plans, as well as recognition of their roles in delivering them and targeted support for a range of sub-national actors in order to build consistent multi-level governance (CoR 2019a).

In view of the ongoing review of the Covenant of Mayors, which has been carried out ahead of its first target deadline in 2020, and as a means of adapting the Covenant to the rapid evolution of EU and global climate policies, the CoR was also compiling new suggestions for the further development of the Covenant (CoR 2019b). Considering the remarkable success of the Covenant in terms of signatories (more than 9500 by 2019), but also some concerns about its geographical balance (the spread of Covenant signatories is rather uneven, ranging from just 74 in Poland, to more than 4800 in Italy),[7] and the ability and willingness of all signatories to sign up to more demanding targets for 2030, the Committee insists on the need for more coordinated action from the European Union to support the signatories, and particularly smaller communities. The CoR has also successfully lobbied to involve regions in the Covenant structures, giving them special tasks to coordinate the participation of 'their' cities, towns and villages, thus bringing to bear the Committee's own representation of multiple and diverse layers of governance.

This example of the CoR's activity in the area of climate change serves to illustrate how the institution managed to exploit 'opportunity structures' (in the shape of the European Commission's recognition of the role of local and regional authorities in developing and implementing climate policy) and to progressively gain attention and build credibility as a partner (Princen 2011). This made it possible for the CoR to enhance its own political and institutional role as part of the EU's policy-making structures, while also promoting the very concept of practical multi-level governance. The issue of climate change as an emerging and rapidly developing policy area for the European Union provides particularly fertile ground to experiment with new solutions, and for a relatively new player such as the CoR to bring both the local expertise of its members and their political capital into an institutional framework of multi-level governance, thereby also expanding its own role.

---

7   Figures taken from the Covenant's own website https://www.covenantofmayors.eu/about/covenant-community/signatories.html (Covenant of Mayors 2019c)

The RegHubs and Implementing 'Active Subsidiarity'

The CoR's pilot project of a 'network of regional hubs for EU policy implementation review (RegHubs)' is a second area of activity where the CoR's role as an important link between the multitude of sub-national entities in the EU and the EU institutions is visible.[8] The project was launched in 2018 as a follow-up to the CoR's participation, with three members, in the European Commission's task force on subsidiarity and proportionality, and aims to promote the new notion of 'active subsidiarity' developed by the Task Force (Lambertz 2018). In fact, the Committee of the Regions has seen itself as an important institutional player in the attempts to fill the EU's contested notion of subsidiarity with life from its beginnings in 1993 (contemporary with the inclusion of 'subsidiarity' in the EU Treaties) (Piattoni/Schönlau 2015: 91-98). Moreover, for the CoR, subsidiarity has always been closely linked to the concept of multi-level governance; from the CoR's perspective, both include all levels from the local to the EU, not just the division of competencies between the EU and the member states (Piattoni/Schönlau 2015: 49-54).

The particular institutional role of the Committee in this respect was, of course, formally recognised with the addition of the explicit reference to local and regional authorities in Art 5 (3) of the TEU and the addition of 'Protocol No2' on subsidiarity to the Lisbon Treaty. These grant the CoR the right to take action before the European Court of Justice in cases of presumed breaches of subsidiarity (interestingly not on proportionality!). In an attempt to operationalise this role, and to feed into the subsidiarity-compliance assessment through CoR opinions, in 2007, the Committee created a network of regions, intermediary and local authorities (at legislative or executive level), national parliaments, regional associations and other partners who voluntarily participate in subsidiarity assessments based on a 'grid' of questions developed by the CoR administration (Piattoni/Schönlau 2015; Lambertz 2018). These consultations should, in parallel to the Early Warning Mechanism for National Parliaments, provide the basis for delivering political messages on subsidiarity compliance, and, in extremis, for legal action by the CoR. Yet, similarly to the national parliaments' role, the CoR has only very rarely formulated concrete subsidiarity concerns supported by a majority in its plenary, and only in two concrete cases has even 'threatened', but never taken, legal action (Pazos-Vidal 2019).

This situation, and the debate about whether it proves that the subsidiarity principle is, by-and-large, respected by the EU's legislative action, or rather that the subsidiarity control systems are ineffective, formed the backdrop to EU Commission President Jean-Claude Juncker's 2017 initiative to launch a Task Force (TF) on subsidiarity and proportionality under the leadership of Commission 1st Vice President Frans Timmermans. The TF was to be composed of three representatives

---

8   https://cor.europa.eu/en/our-work/Pages/network-of-regional-hubs.aspx (CoR 2019c)

each of the European Parliament, the national parliaments and, significantly, the Committee of the Regions (Juncker 2017). While the European Parliament decided eventually not to participate in the exercise, the Committee of the Regions, in the persons of its president, Karl-Heinz Lambertz, the chairman of its own subsidiarity steering group, Michael Schneider, and the 1st vice-president of its Commission responsible for governance issues, Francois Decoster, took up the opportunity enthusiastically (Lambertz 2018). The Task Force elaborated a series of recommendations and proposals during its six-month term, which were published in July 2018 (European Commission 2018a) and further discussed in a European Commission Communication on subsidiarity and proportionality (European Commission 2018b) and in the Commission's 2019 report on better law making (European Commission 2019). Both in the assessments of those directly involved in the task force (Lambertz 2018, Schneider 2019), and upon analysis of the CoR's contributions to the debates of the task force, it appears that the Committee's representatives did have a substantial impact on the overall results. In fact, numerous recommendations of the TF are addressed directly to the CoR (eight out of 36 proposed 'follow-up actions'), or to local and regional authorities (15 out of 36) (Lambertz 2018: 83).[9]

Among these recommendations, No 8 is particularly relevant for our investigation. It calls on the European Commission to 'develop a mechanism to identify and evaluate legislation from the perspective of subsidiarity, proportionality, simplification, legislative density and the role of local and regional authorities' (European Commission 2018a: 20). The proposed follow-up actions contained within this recommendation include the suggestion that the 'Committee of the Regions should launch a pilot project for a new network of regional hubs to collect and channel systematically the views and hard information about the implementation of legislation' (ibid). This proposal, put forward by the CoR members themselves in the TF, now forms the basis for the pilot project set up in late 2018 (CoR Bureau Decision of 08.10.2018). Under this project, the Committee has called primarily for regional authorities to put themselves forward with a commitment to cooperate in the network. According to a method similar to that used in the subsidiarity monitoring network, the CoR has develop detailed questionnaires on issues arising from the implementation of existing EU legislation. The network partners each identify a 'contact point', who is responsible for linking with a variety of stakeholders in each region (not only the relevant parts of the administration, but also associations, research institutions and civil society organisations involved in, or affected by the legislation in question) and compiling the answers (RegHub Code of Conduct).[10]

---

9   The Task Force report contains five broad 'conclusions', nine 'recommendations' and no less than 36 'follow-up actions' to be taken by various institutions.

10   Available at https://cor.europa.eu/en/events/Documents/ECON/reghub.pilotphase.codeofconduct.final.pdf (CoR 2019e)

The pilot project (for the years 2019-20) foresees the development of a working programme by the CoR under the guidance of its political 'subsidiarity steering group' in which all five political groups in the CoR are represented, in dialogue with the network partners. At least three consultations are foreseen per year. The responses to the selected topics (at the time of writing, a first consultation on public procurement has been concluded and a second one on cross-border healthcare is under way) are to be discussed among the network-representatives in workshops organised (and funded) by the Committee of the Regions, and then compiled into a technical implementation report to be transmitted to the European Commission.[11] The CoR clearly hopes that, if the pilot phase is evaluated positively and the results and input from sub-national governments are considered useful, the RegHub network could eventually be expanded to cover all EU member states and a much larger number of regions. For the pilot project, the CoR received 53 applications involving 88 regions, and selected 36 participants covering 18 member states. Such an extension would, however, require direct administrative and financial support from the European Commission, both for the processing of the input at EU level, and to assist smaller and administratively weaker sub-national units in participating.

While it is still early to judge on the final outcome of the consultation processes and the evaluation of the usefulness and feasibility of the pilot project both in terms of time and of geographical and thematic reach, the example of the RegHubs shows how the idea of involving local and regional authorities through the CoR more directly in EU policy making is taking hold. Following on from the intense debates in the TF on subsidiarity and proportionality, where the CoR was responsible for a key part of the operational input and ideas,[12] and where it was somewhat disproportionally represented with three out of six task force members due to the European Parliament's decision not to join, this pilot project seeks to demonstrate the added value of multi-level governance in action. By focusing on the retrospective evaluation of difficulties faced by a range of sub-national players in implementing EU legislation, the CoR aims to tap into the first-hand experience of the network partners. It is also actively promoting the creation of sub-networks involving a number of institutional and non-institutional actors, in the interest of improving the effectiveness and thus also the legitimacy of European policy making.

---

11   See the section of the RegHub Website titled 'How does it Work?' At https://cor.europa.eu/en/our-work/Pages/network-of-regional-hubs.aspx (CoR 2019c)
12   See the CoR's own website on its contributions to the Task Force, at https://portal.cor.europa.eu/subsidiarity/TaskForce/Pages/welcome.aspx (CoR 2019f)

Conclusion: Multi-Level Governance to Meet the Challenges of Diversity and Complexity

The European Committee of the Regions reflects in its composition and the multitude of views, experiences and propositions of its 350 members (and 350 alternate members)[13] the diversity of sub-national governance in the European Union. While being conceived, and often expected, to deliver 'the view' of the EU's cities and regions, it has to try to aggregate and balance these differences through democratic processes and transform diversity into constructive and concrete policy action to promote effective multi-level governance, and through it the legitimacy of the European integration process. Being formally limited to an advisory function, the CoR has sought over the years to expand its impact on EU policy making in various ways. This chapter has presented two examples of this, both of which build on the same resources (i.e. the experiences and the political legitimacy) belonging to a range of sub-national structures of governance, which the CoR seeks to bring to bear on different parts of the EU's functioning.

The current debates on the EU's emerging and rapidly evolving climate policy require innovative tools to involve villages, cities, provinces and regions in the extremely complex processes of transition that are necessary. Through its involvement in, and support for, a structure like the Covenant of Mayors, the CoR, in close cooperation with the European Commission and key stakeholders at EU level, tries to push for appropriate mechanisms of multi-level governance to be built, involving not just the European, but also the national and global levels. The potential of cities and regions across the EU to experiment with new solutions on climate change and the still constantly changing policy frameworks allow the CoR to build on its own role and experience as a network facilitator and communication channel.

At the same time, the ongoing discussions on the EU's legitimacy and in particular its respect for the principle of subsidiarity have directed the CoR's attention towards a different aspect: the question how to open the 'black box of EU law in action' (Versluis 2007). By offering to set up a network of institutions and organisations affected by EU legislation in order to gather first-hand information on its implementation at the lowest levels, the CoR underlines the need for effective communication and information links vertically across all levels. While this activity is so far just a pilot project, it seems to hold significant potential to build new structures, which could significantly reinforce traditional notions of multi-level governance.

Based on these two examples, the Committee of the Regions indeed appears to be a significant agent in efforts to institutionalise multi-level governance while reaping the benefits of regional diversity, and thus to support the good functioning and ultimately the legitimacy of the European integration project.

---

13   After the Brexit the CoR has now 329 members and 329 alternates.

References

Betsill, Michele/Bulkeley, Harriet (2007): "Looking Back and Thinking Ahead: A Decade of Cities and Climate Change Research." In: Local Environment 12/5, pp. 447–56.
Christiansen, Thomas (1996): "Second Thoughts on Europe's 'Third Level': The European Union's Committee of the Regions." In: Publius 26/1, pp. 93–116.
Christiansen, Thomas/Lintner, Pamela (2005): "The Committee of the Regions after 10 Years: Lessons from the Past and Challenges for the Future." In: EIPAScope 2005/1, pp. 7–23.
CoR [Committee of the Regions] (1997): 0140 – Opinion of the Committee of the Regions on Climate Change and Energy.
CoR [Committee of the Regions] (2001): 0458 – Opinion of the Committee of the Regions on Conclusion of the Kyoto Protocol to the United Nations Framework Convention on Climate Change.
CoR [Committee of the Regions] (2008): 0241 – Opinion of the Committee of the Regions on How Regions Contribute to Achieving European Climate Change and Energy Goals, with a Special Focus on the Covenant of Mayors.
CoR [Committee of the Regions] (2011): 0005 – Opinion of the Committee of the Regions on the Role of Regional and Local Authorities in Promoting Sustainable Water Management.
CoR [Committee of the Regions] (2012): 0190 – Opinion of the Committee of the Regions on the Environmental Noise Directive – the Way Forward.
CoR [Committee of the Regions] (2015a): 02592 – Opinion of the Committee of the Regions on the Future of the Covenant of Mayors.
CoR [Committee of the Regions] (2015b): 05369 – Opinion of the Committee of the Regions on Delivering a New Deal for Energy Consumers.
CoR [Committee of the Regions] (2016): "Sustainable Energy Action Plans Report", July 2, 2016 (http://cor.europa.eu/en/events/Documents/SEAP.pdf).
CoR [Committee of the Regions] (2017): 0836 – Opinion of the Committee of the Regions on the Environmental Implementation Review.
CoR [Committee of the Regions] (2018): 01230 – Opinion of the Committee of the Regions on Reflecting on Europe: the voice of local and regional authorities to rebuild trust in the European Union.
CoR [Committee of the Regions] (2019a): 0618 – Opinion of the Committee of the Regions on Implementing the Clean Energy Package: the INECPs as a tool for a transversal approach to climate, active and passive energy (to be adopted during CoR plenary Oct 2019).
CoR [Committee of the Regions] (2019b): "Working Document for opinion ENVE-VI/042 on the Covenant of Mayors Beyond 2020", July 15, 2019 (https://cor.europa.eu/en/events/Pages/envestakeholdercovenantofmayorspost2020.aspx).

CoR [Committee of the Regions] (2019c): "Network of Regional Hubs", July 15, 2019 (https://cor.europa.eu/en/our-work/Pages/network-of-regional-hubs.aspx).

CoR [Committee of the Regions] (2019d): "Local and regional leaders become new EU climate action ambassadors", July 2, 2019 (http://cor.europa.eu/en/news/Pages/Local-and-regional-leaders-become-new-EU-climate-action-ambassadors.aspx).

CoR [Committee of the Regions] (2019e): "RegHub. Code of conduct for the pilot phase [2019-2020]", July 2, 2019 (https://cor.europa.eu/en/events/Documents/ECON/reghub.pilotphase.codeofconduct.final.pdf).

CoR [Committee of the Regions] (2019f): "Task Force on Subsidiarity and Proportionality and 'Doing Less More Efficiently'", July 2, 2019 (https://portal.cor.europa.eu/subsidiarity/TaskForce/Pages/welcome.aspx).

Covenant of Mayors (2019a): "Covenant of Mayors FAQ", July 15, 2019 (https://www.covenantofmayors.eu/support/faq.html).

Covenant of Mayors (2019b): "Alleviating energy poverty", July 15, 2019 (https://www.covenantofmayors.eu/support/energy-poverty.html).

Covenant of Mayors (2019c): "Covenant community", July 15, 2019 (https://www.covenantofmayors.eu/about/covenant-community/signatories.html).

Decoster, Francois/Delhomme, Vincent/Rouselle, Jennifer (2019): "The Committee of the Regions and the European Parliament: An Evolving Relationship?" In: Costa, Oliver (ed.), The European Parliament in Times of Crisis – Dynamics and Transformations. London: Palgrave Macmillan.

Di Martino, Luigi Alberto (2016): "The Covenant of Mayors: Multi-Level Governance of Energy Policy Implementation in the European Union." Research Paper (unpublished), October 27, 2019 (http://www.setsunan.ac.jp/~k-yagi/2013intrrep9DiMartino.pdf).

Domorenok, Ekaterina (2009): "The Committee of the Regions: In Search of Identity." In: Regional & Federal Studies 19/1, pp. 143–63.

European Commission (2006): Action Plan on Energy Efficiency – Realising the Potential, Brussels.

European Commission (2018a): "Report of the Task Force on Subsidiarity, Proportionality and 'Doing Less More Efficiently'", October 27, 2019 (https://ec.europa.eu/commission/sites/beta-political/files/report-task-force-subsidiarity-proportionality-doing-less-more-efficiently_1.pdf).

European Commission (2018b): "The principles of subsidiarity and proportionality: Strengthening their role in the EU's policymaking. COM(2018) 703 final", October 27, 2019 (https://ec.europa.eu/info/sites/info/files/communication-principles-subsidiarity-proportionality-strengthening-role-policymaking_en.pdf).

European Commission (2018b): "Better regulation taking stock and sustaining our commitment", October 27, 2019 (https://ec.europa.eu/info/sites/info/files/better-regulation-taking-stock_en_0.pdf).

Hönnige, Christoph/Kaiser, André (2003): "Opening the Black Box: Decision-Making in the Committee of the Regions." In: Regional & Federal Studies 13/2, pp. 1–29.

Juncker, Jean-Claude (2017): "State of the Union 2017 address", October 27, 2019 (https://audiovisual.ec.europa.eu/en/video/I-143451).

Lambertz, Karl-Heinz (2018): "Das Subsidiaritätsprinzip in Der Politischen Praxis Europas" In: Boll, Christoph (eds.), Europa–Subsidiarität Und Regionen. Ibbenbühren: Stiftung Westfalen Initiative.

Marks, Gary (1993): "Structural Policy and Multi-Level Governance in the EC" In: Cafruny, Alan W./Rosenthal, Glenda G. (eds.), The State of the European Community : The Maastricht Debates and Beyond, Harlow: Longman, pp. 391–411.

Pazos-Vidal, Serafin (2019): Subsidiarity and EU Multilevel Governance: Actors, Networks and Agendas, London: Routledge.

Piattoni, Simona (2009): "Multi-level Governance: A Historical and Conceptual Analysis." In: Journal of European Integration 31/2, pp. 163–180.

Piattoni, Simona/Schönlau, Justus (2015): Shaping Policy From Below – EU Democracy and the Committee of the Regions, Cheltenham: Edward Elgar.

Princen, Sebastiaan (2011): "Agenda-Setting Strategies in EU Policy Processes." In: Journal of European Public Policy 18/7, pp. 927–943.

Schneider, Michael (2019): "Europe Must Deliver at the Level Closest to the Citizens Subsidiarity: Past, Present and Future." In: European View 18/1, pp. 16–25.

Schönlau, Justus (2017): "Beyond Mere 'Consultation': Expanding the European Committee of the Regions' Role." In: Journal of Contemporary European Research 13/2, pp. 1166–1184.

Versluis, Esther (2007): "Even Rules, Uneven Practices: Opening the 'black Box' of EU Law in Action." In: West European Politics 30/1, pp. 50–67.

Warleigh, Alex (1999): The Committee of the Regions: Institutionalising Multi-Level Governance, London: Kogan Page.

Wassenberg, Birte (2020): History of the European Committee of the Regions, Study on the Occasion of the 25th Anniversary of the Inaugural Plenary Session 1994.

Small is Beautiful?
Identity and Placism in Europe

Claire Wallace

Introduction

For some decades, increasing European integration has occurred alongside enlargement inspired by a 'European Dream' of spreading peace, tolerance and human rights through developing a common set of values, currency, mobility and a social model. This dream was to a great extent shattered by first the financial crisis and then an immigration crisis. The re-emergence of nationalism as a threat to the European Dream means that an alternative vision of Europe has emerged. However, in addition to national identification, regional identification at a sub-national level appears to have grown. This contribution is going to discuss the examples of Russians in Latvia and Scottish regions to exemplify these trends. However, these identities have not necessarily displaced either national or European attachment, as analysis of the Eurobarometer illustrates. Rather, we could point to an increasing sense of the importance of place in people's sense of belonging, which seems to encompass all geographical scales.

The increasing recognition of localism in regional governance and in academic writing is also reflected in people's sense of identity in European countries (Roudometof 2019). Meaningful identities are constructed around local communities, giving rise to a sense of localism, which we might also describe as 'placism'. This sense of local place-making is encouraged by EU policies and funding such as LEADER and also by national governments, such as in the UK, that are keen for civil society to compensate for cuts in state spending. For example, if local communities organise their own 'litter picking' exercises, it makes it less obvious that the state has cut back on street cleaners. How does this fit with more general long-term tendencies? For decades, the supra-national governance of the European Union as a centrifugal force was seen as a way of eroding the nation state. The rise of various regionalisms could be said to be doing the same thing as a countervailing centripetal force. However, more recently, the rise of nationalism in Europe seems to contradict these tendencies with an increasingly recidivist emphasis on the nation state.

This chapter will examine these pressures with respect to two particular examples: Scotland within the UK and Russian minorities in Latvia. It will then consider more generally the role of place identity in Europe.

The European Dream: The Rise of Post-National Europe

I have been teaching European Studies for two decades. A key question we perennially address is whether European governance might be replacing national governance and what implications this has for identities. One implication is that a new form of supra-national governance is emerging and, along with it, a new kind of post-national cosmopolitan identity. This formed part of the intellectual Zeitgeist of the late 1990s and early 2000s, as many social scientists rode the waves of Europhile optimism. Major social theorists devoted a lot of printed pages to analysing what this might mean both theoretically and empirically (Giddens 2007; Eder/Spohn 2005; Beck 2006). Gerard Delanty, for example, suggested that European identity could only be founded upon a sense of cosmopolitanism (Delanty 2000; 2009; 1995). And this cosmopolitanism was post-national.

More generally, Jurgen Habermas argued that 'constitutional patriotism' was a viable alternative to the dangerous nationalisms that had brought so much ruin to Europe (Habermas 2002). European integration helped to further this rational project of international co-operation based upon Enlightenment ideals. Many people found it convincing. For example, Jeremy Rifkin in his book 'The European Dream' argued that it was 'the most humane approach to capitalism ever invented', embodying a vision of peace, harmony and social solidarity (Rifkin 2004). One element of this dream was the redistribution of resources across different regions – from rich ones to poor ones – with the idea of raising the level of development for all. Another element was the emphasis on cross-border regionalism to help cement links between countries at a sub-national level as part of a project to create a 'Europe of the Regions'. An essential element for the consent to this European solidarity was the idea of European identity, something which was often promoted at a European level. For citizens to share the European Dream, they needed to identify with Europe and the EU project.

However, European identity proved elusive. It was only ever espoused by a minority of people and the idea of cosmopolitanism was a vague ideal pursued by social theorists rather than something embedded in popular consciousness. Neil Fligstein's analysis of the Eurobarometer suggested that in 2004 only 3.9 percent of people identified as European, and this has remained rather consistent ever since the Eurobarometer was introduced in 1973 (Fligstein 2008). Inclusion of the so-called 'Moreno question' in the Eurobarometer helped to boost this figure by allowing people to choose European alongside national identity. This meant that people choosing 'mostly European' (European + own nationality) could be counted as 12.7 percent and 'sometimes European' (own nationality + European) was as high as 56 percent in answer to the question 'In the near future will you think of yourself as...?'. However, 87.3 percent saw themselves as having mostly a national identity (Fligstein 2008: 141).

Nevertheless, there are important national variations. The UK had a consistently low score for 'European' and a correspondingly high score for national identity, while Belgium, Germany, France, Italy and Luxembourg (seen as the core European countries) had lower national identity scores and higher European ones – although this was still a minority perspective. Being at the heart of Europe helped to make people more European, and these countries were among the founders of what later became the European Union. The UK had always been an outlier in this respect with a strong tradition of Euroscepticism.

The most pro-European parts of the population in all countries were young people, the highly educated, the highly mobile and those that spoke more than one European language (Fligstein 2008). Adrian Favell in his book 'Eurostars' suggested that EU mobility, multilingualism and the opening of professional opportunities were creating an elite strata of young cosmopolitan professionals who also married one another, hence cementing this 'post national' social layer based mainly in major cities such as Brussels, London and Paris (Favell 2008). In the natural course of generational replacement, it was believed that European would displace national identities – or at least rival them.

There was a growing realisation that many areas of national life involved cross-border liaisons requiring international mobilisation and regulation. As well as security issues (terrorism, organised crime), this included environmental issues such as pollution, global warming and food security. Migration issues also required cooperation across different countries, taking into account refugee flows, trafficking and uneven settlement. There was a realisation that the regulation of the global forces of capitalism needed to be addressed supra-nationally to avoid countries competing with each other in a race to the bottom. By introducing the regulation of working hours, maternity leave and childcare across the European Union, work standards could be maintained at a higher level than in much of the world, keeping the European Union countries as bastions of 'quality work', as explicated in the publications of the European Foundation for the Improvement of Living and Working Conditions.

This Enlightenment optimism reached its zenith in the Lisbon Treaty of 2000 when, at the start of a new millennium, the EU aimed to become 'the most competitive knowledge economy in the world' and further European integration appeared to be inevitable. Concern with the quality of work infused welfare models and the idea of the 'European Social Model' was born as a universal safety net to cover European populations. Those countries that had lacked a comprehensive welfare state (such as Greece) started to introduce one, although there were variations in how this was done (Taylor-Gooby, Leruth et al. 2017). The EU set out its European Pillar for Social Rights as a framework for subsequent legislation in 2017, focusing mainly on working conditions and equal opportunities for women and childcare for the moment but also including more vaguely defined access to old age pensions, health care, decent housing, social protection, childcare support and a minimum income as a set of rights. The Lisbon Treaty itself has been modified to improve and streamline the European institutions.

One form of post-national integration was through the 'Cohesion funds', which aimed to redistribute funds towards more deprived regions and was one of the largest elements of EU funding. It took money from richer countries to support poorer ones on a regional basis according to a model of social cohesion introduced by Jacques Delors in the early 1990s.

Finally, an important aspect of European integration for some countries was the introduction of the Euro in 2001, which introduced a common currency alongside fiscal and other controls. These were monitored by the European Central Bank, which aimed to maintain the stability of the Euro across all the widely divergent economies of Europe. Despite the threats to the Euro over the years, the currency has remained strong. Euro coins represent the principle of 'Unity in Diversity' by being both internationally homogeneous and nationally various in terms of the pictures and logos found on them. Economic integration was balanced by cultural integration through introduction of a rousing European anthem, flag, cultural heritage data base,[1] an increasingly comprehensive central statistical agency (Eurostat) and educational exchange programmes such as ERASMUS, which soon become widely established.

These integrationist tendencies were especially reassuring for small member states, many of them in Eastern Europe. Their guarantee of security was to become part of a supra-national defence force (NATO) and the EU also took care of many onerous and expensive aspects of national sovereignty, such as embassies and delegations, trade negotiations, transport and cross-border relations, as well as relations with external powers.

The increasingly complicated accession process forced states hoping to become members to recognise the rights of national minorities within their borders. This was enshrined in the mantra of peace, tolerance and human rights which formed the guiding principles of both the EU and the Council of Europe – a larger and even more idealistic collaboration of European states that also included Russia.

Enlargement had been welcomed as a way of spreading the European social and economic model to Eastern European countries, forming a bulwark against the still threatening East (especially a newly resurgent Russia) and guaranteeing adherence

---

[1] https://www.europeana.eu, 1 September 2019.

to democracy and a liberal market economy. This was seen as a contrast to the authoritarian and dysfunctional neighbouring countries such as Ukraine, Belarus and Moldova, who seemed to be moving in a different direction. The aim was to make everybody in Europe more prosperous, as this also offered market opportunities for Germany, the UK and other exporting countries that would help to boost their economies. By taking on a raft of much poorer countries (and often vary small ones), the aim was to raise the level of all of them up to more 'European' standards. The 'cohesion funds' that redistributed wealth within the European Union were often spent first of all on infrastructure projects such as road building, but also on modernising state and welfare services. The trend continued with the accession of Romania and Bulgaria in 2007 and then Croatia in 2015. Many other countries are still on the pre-accession waiting list, including Turkey, Serbia, Bosnia-Herzegovina and Macedonia, so there is still a great appetite to join the EU. Furthermore, the policies and principles of the EU could be spread through normative encouragement and 'moral example' to a widening circle of countries such as those of North Africa and Eastern Europe via the European Neighbourhood Policies and the 'soft power' of science and cultural diplomacy (Whitman 2011).

Altogether then, the 'European Dream' of post-national integration seemed to be reflected in an inevitable process of consolidation around a work-based social market economy that drew elements from German, French and Scandinavian welfare states. With this extensive infrastructure in place, what remained was for European citizens to see themselves as European. But this did not seem to happen quite so easily. This dream was also reflected in real improvements in living standards and life satisfaction across European countries, with the poorer and newer states starting to converge with the rest (Mascherini 2018), widening the gulf between them and neighbouring countries that did not join the EU.

Return of the Native: The Nationalist Backlash

The European Dream started to fracture after 2008, when the various cracks started to become canyons. The economic crisis, originating in the US, had drastic repercussions in Europe that led to the crisis of the Euro currency. Desperate attempts to shore up the Euro took place through the European Central Bank, but the fiscal crisis particularly affected some of the smaller and weaker economies such as Hungary, Greece and Ireland. The stronger economies who bailed them out were keen to impose fiscal austerity, resulting in substantial cuts to welfare and rising unemployment (Tsoukalis 2016). This threatened the dream of the 'European Social Model' along with the idea that a broad and well cushioned safety net would be spread universally across European countries. Now in some European countries, this net was snatched away again (Taylor-Gooby, Leruth et al. 2017). Altogether, the

European Dream of solidarity, cohesion and co-operation across European regions was under threat, as tax payers in wealthier European countries such as Germany and Britain resented paying for poorer ones.

Mobility of labour had been a key ambition of EU economic policy with the aim of balancing labour supply and demand within its borders. In the early years of the free movement of labour, there was disappointment in Brussels that more labour mobility had not occurred. Yet after the ten new accession countries joined the EU in 2004 and the UK, Sweden and Ireland opened their doors to them, there was a large influx of workers from the Baltic States and Poland, especially to Ireland and the UK. Other countries had restricted this mobility by means of a phased programme of gradual opening. The influx of so many East European workers, where there had been no previous migration system of traditions in place, took many in the UK by surprise, and the Labour Party under Tony Blair, whose liberal social policies had allowed this movement, later regretted it. The UK, also faced with strong fiscal austerity after bailing out the banks with vast sums of money known as 'quantitative easing', was not prepared for this influx.

Hardly had this crisis been mitigated when an immigration crisis hit the EU in 2015. The ranks of migrants trying to penetrate fortress Europe were joined by one million asylum seekers who turned up at the EU borders following the collapse of regimes in Afghanistan, Libya, Iraq and Syria – where protracted civil war and failed states replaced authoritarian regimes. The arrival of these migrants, sometimes on boats across the Mediterranean, sometimes through well established trafficking routes through the Balkans, brought about the collapse of the already weak European system for refugees and asylum seekers.

The various Dublin Regulations were designed to delegate authority for processing asylum seekers according to a common convention and distribute the refugees around Europe on a principal of solidarity. However, the borderland countries of the EU were soon overwhelmed with the numbers of extra-EU migrants and were unable to process their applications, let alone support them while they waited. These were also, coincidentally, the poorer countries of the EU and those most hurt by the economic recession – countries such as Greece and Hungary. The asylum seekers themselves preferred to head for wealthier countries, so they were often in practice just ushered through. Then Angela Merkel, the Chancellor of Germany, aware of the fact that asylum seekers were arriving in increasing numbers anyway, opened the doors to this new wave of refugees in a gesture of 'Wilkommenspolitik'. The result was an influx of one million asylum seekers into Germany. Accommodation prepared for them in other countries to spread the load remained empty. Although the numbers subsequently declined (partly due to better management of the external borders of the EU through agencies such as Frontex), it created a political crisis for Angela Merkel and other mainstream politicians.

These developments fuelled the popularity of anti-immigrant, anti-Muslim parties. But this was also a turn against the liberal globalised capitalism that the EU represented (albeit a 'social' version of it). Populist parties cried out for protection of jobs and living conditions for native workers, welfare chauvinism and increased protectionism.

Hence, history, rather than ending in a universal globalised liberalised market economy, as had been predicted by Francis Fukuyama (Fukuyama 1992), was rediscovered. Nationalism based on nativist sentiments came boiling to the surface everywhere, and nationalist parties were in the ascendancy in EU countries.

In Britain, this populist, anti-EU current of opinion helped the UK Independence Party (UKIP) to enjoy a surge in popularity. With pressure from UKIP, the Conservative Party tried to capture some of this popularity by offering a referendum on leaving the EU. Against the expectations of David Cameron, the Tory leadership and most experts, Britain voted to leave the EU on 23 June 2016. This miscalculation led to a seismic shift in British politics. The strident anti-EU rhetoric that haunted the referendum burst into mainstream politics, with politicians on all sides expressing extreme and uncompromising views in colourful language and even making blatantly false claims. The protracted withdrawal negotiations proved more difficult than many had expected, during which the divisions in the Conservative Party were ripped open rather than healed.

The call to leave was led by capricious and charismatic politicians such as Boris Johnson and Nigel Farage. There were demands to 'take back control' of national sovereignty as a way of controlling immigration, fishing rights and trade. Taking back control was seen as anti-EU but also borrowed anti-French and especially anti-German rhetoric in popular media. Calls for a revival of the 'Blitz spirit' and the use of swastikas in social media recalled victory in the Second World War (but of course only the British part of it), building on comic stereotypes of continentals popularised in comedies such as *Monty Python*, *Dad's Army* and *'Allo 'Allo*. One of the characteristics of the social media revolution is its ability to blend apparently contradictory images, memes and tropes in convenient sound bites to reinforce popular prejudices. The idea was promulgated that Britons would be better off if they didn't have to send a share of their national budget to be redistributed in Brussels (even though many British regions benefited from these funds, especially in leave-voting areas).

The referendum exposed fundamental divisions in British society as well. While young people, and especially students, had voted to remain in the EU, older people and those from traditional working class areas voted to leave (Clarke et al. 2017; Evans/Menon 2017). New divisions along generational and educational lines joined the more traditional ones of social class. These new divisions suggest that with the replacement of older cohorts with younger ones and the general spread of education, these anti-EU sentiments might fade, and an EU identity might strengthen in the fullness of time (see our analysis in the next section). However, the people who espouse anti-EU sentiments were often the victims of globalisation, and could recall an imaginary past when the Second World War was seen as a glorious victory for England while Britannia ruled the waves through the British Empire (Dorling/Tomlinson 2019). The view of the Second World War as a catastrophe for European nations, especially Eastern Europe, which paid the highest price in terms of loss of life, was not accepted north of the English Channel. Rather, vitriolic social media flaming on these historical tropes stoked nationalist fires and an ascendant English nationalism was reborn out of them.

Frank Furedi, writing mainly about Hungary, suggested that two different historical narratives had emerged and were in conflict with one another (Furedi 2018). On the one side was the EU narrative of an Enlightenment, rationalist administration built on of the smoking ruins of a Europe destroyed by nationalism in the Second World War. The EU 'founding fathers' looked around them in 1945 and vowed to never let this happen again. Instead of being built on conquest, the new Europe was built out of treaties and negotiations, which were often slow-moving and obscure. These took a long time to implement and sometimes failed to be ratified, due to the problems of managing consensus among a large collection of countries. This trend was followed by post-War politicians, with France and Germany leading the way. For this EU narrative, history begins after the Second World War and continues through a series of deals and compromises often named after the places in which they were negotiated (the Schengen Treaty, the Lisbon Treaty and so on). It represents the march of progress through increasing co-operation, legal frameworks, integration and enlargement. This version of history, however, often fails to connect with people's emotions and primary loyalties.

The second narrative of history is represented by the more nationalist movements and refers back to an historical continuity with the past. This does connect with a visceral emotional sense of identity rooted in a particular national narrative. This reconnection with the past helps to provide a sense of anchoring and continuity, even when it celebrates selective national traditions. In Britain for example, the more glorious parts of history, such as the Elizabethan and Victorian ages, are taught in school and evoked in popular rhetoric. This is reinforced by a seemingly bottomless appetite for films, box sets and mini-series celebrating the Royal Family. Even more distant and mythical ideas of the past, such as that of King Arthur and so on, are also presented as popular tropes. These have a much more powerful appeal, because, in the words of Furedi 'On their own administratively created rules and procedures [for example by the EU] lack the moral resources to motivate and give meaning to human life, and the major questions about the meaning of existence are left unresolved.' (ibid.: 99). He points out that, for Eastern Europeans, history is of special significance in their nationalist movements against the former Communist regimes.

So the revival of nationalism has had a particularly powerful resonance in contemporary Europe. It is often counterposed to EU post-nationalist centralisation. But what about the regionalism encouraged at the other end of the 'place-making' spectrum. Where does it leave us?

It is clear by now that the creation of a Europe of the regions in the sense of cross-national coalitions of sub-regions was largely a failed project. Despite sponsorship of various cross-border co-operation projects, these alliances have not made deep impressions compared with more primordial ethnic and national identifications. Cross-national ties between ethnic minorities and kin states may have the potential to mobilise popular sentiments, but as we shall see, ethnic minorities are more keen to build identities around their own ethnically and culturally defined geographical areas. So in practice, place-making regionalism takes place mainly at a sub-national level.

Here we will look more closely at two examples: Latvia and Scotland. Although Latvia is strongly regionally and ethnically polarised, there are signs that this is decreasing. On the other hand, recent events have pushed Scotland in the direction of further regional differentiation from the other "nations" of the UK.

Latvia: Weakening of Regional Identities?

Historically, Central and Eastern Europe comprised a patchwork of ethnic groups. After the First and Second World Wars, many of the borders were moved or crystallised, leaving some ethnic minorities in the 'wrong' country. While the Communist powers that dominated the region recognised some ethnic minorities in a formulaic way, they forcibly suppressed or assimilated others. The ending of Communism saw a resurgence of nationalism in the 1990s, as both nation states and ethnic minorities clamoured for recognition, leading to new conflicts, as in the former Yugoslavia, and new nation states, as in the breakup of Czechoslovakia.

Rogers Brubaker, in his seminal studies, characterised these tensions as ones between ethnic minorities, host states (where ethnic minorities were situated) and kin states, to which the ethnic minorities were related by language, ethnicity and culture (Brubaker 1996). The host states and kin states with nationalising tendencies tended to problematise the ethnic minorities. For the host state, they could be seen as a 'fifth column' of unreliable citizens with loyalties elsewhere, whilst for the kin state they could be seen as a wider group of citizens for aggrandising national political leaders. Some Hungarian leaders, for example, started to envisage a 'greater Hungary' and gave some citizenship rights to the Hungarian diaspora. Brubaker's studies focused mainly on the Hungarian population within Romania. However, his concepts can also be applied to the Baltic States. In Latvia, the disintegration of the Soviet Union in 1991 also meant the end of Soviet occupation, as ethnic Latvians saw it, enabling them to win their sovereignty after many decades of domination by foreign powers. However, this left many ethnic Russians still living within the borders of the new states, amounting to around one quarter of the population in Latvia and around one third in Estonia. To these small states with a large and threatening neighbour (now the Russian Federation), this was regarded as a potentially de-stabilising situation.

The ethnic Russians in Latvia are in fact comprised of a variety of nationalities sharing a common language and reflected in different waves of settlement. Some have been there for centuries as dissident 'Old Believers' from the Orthodox Church. Some arrived with the Soviet armies of occupation and then stayed on, and their backgrounds reflected the ethnic diversity of the former Soviet Union, including Ukrainians, Armenians, Georgians, Belarusians and so on. Others had arrived to staff the factories built by the Soviet Union, which was also keen to colonise the Baltic States with ethnic Russians. Still others had retired to the Baltic States, whose gentle climate and sandy, pine-fringed beaches lapped by the Baltic Sea were regarded as the Russian Riviera. For this reason, 'New Russians', rich with post-communist booty, bought and renovated villas in spa resorts such as Jūrmala or enjoyed holidays and honeymoons there. For Russians, the port of Riga was originally a Russian port. They did not see themselves as occupiers, but rather as having liberated this region from German occupation after the Second World War.

These different readings of history and identity lead to tension when Latvia and Estonia made their native languages the official ones and a condition of citizenship. While some Russians left at this time, most felt that this was their Baltic homeland, and many of the older population were unwilling or unable to learn a new language. They remained in Russian-speaking enclaves with their own news channels and media. However, gradual integration of ethnic minority populations is being achieved through the introduction of Latvian and Estonian as languages of education in schools, starting with primary schools. So children at least grow up bilingual.

The Accession of the Latvia firstly to the Council of Europe in 1995 and then to the European Union in 2004 forced the Latvian state to recognise national minorities. Indeed, this was a condition of membership of the EU. This meant that, in addition to the triadic tension between kin state, host state and ethnic minority, there was now a supra-national actor setting the rules – the European Union (Galbreath 2006). The recognition of non-Latvian speaking minorities was a problem in this respect, and a compromise was reached by according them the status of 'non-citizens' who nevertheless held various rights and responsibilities as members of the European Union. These non-citizens numbered 365,417 in 2019.

An unexpected effect of this enlargement was the spread of English as the lingua franca in European countries and the opening of opportunities to work in the UK and Ireland, two of the few countries to fully open their labour markets to new

EU migrants in 2004. The result was that large numbers of Latvians went to work abroad, especially in the UK, whose strong economy and higher wages (at the time) were attractive to Latvians struggling in a transition economy. As a result of this and of demographic changes, the population of Latvia has shrunk by one fifth since it joined the EU, according to the EU information news website POLITICO.[2] The dominant languages were no longer only Latvian and Russian, but for young people (who could mostly speak both these languages anyway), English offered a passport to travel.

Research carried out into ethnic minorities on the European borderlands between 2008 and 2011 as part of the European Framework Programme[3] investigated the situation of the Russian minority in Latvia. The research revealed generational differences, with the mental geography of younger Latvians being focused on the European Union rather than the Soviet Union, as was the case in earlier generations (Patsiurko & Wallace 2014). Joining the Euro currency in 2014 reinforced these tendencies. However, even the older generation of Latvians did not see themselves as wanting to join Russia. Rather, they sought recognition as Russian speakers within Latvia. Respondents in our surveys and interviews expressed a fierce loyalty to their Latvian region rather than to Russia, even when they felt alienated by the nationalising host state. The concentration of traditional Russian-speaking minorities around the Latvian region of Latgale was reinforced by the settlement patterns around the factories where they were brought to work, or religious centres where Orthodox rather than the dominant Protestant churches could be found. This reinforced the idea of Latvia as a multicultural state that also includes Poles, Belarusians and Germans, which was enshrined in the constitution, even if this was not always enthusiastically embraced by a country that had recently established its independence with an appeal to nationalist struggle.

The situation was helped by the fact that the Russian Federation did not actively promote the position of the Russian minority in the same way that Hungary and Poland did for theirs. The new newly resurgent Russian Federation, however, felt threatened by the growing westernisation of the Baltic States, especially when they joined NATO in 2002. There is evidence of a strategy to bombard receptive populations with cyber-attacks and fake news as a new kind of destabilising propaganda, for which the Russian-language media was particularly appropriate. For the Baltic nations, even the austerity that resulted from EU integration was an acceptable compromise for the guarantee of security vis-a-vis their big neighbour.

---

2   https://www.politico.eu/article/latvia-a-disappearing-nation-migration-population-decline/ (Sander 2018)
3   ENRI-East European National and Regional Identities on Europe's Borderlands Project number 217227. April 2008-September 2011. (clairewallace.info 2019)

Nevertheless, there was an uneasy reconciliation of Latvian and Russian populations. This is exemplified in the two different celebrations of the end of World War II that take place in Riga every year – one on March 16 to commemorate soldiers that fought in the Latvian Legion and one on May 9, the traditional day for Russians (Beitnere-La Galla 2016).

The EU has thus enabled the recognition of the Russian-speaking minorities in Latvia who have strong regional identification. The reforms carried out since independence, including schooling in Latvian, have helped to integrate at least the younger generations of Latvians into the Latvian state. Differences in language, religion and historical memory, however, mean that this is a partial integration, but it is one that has remained peaceful. The mantra of tolerance, peace and human rights has been implemented, albeit not without tension. However, the tensions have not erupted into hostility.

The UK: Strengthening Regional Identities

On June 23, 2016, 51.9 percent of those voting in the UK-wide referendum opted to leave the European Union. This slight majority resulted in an effervescence of nationalist feeling. Analysis of voting patterns suggests that was older people, working class people, people with lower levels of education and poorer people who helped to tip the balance (Clarke et al. 2017). The vote was a response to unprecedented and unexpected EU immigration, globalisation and alienation from elite technocratic politics as represented by the EU (Evans & Menon 2017). This English nationalism was encouraged by populist parties such as UKIP. It was seen as a 'howl of protest' from marginalised groups.

There were strong regional differences in voting patterns. The majority of people in London, Scotland and Northern Ireland voted to remain in the European Union. The political differentiation between Scotland and England started to widen, as the majority party in Scotland, the Scottish Nationalist Party (SNP), supported remain, and there are pressures for a second referendum on independence. By virtue of this vote, the United Kingdom became less united than ever. The independence referendum that had taken place in Scotland in 2014 had only been marginally rejected, and one of the arguments at the time was that an independent Scotland could not be part of the EU unless it had petitioned to re-join. Other countries faced with secessionist regions, such as Spain, were strongly opposed.

Ironically, the re-emergence of a specifically English nationalism was in part a response to the rise of Scottish nationalism some decades earlier. However, Scottish nationalism – at least in its present incarnation – attempts to be a civic and inclusive style of nationalism. It is championed by the SNP, which consistently holds the majority in the devolved Scottish Parliament and sends a significant number of MPs to Westminster. One of the long-term aims of the SNP is independence. Hence, Brexit paves the way for the break-up of the United Kingdom, with the new Brexit deal granting Northern Ireland a special status that is more closely aligned with the Republic of Ireland and the Scots feeling that their needs have been consistently ignored.

This regionalisation of identities taking place within the UK disguises the fact that there are also strong place loyalties within Scotland. Our research into digital place-making took us to the Outer Hebrides, where a very strong sense of regional identity is reinforced by the relative isolation of small crofting communities and use of the Gaelic language. The strong sense of place was developed partly by the active role of the local historical associations, known as *comainn eachdraidh*, which form a central part of the community, with a large proportion of each community being members. Several of the *comainn eachdraidh* took over the old school houses in the centre of the village and converted them into museums, cafes, local shops and meeting places for young and old. The flowering of this kind of civil society encouraged a sense of place-making. The importance of a sense of history and ownership is sometimes extended to community buy-out of the land surrounding the hamlets, something that is enabled under Scottish law (Beel & Wallace 2018). The historical associations were evidence of the construction of a very strong sense of place identity.

This regionalisation of identities at a sub-national level is clear in the different examples. But how generalisable is it?

Changing Place Attachments in Europe

In order to answer this question, we can turn to the Eurobarometer, and for this purpose we shall analyse the 'attachment' question, since it has been repeated in every EB and we have a good time series. Here we compare Latvia, the UK and the EU average. Unfortunately, there are no separate figures for UK or Latvian regions when comparing this time series, so instead we have looked at 'attachment to town, country village' as the nearest proxy measure.

Figure 1 shows attachment to Europe. We can see that although attachment to Europe fell after 2006, following the financial crisis and the subsequent rise of anti-EU populist parties, there has been a steady increase in attachment since 2014. In the UK, attachment to Europe has in fact risen since the referendum – before that, people in the UK had little opinion about Europe. Indeed, attachment to Europe is the highest that it has ever been in the UK – at the very time that Britain is about to leave! This paradoxical finding needs to be seen in the context of the polarisation of public opinion within the UK, with anti-EU feeling also being strong among different subsets of population (Clarke et al. 2017).

Figure 1: Attachment to Europe

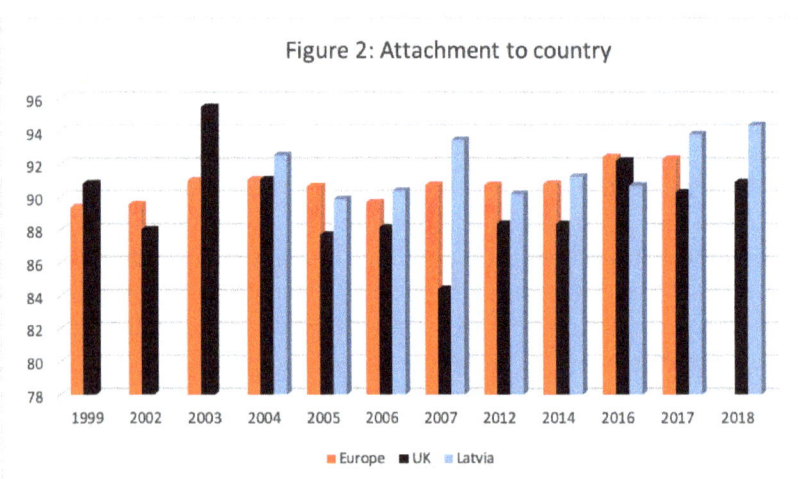

Figure 1: Attachment to Europe

Source: European Commission/European Parliament (2019)

Figure 2: Attachment to country

Figure 2: Attachment to country

Source: European Commission/European Parliament (2019)

Figure 2 shows attachment to country among the populations of the EU, UK and Latvia. It is undoubtedly the case that the attachment to one's own country is the strongest of these place attachments, with more than 90 percent expressing attachment to their country in 2018. However, while attachment to one's country is on the rise in Europe, it is down in the UK from just over 92 percent in 2016 at the time of the referendum to nearer 90 percent in 2017 and 2018. In 2007, there was an exceptionally low score for attachment to the UK. In Latvia there has also been a rise in attachment to country since 2012, rising to its highest point in 2017 and 2018.

Figure 3 shows another option: attachment to village, town or city as a proxy for regional identity. Here we see that this place identification has also been on the rise since the mid-2000s. Whilst there is a rise in Europe generally, there is a steady climb in the UK and a rather dramatic rise in regional attachment in Latvia. Does this reflect the resurgence of regionalism or a rise in place attachment as a source of identity more generally? It is difficult to verify either question from this data.

Figure 3: Attachment to village/town/city

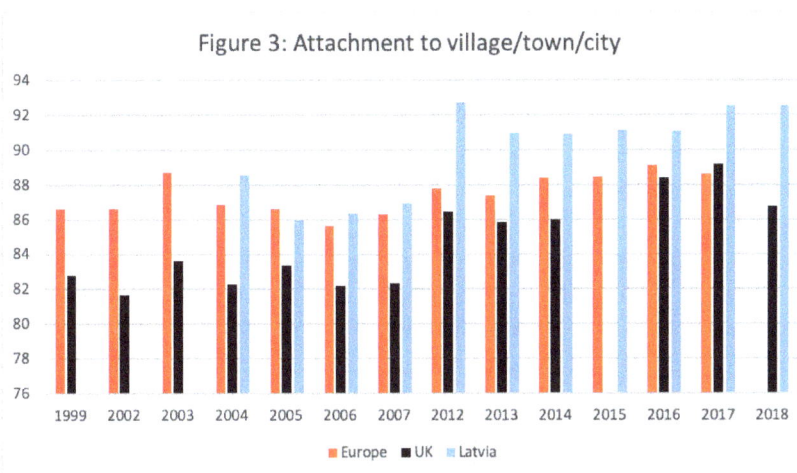

Source: European Commission/European Parliament (2019)

Conclusions: More Local, More National AND More European?

It could be that what we are seeing is a rise in 'localism' in tandem with globalisation, reinforcing the phenomenon of 'glocalisation' as identified by Roland Robertson (Robertson 2012). As people become more disembedded by globalisation, so local attachment or regional and ethnic identities become more important for them. However, this is not necessarily a primordial attachment. Savage and colleagues have identified the importance of 'elective affinity' among incomers in terms of placement attachment to places of settlement rather than places of origin (Savage, Bagnall et al. 2005; Wallace/Vincent 2017). It is not clear from this data if there are ethnic, religious or cultural elements to this place attachment, but they may play some part. Research on local social relations and social networks and how they influence place attachment in the context of globalisation needs to be undertaken. There are calls for the idea of 'place' to be reintegrated into sociological studies, especially in understanding the role of new media and communications (Roudometof 2019).

There are a number of factors that might help to promote localised place attachments. First of all, social media has a strong local component in the form of Facebook groups and pages and buy, sell and swap-type sites. Hence, social media can help to reinforce a sense of place (Miller 2016). Secondly, while national media have been in decline, local media have often taken on a hyperlocal dimension, including stories, news and posts with purely local significance alongside local newsletters and events. Local social media have replaced village noticeboards for passing on information and events (Wallace/Townsend 2019; Wallace/Vincent 2017).

This corresponds with recent analysis carried out by the World Values Survey, which suggests that although vertical trust in political institutions has declined throughout Europe, horizontal trust of those around you, including both known and unknown people, people of the same nationality and other nationalities, and people of other religions, has in fact increased (Wallace/Haerpfer 2019). In fact, the world is becoming more rather than less tolerant despite the recent 'cultural backlash' of authoritarian populism (Norris/Inglehart 2019).

We might conclude that this ever more local focus in the development of 'placism' represents the rise of increasingly narrow regionalisms. However, this takes place within the general oversight of supra-national institutions such as the EU. The EU offers some guarantee of security for small states and regions that have been overrun by larger aggressive neighbours for many centuries.

The EU also provides a regulatory framework – for example for food, trade and research – that small states and regions would find difficult to accomplish alone. The larger structure of the EU is therefore the guarantor for the existence of smaller states and regions.

EU governance also secures the protection of national minorities such as Russians in Latvia from oppression by nationalising host states. This might not always be very successful, as the partial integration of Russian speakers in Latvia suggests. However, it can help to prevent the escalation of hostilities.

We might call this identification with geographical regions 'placism'. There is an increasing attachment to places large and small, but also an increased sense of localism. Therefore, it is not just small that is beautiful. Large can be beautiful, too, by offering small nations and sub-regions security and affirmation. In fact, it is these larger configurations that make placism possible and give it a new impetus.

References

Beck, Ulrich (2006): The Cosmopolitan Vision, Cambridge: Polity Press.
Beel, David/Wallace, Claire (2018): "Gathering Together: Social Capital, Cultural Capital and the Value of Cultural Heritage in a Digital Age." In: Social & Cultural Geography, 1–21.
Beitnere-Le Galla, Dagmāra (2016): "Second World War History: Memory Conflict and Dialogue." In: Sociology and Anthropology 4/7, pp. 536–545.
Brubaker, Rogers (1996): Nationalism Reframed: Nationhood and the National Question in the New Europe, Cambridge: Cambridge University Press.
Clairewallace.info (2019): "European, National and Regional Identities: nations between states along the new eastern borders", October 2, 2019 (https://clairewallace.info/ceeenri).
Clarke, Harold D./Goodwin, Matthew/Whiteley, Paul (2017): Brexit: Why Britain Voted to Leave the European Union, Cambridge: Cambridge University Press.
Delanty, Gerard (1995): "Inventing Europe: Idea, Identity, Reality". Book, Whole. Basingstoke: Macmillan.
Delanty, Gerard (2000): Citizenship in a Global Age: Society, Culture, Politics, Buckingham: Open University Press.
Delanty, Gerard (2009): Cosmopolitan Imagination, Cambridge: Cambridge University Press.
Dorling, Danny/Tomlinson, Sally (2019): Rule Britannia: Brexit and the End of Empire, UK: Biteback Publishing.
Eder, Klaus/Spohn, Willfried (2016): Collective Memory and European Identity: The Effects of Integration and Enlargement, London/New York; Routledge.
European Commission/European Parliament (2019): Eurobarometer 91 (2019), TNS opinion, Brussels [producer].
Evans, Geoffry/Menon, Anand (2017):"Brexit and British Politics". Cambridge/Medford, MA: Polity Press.
Favell, Adrian (2008): Eurostars and Eurocities: Free Movement and Mobility in an Integrating Europe, Malden: Blackwell.
Fligstein, Neil (2008): Euroclash: The EU, European Identity, and the Future of Europe, New York/Oxford: Oxford University Press.
Fukuyama, Francis (1992): The End of History and the Last Man, London: Penguin.
Furedi, Frank (2018): Populism and the European Culture Wars, London: Routledge.

Galbreath, David J. (2006): "European Integration through Democratic Conditionality: Latvia in the Context of Minority Rights." In: Journal of Contemporary European Studies 14/1, pp. 69–87.

Giddnes, Anthony (2007): Europe in the Global Age, Cambridge: Polity Press.

Habermas, Jürgen (2002): "Toward a European Political Community." In: Society 39/5, pp. 58–61.

Mascherini, Massimiliano (2018): Progress on Convergence in the Socioeconomic Area, Eurofound.

Miller, Daniel (2016): Social Media in an English Village, London: UCL Press.

Norris, Pippa/Inglehart, Ronald (2019): Cultural Backlash: Trump, Brexit, and Authoritarian Populism, Cambridge: Cambridge University Press.

Patsiurko, Natalka/Wallace, Claire (2014): "Citizenship, Europe and Ethnic Boundary Making among Russian Minorities in Latvia and Lithuania." In: Migration Letters 11/2, pp. 187–205.

Rifkin, Jeremy (2004): The European Dream: How Europe's Vision of the Future Is Quietly Eclipsing the American Dream, Cambridge: Polity.

Robertson, Roland (2012): "Globalisation or Glocalisation?" In: The Journal of International Communication 18/2, pp. 191–208.

Roudometof, Victor (2019): "Recovering the Local: From Glocalization to Localization." In: Current Sociology 67/6, pp. 801–817.

Sander, Gordon F. (2018): "Latvia, a disappearing nation. Since it joined the EU, the country has lost one-fifth of its population", October 2, 2019 (https://www.politico.eu/article/latvia-a-disappearing-nation-migration-population-decline/).

Savage, Michael (2005): Globalization and Belonging, London: SAGE.

Taylor-Gooby, Peter/Lereuth, Benjamin/Heejung, Chung (eds.) (2017): AFTER AUSTERITY : WelfareState Transformation in Europe after the Great Seccession, Oxford: Oxford University Press.

Tsoukalis, Loukas (2016): In Defence of Europe. Can the European Project Be Saved?, Oxford: Open University Press.

Wallace, Claire/Haerpfer, Christian (2019): "Changing Patterns of Trust and Social Cohesion in Europe.". Presentation to the Social Indicators Meeting. Villa Vigioni.

Wallace, Claire/Townsend, Laenne (2019): "Community Development, Wellbeing and Technology: A Kenyan Village." In: Phillips, Rhondaa (ed.), The Research Handbook on Community Development, Cheltenham: Edward Elgar.

Wallace, Claire/Vincent, Kathryne (2017): "Community Well-Being and Information Technology." In: Wong, Cecilia/Phillips, Rhonds (eds.), Handbook of Community Well-Being Research, Dordrecht: Springer, pp. 169–188.

Whitmad, Richard G. (2011): Normative Power Europe. Empirical and Theoretical Perspectives, London: Palgrave Macmillan.

List of Tables and Figures

Figure 1: "Attachment to Europe." Taken from European Commission/European Parliament (2019).
Figure 2: "Attachment to country." Taken from European Commission/European Parliament (2019).
Figure 3: "Attachment to village/town/city." Taken from European Commission/European Parliament (2019).

'Europe of the Regions'
A Genealogy of an Ambiguous Concept

Ulrike Guérot

Once again, the future of the EU is up for debate. Ursula von der Leyen, who took over the EU Commission in late 2019, has announced a Conference on the Future of Europe, starting in 2020 and lasting for two years. Citizens and civil society are to have their say as equal partners alongside European institutions. While the concrete scope and objectives of the conference still have to be agreed on, von der Leyen has already declared her readiness to follow up on what the conference decides – be it legislative action or even treaty changes. While the latter requires consensus among member states – something hard to imagine in the current situation – the public space was already flooded with manifestos and proposals for a European Constitution[1] in the weeks around the May 2019 European Parliament elections.

Before that, in March 2017, EU Commission President Jean-Claude Juncker had presented five scenarios for the future of the EU in a white paper and put them up for discussion.[2] Without awaiting the outcome of the ongoing consultation process, Juncker set up the Task Force on Subsidiarity, Proportionality and 'Doing Less More Efficiently' a few months later, which presented its recommendations in July 2018.[3] Those who can still remember the last major debate on the future of the EU, which was officially opened by the Laeken Declaration in 2001 and resulted in the EU Constitutional Treaty of 2004, cannot help wondering about the contrast: hopes of a better, more democratic Europe have given way to fear of the future and short-sighted cost-benefit thinking or even national egoism, while visionary drafts have been replaced by half-hearted reform proposals. The rejection of the EU Constitutional Treaty by French and Dutch voters in 2005 and more than ten

---

1 See, for example: the Amsterdam Declaration of the Pan-European Party VOLT (Volt 2019) (https://www.volteuropa.org/amsterdamdeclaration) and many more. For an overview, see Ulrike Guérot (2019), Was ist die Nation?, Part III, Hannover: Steidl, or Ulrike Liebert (2019), Europa erneuern. Eine realistische Vision für das 21. Jahrhundert, Bielefeld: transcript.
2 See: European Commission (2017): White Paper on the Future of Europe. Reflections and scenarios for the Eu27 by 2025, 1 March 2017, COM(2017)2025.
3 See: Report of the Task Force on Subsidiarity, Proportionality and 'Doing Less More Efficiently', 10 July 2018. (CoR 2019b)

years of permanent crisis – economic and financial crisis, euro and sovereign debt crisis, Ukraine conflict, refugee crisis, Brexit – have left deep marks and further undermined the already precarious legitimacy of the EU.

Significantly, the Commission's white paper and the final report of the Subsidiarity Task Force do not mention the EU's democratic deficit or European citizens at all. Instead, the discussion once again focuses on the position of the member states in the EU, as it did in the 1990s, when the treaties were subject to constant reforms. Thus three sets of questions are at the forefront: 1. the distribution of competences between the EU and the member states (*'how much* or *what* should be decided at European level?'); 2. the design of the European decision-making process and, in particular, the relationship between intergovernmental and supranational institutions and procedures (*'how* and *by whom* should decisions be taken in the EU?'); 3. the scale and speed of European integration for individual member states, that is, the room for differentiated (dis)integration ('which states *may*, which states *should* take what steps towards integration?'). However, one thing is never questioned in these never-ending discussions: that the EU is and should remain primarily a union of (national) states. Though – unfortunately – a political reality so far, this view clearly neglects an important aspect that has been enshrined in the constitutional foundation of the EU itself since the adoption of the Maastricht Treaty in 1992, namely that the EU is not only a Union of *States*, but also a Union of *Citizens*.[4] As German historian Hartmut Kaelble recently put it, European citizens, although they are the sovereign of the political union of Europe, have also so far been the 'dismissed subjects' of European integration.[5]

The EU – Still Only a Union of (Nation) States?

After years of European integration and despite persistent complaints about 'being bossed around' by 'Brussels bureaucracy', the member states do indeed remain the key players in the EU – and they are not thinking of disempowering themselves for the sake of the European idea by merging into a full-blown European political union. The German constitutional lawyer Josef Isensee sums up the prevailing legal opinion with a vivid metaphor: The member states are not only the builders of the European Union, but also provide "the building land" and "the building material, which they take from their own houses. The Union is the work of its member states." (Isensee 2016: 7, author's translation)

The member states are the 'masters of the treaties'. They decide which competences to transfer to the European level. In most cases, however, this does not

---

4   Cf. especially Art. I-XII of TEU.
5   Hartmut Kaelble (2019).

mean that they would *give away* these competences, but simply that they *exercise* them *jointly*, with the participation of the Commission and the European Parliament. In any case, with their seats in the European Council, which (unanimously) lays down the strategic guidelines for European policy, and in the Council of the EU, which is involved in most law-making procedures, the member states are guaranteed control over the European political process. This is even more true of key financial and personnel issues such as the negotiation of the multiannual financial framework and the filling of top positions.

Hence the EU merely provides the framework within which the member states pursue common objectives. The transfer of competences to the EU is a permanent loan, which, as Brexit shows, can in principle be revoked at any time. Moreover, member states are wary of handing over policy areas that are at the core of national sovereignty (e.g. defence, taxation – with the important exception of currency) or critical to securing citizens' loyalty (e.g. welfare and social affairs). Last but not least, European integration in no way challenges the member states' monopoly on the use of force. Instead, the EU depends on the provision of resources by the member states for its defence and security policy.

Nation-state thinking permeates even utopian blueprints for the future of Europe. Significantly, the final point of the 'ever closer union' is conceived of in statist terms, namely as 'United *States* of Europe', a 'European federal *state*' or a 'confederation of nation states'. These old debates, which were particularly relevant in the 1990s, focus exclusively on relations between the *European* level, on the one side, and the *nation state*, on the other. They thus completely dismiss two things: first, the role of the citizens themselves in the European polity; and, second, the role of sub-state entities in large federal states, such as Germany and Italy.

The first source of dismay – the lack of the republican component in the EU – can only be touched upon briefly here: In essence, during the past seventy years of European integration, much focus was spend on the question of the *federal* structure of the EU. But little if any energy was spent to reflect on the necessary *republican* component of a political union of Europe – i.e. the necessary legal equality of its citizens. Independently of whether a state is centralized (France) or federal (Germany), any political union must comply with the general principle of the political equality of all its citizens, which is not the case in today's EU, where European citizens remain fragmented in national 'law containers' (Ulrich Beck). Federalism only organises the competition *and* cooperation between sub-state entities. In itself, it does not provide legal equality for citizens, which is the necessary, though not sufficient condition for any democracy. Going forwards, the *federal* and the *republican* principle must be interlaced in the EU if it really wants to become a democratic, political union. This discussion emerged already during the talks around the European Constitution of 2003, especially between Germany and France,[6] but is not the focus of this contribution.

This chapter rather focuses on the *level* of (European) federalism, by questioning whether today's EU member states in their current state are the only possible entities that can 'carry' the political edifice of the EU. This becomes evident when looking at the battle for political independence in Catalonia and Scotland. Though the two cases differ strongly in terms of political context, political leaders of both these sub-national regions have openly proclaimed the goal of 'individual' EU membership for Catalonia and Scotland, respectively, alongside the political independence they seek. Sub-state entities or regions are also vigorously coming back to the European discussion table in other cases, as, for instance, when all of Europe focused on Wallonia in 2016 in the context of the debates about CETA, the EU trade agreement with Canada. There is thus a growing desire on the part of sub-entities of federal EU member states to increase their ability to act on their own in matters of European governance, i.e. independently of the channels provided through their federal states.

The discussion of the role of regions in Europe is, however, not new. It already peaked in the early 1980s, when, for instance, the – at that point new – German Green Party sought to strengthen regional Europe in order to foster regional agriculture and the promotion of 'sustainable farming methods' as well as decentralised energy provision. Conservative parties such as the EPP also began to hold regional party gatherings as early as the time of the Maastricht Treaty in 1991, claiming that European regions, not today's member states, should be the constitutional carriers of a political union of Europe.[7] This concept of a 'Europe of the regions' did indeed challenge the prevailing paradigm of Europe as a union of today's (nation) states. As the EU seems to have reached a dead-end and there is a need for alternative visions for European integration, it might be worth taking a closer look at the now widely forgotten concept of the 'Europe of the regions' and its intellectual history.

'Europe of the Regions' in the EU Political Debate

The 'Europe of the Regions' refers to a wide range of ideas and reform plans that are more or less compatible with the existence of the EU in its current form.

---

6   Cf. Pascal Savidan (2004) La République ou Europe? For details of this discussion cf. Ulrike Guérot (2016, 2019).

7   In 1991, 178 conservative representatives of European regions gathered in Düsseldorf and prepared a 'Regional Manifesto' for a political union of Europe, among them Jordi Pujol. This document still can be found in the Landesarchiv Düsseldorf. This shows that the Catalan question, in particular, is hardly new. (Landtag Nordrhein Westfalen 1991)

Demands for a mere **political upgrading of the regions** through earlier and closer integration in the decision-making process of the EU – whether at European or member-state level – can be quite easily accommodated within the current institutional architecture of the EU. The proposals of the Subsidiarity Task Force[8] and the Committee of the Regions (CoR)[9] currently under discussion clearly fall into this category. Most of these proposals revolve around the principle of subsidiarity, which was enshrined in European primary law with the Treaty of Maastricht. The Task Force and the CoR have called for existing control mechanisms such as the 'subsidiarity early warning system' to be improved by extending deadlines or introducing a standardised test grid. Under the new concept of 'active subsidiarity', work is also underway on new procedures for the consultation of local and regional policy actors at earlier stages of the law-making process. By contrast, the current President of the CoR, Karl-Heinz Lambertz, has proved more innovative with his recent push for the creation of a 'permanent EU mechanism for structured citizen consultations and dialogues'[10] in which regions and cities would play a key role as the transmission belt between citizens and EU institutions. However, it remains to be seen how this initiative will be welcomed by the member states. Hence it is interesting to note in this context that the two above-mentioned essential flaws of the classical federal discussion of the EU, which focuses only on 'Europe vs. the nation state' – the *regional* (sub-state) dimension of Europe and the missing *republican* component, i.e. the linkage of the EU with its citizens – seem closely linked: the regions and towns are where citizens live, and that is where citizens increasingly want to decide about European issues.

A more comprehensive understanding of the 'Europe of Regions' is advocated by proponents of a decentralisation or 'federalisation' of the EU with **regions as actors in their own right in the European multi-level system**. In the 1980s and early 1990s, German *Bundesländer* – above all Bavaria, Baden-Württemberg and North Rhine-Westphalia – championed this concept and contributed to its (short-lived) popularity in regionalist circles. By doing so, they reaffirmed their claim to be recognised as fully fledged political actors in the emerging European polity alongside the member states, at least in those policy areas that traditionally fall within the competence of federated states and legislative regions. These efforts resulted in

---

[8] See: Report of the Task Force on Subsidiarity, Proportionality and 'Doing Less More Efficiently', 10 July 2018. (CoR 2019b)
[9] See, in particular: Karl-Heinz Lambertz (2018): State of the European Union: The View of its Regions and Cities, 9 October 2018, and European Committee of the Regions (CoR 2019a): Building the EU from the ground up with our regions and cities (Bucharest Declaration), 15 March 2019.
[10] See: Karl-Heinz Lambertz and Luca Jahier (2018): Bringing the EU closer to its citizens: The call for an EU permanent mechanism for structured consultations and dialogues with citizens, 14 December 2018.

important legal and political innovations, namely the inclusion of the principle of subsidiarity in the treaties and the creation of the Committee of the Regions by the Maastricht Treaty. However, this lagged behind the original concept and did not affect the structure of the EU as a union of states.

(Some) regional actors have thus embraced the concept of a 'Europe of the Regions' with a view to regaining ground lost to national governments in the course of European integration. However, the initial advocates of the concept had much more in mind than merely strengthening the regions in a union dominated by nation states. What they demanded instead was no less than a paradigm shift: overcoming the nation state and **building a European federation based on independent regions**. The original concept thus involved a radical territorial reorganisation of Europe involving the dismantling of (large) nation states and – where appropriate – the redrawing of regional borders along historical, cultural, linguistic and functional lines. These utopian and revolutionary ideas date back to the beginnings of European unification – or even precede them in some cases – at a time when the memory of the political and moral bankruptcy of nationalism was still alive after two devastating world wars. Interestingly, this initial conception of the 'Europe of the regions' is now experiencing a renaissance with the work of Robert Menasse (2016) and myself (Ulrike Guérot 2016) reacting to the current crisis of the EU, the revival of nationalism and the return of the 'regional question' in (Western) Europe (e.g. Scotland, Catalonia, Tyrol).

'Europe of the Regions' – A Polysemic Concept

The first proponents of a 'Europe of the Regions' share the same criticism or rejection of the nation state. In their view, modern nation states are artificial entities, the random outcome of history, violence and power politics, which compensate for their lack of territorial and cultural cohesion by imposing a homogeneous 'national' identity on their citizens through linguistic, educational and cultural policies. By being integrated into nation states, voluntarily of by force, as the case may be, regions are thus bound to lose their political autonomy and cultural specificity. Beyond this common anti-nationalist and anti-centralist stance that the early advocates of the 'Europe of the regions' have in common, three different understandings of the concept can be identified, rooted in different intellectual traditions:

- the personalistic conception;
- the ethnic conception;
- the anti-authoritarian (*herrschaftskritisch*) conception.

The Personalistic Conception

The idea of a 'Europe of the regions' originated in French intellectual circles of the 1930s among the group known as 'personalists'. This group of young intellectuals around Alexandre Marc saw in the deeply troubled times of the interwar period a crisis of civilisation. Distancing themselves from both rampant totalitarian ideologies and liberal individualism, they claimed to represent a 'third way', beyond left and right, communism and capitalism. The 'new order' (*ordre nouveau*) they were calling for combined conservative concepts, in particular organic and corporatist views of society, with forward-looking ideas, such as the need for European unification, in an original synthesis. The basic element of this new order is the concrete human being (in contrast to the abstract individual of liberalism) considered as an autonomous and responsible person integrated into various organic or natural units: the family, the community, the profession and the region. Accordingly, the personalists advocated federalism as a basic principle for the organisation of society as a whole, that is, not only in the political realm but also in the economy, social relations and all other areas of society (integral federalism). Hence, the social and political order should be built 'from below', according to the principle of subsidiarity – from the corporatist 'intermediary bodies' (*corps intermédiaires*) and the 'regional homeland' (*patrie régionale*) up to the European continent. In this respect, it is very important to note that the renowned liberal thinker Hannah Arendt was deeply influenced by Alexandre Marc and his *non-ethnic* concept of a 'federation of small federations' (borrowing from Montesquieu) in Europe, when sketching out her political grammar for the founding of federal entities.[11]

After the Second World War, the Swiss writer Denis de Rougemont (1906–1985), who had joined the personalists in the early 1930s and became a central figure in the pro-European movement, elaborated on personalist thought. Rougemont inspired the creation of the Union of European Federalists (UEF) in 1946–1947 and took part in the Haagen Congress in May 1948, where his 'Message to Europeans', a passionate plea for European unification, was adopted by acclamation. Although the UEF soon lost momentum, and the dream of a supranational European federation gave way to the realpolitik of the Cold War, Rougemont tirelessly continued to campaign for a federal Europe.

In view of the stagnation of the European unification process and the continuing primacy of national interests in the young European Economic Community, he intensified his criticism of the nation state from the 1960s onwards. According to Rougemont, nation states are a relic from bygone times and either too large or too small, as the case may be, to cope with current challenges: '*L'Europe unie ne peut avoir réponse à tout, mais [...] les souverainetés nationales ne peuvent plus avoir réponse à rien,*'

---

11   Cf. Wolfgang Heuer (2016).

he summed up in 1979.[12] Moreover, as sovereign entities, the member states would never be willing to merge into a European federation, whose creation Rougemont regarded as a historical necessity. Deeply disappointed by the intergovernmental process of European integration, he then pinned his hopes on the young regional movements that were starting to gain political momentum in the 1960s and advocated the creation of a European Federation based on the regions. This shift of emphasis is reflected in the term 'Europe of the Regions', which he introduced in 1962 and continued to develop.

Rougemont's definition of the region is quite original – today no less than five decades ago – and deserves a more detailed description. It does not coincide with the existing political-administrative regions, nor with the old historical provinces and territories, nor with the so-called 'ethnic regions', which are defined by language and culture. In his view, regions are rather 'multifunctional associations of persons that are formed on the basis of economic, social and cultural interdependencies [...]'. (Ruge 2004: 505, author's translation) The regions thus do not constitute 'nation states on a smaller scale' (*mini États-nations*). As '*clusters of municipalities*', they are supposed to support the municipalities in carrying out concrete tasks in the service of the citizens (e.g. provision of basic needs) which exceed their material and political capacities, in accordance with the principle of subsidiarity. This being so, the municipalities are free to decide how they want to associate – possibly across national and administrative borders – so that regional boundaries may vary (*géométrie variable*) depending on the policy area at hand.

Thus, while functional aspects are important to Rougemont, preserving local autonomy is even more crucial. The region should enable the municipalities to remain as autonomous as possible despite their limited size and resources, attempting to solve the equation: '*Comment être assez grand pour être fort, tout en restant assez petit pour rester libre?*'[13] In line with the key role played by autonomy and responsibility in personalist thought, Rougemont conceives of the regions as areas of civic participation. The human desire for political self-determination can only be fulfilled at the local and regional level, as it is only there that the citizens can have a real influence on problems they understand and that directly concern them. National centralism and bureaucracy, by contrast, generate political passivity and cultural homogenisation.

Just as nation states cannot meet the diversity of local and regional needs, they cannot, conversely, cope with tasks of a larger scale. '*Aujourd'hui, il faut penser par problème, pas par nation*', posits Rougemont.[14] Transnational or continental problems therefore require European solutions. Such solutions can only be provided by a

---

12   Cited in Reszler 2008.
13   Quoted in Saint-Ouen (2000).
14   Quoted in Saint-Ouen (2000).

European federation that does not consist of national sovereign states but is rather conceived of as a free association of functional regions. In such a 'Europe of the regions', Rougemont expects nation states to eventually become redundant, their powers being transferred 'upwards' to the European level and 'downwards' to the regions.

The Ethnic Conception

While Rougemont was sceptical about ethnic claims and warned of the danger of 'ethnic regions' turning into culturally homogeneous and centrally governed 'nation states on a smaller scale' (*mini États-nations*), other thinkers pushed the emerging regionalist discourse in a clearly ethnic or culturalist direction. The most influential of them, Guy Héraud (1920-2003), a French constitutional lawyer and ardent supporter of the Occitan cause, was close to Alexandre Marc and Denis de Rougemont, with whom he occasionally collaborated. However, his worldview and thinking were fed by other sources: the protection of European minorities and 'ethnic groups'. Héraud thus engaged in the 'Federalist Union of European Ethnic Groups' (FUEV) and was co-editor of the journal *Europa Ethnica*, which was founded in 1961.

Héraud advocated a 'Europe of ethnic groups', a term he introduced in 1963 – almost at the same time as Rougemont's 'Europe of Regions' – in his book *L'Europe des ethnies*. There, Héraud laid down his plans for a three-tiered federation consisting of (linguistically and culturally homogeneous) ethnic groups, which would be members of the European Federation, on the one hand, and subdivided into smaller 'mono-ethnic' regions, on the other. In later drafts, he made regions the direct constitutional units of the European Federation. According to Héraud, ethnic groups are defined and united primarily by common language and culture (and, in his earlier writings, by mentality ['*ethnotype*']). In this sense, individuals or even entire ethnic groups have only limited freedom to decide for themselves which ethnic group they belong to: '[…] a people is what it is. No one can change their ethnotype. It is therefore wrong that by an arbitrary profession of ethnicity (usually based on complexes) one should take oneself for what one is not and attaches oneself to a community that is not, in nature, one's own.'[15]

Despite his undeniable proximity to Rougemont – both shared the rejection of the sovereign nation state and the idea of a strongly decentralised federal Europe – Héraud's theses are permeated by a very different spirit. While Rougemont focuses on the autonomous and responsible person, Héraud subordinates individual self-determination and democracy to the right of existence and self-determination of ethnic groups. Unlike Rougemont's, Héraud's criticism of the nation state is not of

---

15   Quoted in Melkevik (1994), author's translation.

a principled nature, but due to the historical fact that the formation of nation states in Europe went hand in hand with the suppression of 'stateless ethnic groups' and other minorities. The right to self-determination of ethnic groups he advocated involves the right to, and indeed the demand for 'a state of one's own' as a guarantee of the collective existence and independence of ethnically homogeneous groups. Héraud's 'Europe of ethnic groups' and all similar concepts of Europe based on ethnicity[16] are thus fundamentally ambivalent: A European Federation appears less as a goal to be pursued for its own sake than as a mean for the emancipation of stateless peoples and ethnic minorities from the supposedly oppressive grip of the nation state. Héraud therefore seems to be more concerned with the dismantlement of existing, mostly polyethnic nation states than with overcoming the idea of nation state as such.

The Anti-Authoritarian (herrschaftskritisch) Conception

Leopold Kohr (1909-1994), a political scientist and national economist of Austrian origin, is not always counted among the spiritual fathers of the 'Europe of the Regions', perhaps because he did not use the *term* 'Europe of the regions'. He nevertheless anticipated the *idea*. In an article from 1941, 'Disunion Now', Kohr advocated the unification of Europe according to the Swiss model, i.e. not along linguistic or national boundaries, but on the basis of a balance between smaller independent units (Kohr 1941). This, however, would require the division of the major European states – above all Germany, but also France, Italy and others – into smaller states of seven to ten million inhabitants, which would then be unified under the umbrella of a 'Pan-European Union'. 'If Europe is to be united', he later wrote in his main work, The Breakdown of Nations, 'great powers must first be dissolved to a degree that [...] none of its component units is left with a significant superiority in size and strength over the other.' (Kohr 1978: 183) For federations of states to be successful, they must consist of smaller units of relatively equal size and power. Where this condition does not hold, Kohr warns, a federal union cannot last: 'If a federation has several great-power participants, it will break apart. It will end in disintegration. If it has only one, it will turn the smaller members into tools of the biggest. It will end in centralization.' (Kohr 1978: 179)

Unlike Rougemont and Héraud, Kohr's call for small political units is based on empirically verifiable (or at least 'falsifiable') statements about the influence of state size on democratic government, international relations and the stability of federal unions. His critique of excessive size – '*oversize*' in his terminology – as the root of all evil plays a central role here. Thus, he states concisely – although admittedly in a

---

16   See, in particular, Fouéré (1968).

somewhat undifferentiated fashion: '[...] there seems to be only one cause behind all forms social misery: bigness. [...] bigness, or oversize, is really much more than just a social problem. It appears to be the one and only problem permeating all creation. Wherever something is wrong, something is too big.' (Kohr 1978: xviii)

The harmful effects of oversize *are* particularly obvious in the field of international relations, as Kohr explains in his 'power theory of aggression'. In his view, the primary cause of war does not lie in political, ideological or economic conflicts, but simply in the accumulation of a 'critical' mass of power. Power is often abused and rarely remains unused: Whenever a society is large enough and has accumulated a critical mass of power, it will use it, especially when it feels safe from reprisal. According to Kohr, this explains why most nations, regardless of racial background, degree of civilisation or ideology, have at some point in history committed atrocities. Kohr's proposed solution is as radical as his diagnosis: 'The solution [...] does not seem to lie in the creation of still bigger social units and still vaster governments [...]. It seems to lie in the elimination of those overgrown organisms that go by the name of great powers, and in the restoration of a healthy system of small and easily manageable states such as characterized earlier ages.' (Kohr 1978: xix) Smaller states tend to be more peaceful and conciliative, not because they are more virtuous *per se*, but for the simple reason that they have less power and are more aware of their vulnerability. If small states nevertheless do provoke wars, they can easily be kept in check by coalitions and therefore do only limited damage. Hence, the coexistence of many small states appears to be a prerequisite for peace, or at least the containment of war.

In addition to the concern for peace, Kohr has a number of other arguments against the excessive size and power of states. He is thus part of the long tradition of political thinking about the 'optimal size of states', which, from Plato and Aristotle to Montesquieu and Rousseau, emphasizes the advantages of small states.[17] Kohr's plea for small states is as one-sided as his condemnation of the great powers: 'the worst of small states provides greater happiness to man than the best of large ones' (Kohr 1978: 98). Small states are inherently more democratic, since the government does not confront the individual with the strength and pomp of a powerful state apparatus, but with means of power limited from the outset by the modest size of the country. The government of smaller states is therefore less inclined to lose sight of its true purpose – serving the *individual*. However hard they may try, great powers are, by contrast, constitutively incapable of a truly democratic government because they must serve (mass) society (Kohr 1978: 101). Accordingly, Kohr sets the upper limit for a 'healthy and manageable' society at eight to ten million people (Kohr 1978: 108).

---

17 For more recent contributions to the debate see Dahl & Tufte (1973), Alesina and Spolaore (2003) and Jörke (2019).

Among the advantages of smaller states, Kohr also mentions the fact that the administration of public affairs requires less effort and attention, because they are more straightforward, and stir less ambition and power struggles, the stakes being less high. Largely liberated from the temptations and trouble of 'great politics', individuals have more leisure for the cultivation of the arts and sciences ('the glory of the small'), as the cultural heyday of the Italian and German states in the period *before* national unification shows. Smaller units are also advantageous in the economic sector. According to Kohr, competition between many small economic actors was a decisive factor for the emergence of capitalism in early modern Europe. Today, on the contrary, a few large players, some of which even enjoy monopolies, dominate huge markets, at the expense of diversity and creativity. Thus, according to Kohr, the main cause of the instability and crisis susceptibility of the modern economy is not to be found in the 'immanent laws of the capitalist mode of production' (Marx), but rather in its *vast scale*.

Institutionalised Solidarity

Obviously, this lasting and to some extend idle debate, this increasing arm-wrestling between regions and nations on their place and say in a European polity depends largely on the definition of what a nation state is.[18] This is obviously a vast debate, but stands at the centre of the classical discussion of federalism in Europe. Does a nation state depend on an autochthonous, 'pre-political' substance (identity, ethnicity, language, culture); or is a 'nation state', in the end, more the product of processes of socialisation, of collective law-making and the joint exercise of power? Modern, *functional* definitions of nation states tend to advantage the latter. A nation state, in this view, is basically where the level of solidarity is institutionalised. In other words: independently of 'pre-political' origin, language or culture, a nation – or *demos* – is composed of those who collectively decide on societal affairs.[19]

Reviving ideas and thoughts towards a regional genealogy of Europe, therefore, does not – and should not – aim at making new nations out of old regions, e.g., with respect to Catalonia or Scotland. Rather, the notion is to conceive a horizontal network of European regions and metropolitan areas, protected under the common roof of a political European entity that guarantees not only the same democratic conditions for decision-making for all European citizens in European affairs, but

---

18   Cf. for an overview of this: Ulrike Guérot (2019), Was ist die Nation?, especially parts I & II.
19   On this, cf. Marcel Mauss (2017), Die Nation oder der Sinn fürs Soziale: Frankfurter Beiträge zur Soziologie und Sozialphilosophie, Institut für Sozialforschung, Band 25, Campus: Frankfurt/ New York 2017. Cf. also the ongoing research on the social and not the identitarian dimension of a nation, e.g. in France the writings of the leading experts on Marcel Mauss, Bruno Karsenti & Cyril Lemieux (2017): Socialisme et sociologie.

also the same social rights for all, if they are ultimately supposed to be equal before the law. This 'federation of small federations' should then be constitutionalised as a Federal Republic of Europe.

References

Alesina, Alberto/Spolaore, Enrico (2003): The Size of Nations, Cambridge, Massachusetts: MIT Press.
CoR [Committee of the Regions] (2019a): "Building the EU from the ground up with our regions and cities", December 2, 2019 (https://cor.europa.eu/en/summit2019/Documents/Declaration/NEW_Bucharest_Declaration_template_EN.pdf?utm_source=SharedLink&utm_medium=ShortURL&utm_campaign=bucarest_declaration_en).
CoR [Committee of the Regions] (2019b): "Task Force on Subsidiarity and Proportionality and 'Doing Less More Efficiently'", December 2, 2019 (https://portal.cor.europa.eu/subsidiarity/TaskForce/Pages/welcome.aspx).
Dahl, Robert/Tufte, Edward R. (1973): Size and Democracy, Stanford, California: Stanford University Press.
European Commission (2017): White Paper on the Future of Europe. Reflections and scenarios for the Eu27 by 2025, 1 March 2017, COM(2017)2025.
Fouéré, Yann (1968): L'Europe aux cent drapeux, Paris: Presse d'Europe.
Guérot, Ulrike (2016): Warum Europa eine Republik werden muss! Eine politische Utopie, Bonn: Dietz.
Guérot, Ulrike (2019): Was ist die Nation?, Part III, Hannover: Steidl.
Heuer, Wolfgang (2016): Föderationen – Hannah Arendts politische Grammatik des Gründens, Hannover: Leinebögen 5, pp. 10–11.
Isensee, Josef (2016): "Union – Nation – Region: eine schwierige Allianz." In: Hilpold, Peter/Steinmair, Walter/Perathoner, Christoph (eds), Europa der Regionen, Wiesbaden: Springer, pp. 7–26.
Jörke, Dirk (2019): Die Größe der Demokratie. Über die räumliche Dimension von Herrschaft und Partizipation, Berlin: Suhrkamp.
Kaelble, Hartmut (2019): Der verkannte Bürger. Die andere Geschichte der europäischen Integration seit 1950, Frankfurt: campus.
Kohr, Leopold (1941): "Disunion Now: A Plea for a Society Based upon Small Autonomous Units." In: The Commonweal, 26 Sept. 1941.
Kohr, Leopold (1978) [1957]: The Breakdown of Nations, New York: E.P. Dutton.
Lambertz Karl-Heinz (2018): State of the European Union: The View of its Regions and Cities, 9 October 2018.

Lambertz, Karl-Heinz/Jahier, Luca (2018): Bringing the EU closer to its citizens: The call for an EU permanent mechanism for structured consultations and dialogues with citizens, 14 December 2018.

Landtag Nordrhein Westfalen (1991): 'Düsseldorfer Erklärung', Library Landtag Nordrhein Westfalen, Archiv-Nr. M 28168).

Lauer, Jürgen (2019): "Guy Héraud (1920–2003)." In: Winfried Böttcher (ed.). Europas vergessene Visionäre. Rückbesinnung in Zeiten akuter Krisen, Baden-Baden: Nomos, pp. 492–502.

Liebert, Ulrike (2019): Europa erneuern. Eine realistische Vision für das 21. Jahrhundert, Bielefeld: transcrip.

Melkevik, Bjarne (1994): "Compte rendu de Guy Héraud ‚L'Europe des ethnies." In: Les Cahiers de droit 35/1, pp. 141–143.

Menasse, Robert (2016): "Kurze Geschichte der Europäischen Zukunft." In: Hilpold, Peter/Steinmair, Walter/Perathoner, Christoph (eds), Europa der Regionen, Wiesbaden: Springer, pp. 27–37.

Mauss, Marcel (2017): Die Nation oder der Sinn fürs Soziale, Frankfurt/ New York: Campus.

Mauss, Marcel/Karsenti, Bruno/Lemieux, Cyril (2017): Socialisme et sociologie, Paris: EHESS editions.

Rezler, André (2008): "Denis de Rougemont l'Européen." In: Basil Germon & André Liebich (eds.), Contruire l'Europe. Mélanges en hommage au professeur Pierre du Bois, Paris: Presses Universitaires de France, pp. 87–95.

Ruge, Undine (2004). "Ein konservative Vision - das 'Europa der Regionen'." In: Leviathan, 32/4, pp. 495–513.

Saint-Ouen, François (2000): "Concept des régions chez Denis de Rougemont." In: L'Europe en formation 318, pp. 53–60.

Savidan, Pascal (ed.) (2004): La République ou Europe?, Paris: Livres de poche,

VOLT (2019): "The Amsterdam Declaration. Volts programme for the European Parliament 2019 – 2024", December 2, 2019 (https://assets.nationbuilder.com/volt/pages/6564/attachments/original/1540629281/Amsterdam_Declaration.pdf?1540629281).

Authors Register

Elisabeth Donat

Dr. Elisabeth Donat is a research associate and deputy head of the Department for European Policy and the Study of Democracy at Danube-University Krems. She previously worked as a research associate at the University of Salzburg, Innsbruck and Vienna in their respective institutes of sociology. She has conducted extensive trainings in methodology (qualitative and quantitative) that complete her portfolio. She has passed on her knowledge in more than 50 courses at the aforementioned universities and other colleges. As a research associate within the REGIOPARL project, she is responsible for the conception and execution of surveys with deputies of regional parliaments as well as the evaluation of their responses.

Sarah Meyer

Sarah Meyer is a research associate at Danube University Krems, where she heads the REGIOPARL project studying the role of regional parliaments in EU governance. She previously worked on EU policy affairs at the Austrian Federal Chancellery. Sarah Meyer received a doctorate from the University of Vienna and completed a post-graduate program on European integration at the Institute for Advanced Studies in Vienna. She has worked in different research projects (among others FP7, FWF) at the University of Vienna, Innsbruck and Amsterdam. Her research interests include the role of regional political actors in the EU context, the politicization of European integration, and the (institutional) development of the EU.

Gabriele Abels

Gabriele Abels is professor for comparative politics and European integration at the Institute of Political Science. She holds a Jean Monnet Chair since 2011 and was Director of the Erasmus+ funded Jean Monnet Centre of Excellence PRRIDE from 2015 to 2018. From 2012 to 2015 she was president of the German political science association DVPW). She was visiting fellow at the University of Osnabrück, the European University Institute in Florence, the University of Missouri-St. Louis, USA, St. Petersburg University, Russia, and Harvard University, USA. Her areas of expertise are: democratising the EU, the role of regions in EU decision-making, theorising European integration, comparative parliamentarism, gender studies.

Katrin Praprotnik

Katrin Praprotnik works at Danube University Krems and leads the Austrian Democracy Lab together with Christina Hainzl. She studied political science at the University of Vienna and completed research stays in Paris and Brussels. In her PhD thesis, she examined the program-to-policy-linkage in a representative democracy – i.e. she looked at electoral pledges from Austrian parties and tested whether government (and opposition) parties were able to fulfill these promises. Before she came to Krems, she was a post-doctoral researcher at the German University of Hamburg. Her main research interests are the Austrian political system, parties and elections from a European, comparative perspective, and political representation. Praprotnik's work is published in national and internation political science journals such as the Austrian Journal of Political Science, West European Politics, American Journal of Political Science and Electoral Studies.

Camille Dobler

PhD student in Political Science at the Jagiellonian University in Krakow, in co-supervision with Sciences Po Paris, I am an Early Stage Marie Sklodowska-Curie Fellow for the research project PLATO "The Post-Crisis Legitimacy of the European Union", which brings together in a inter-disciplinary fashion 15 PhD students across 9 European universities. My main research interest is the social integration of the European continent, especially following the debt crisis and refugee crisis, My broad research interests include political theory as well as qualitative methods, borders, identity politics and the role of emotions in politics. I have an education as both a political theorist and social anthropologist, from Sciences Po Lille, the University of Strasbourg and the London School of Economics and Political Science.

Karl Kössler

Karl Kössler is Senior Researcher at the Institute for Comparative Federalism at Eurac Research Bolzano/Bozen (Italy). He obtained a PhD in comparative public law and political science from the University of Innsbruck (Austria) and his main fields of interest and expertise are comparative federalism and autonomy studies and, more broadly, constitutional design in diverse societies. Moreover, Kössler has conducted research on powers and policies in multilevel systems. He has lectured on the above-mentioned subjects in Europe and beyond at universities, as well as in master programmes targeted at post-doc researchers, civil servants and political decision-makers. Kössler is the author of more than 30 peer-reviewed publications on the above-mentioned subjects, including five books, among them Comparative Federalism: Constitutional Arrangements and Case Law (Oxford: Hart Publishing, 2017). Since 2018, he is representative for Austria in the Council of Europe's Group of Independent Experts on the European Charter of Local Self-Government.

Andreas Rahmatian

Andreas Rahmatian is Professor of Commercial Law at the University of Glasgow, Scotland, UK. Originally from Vienna, he obtained a degree and a PhD in law and a second degree in musicology and history there, and continued his studies with an LLM at the University of London. He qualified as a solicitor in London before he became an academic. His research interests comprise commercial law, intellectual property law, property law and property theory, legal history, intellectual history and the law. In 2014-15 he was a Fellow at the Institut d'Études Avancées, Nantes, France. His books include Copyright and Creativity: The Making of Property Rights in Creative Works (2011) and Lord Kames: Legal and Social Theorist (2015).

Roland Sturm

Professor Roland Sturm holds the Chair of Political Science at the Friedrich-Alexander-University Erlangen-Nuremburg. He has published widely in the fields of European Integration, German Politics (federalism), Comparative Politics and Comparative Public Policy, and Political Economy. His most recent research projects focus on "austerity as a political challenge", "the federal second Chamber in Germany" and "decentralization in the Arab World". Roland Sturm was Visiting Professor in Seattle (University of Washington), Beijing (University of Peking), and Barcelona (Pompeu Fabra).

Fabian Landes

Fabian Landes studied political sciences at the University of Bamberg in Germany and graduated from the Nordig Master Programme in Innovative Governance and Public Management at the University of Tampere, Finland and University of Agder, Norway. His research focuses on regional actors in the EU mulit-level governance system of the European Union and on EU regional and cohesion policies. Currently, he works as a research associate in the project "Regional Parliaments Lab

I REGIOPARL" at the European Democracy Lab located at the European School of Governance (EUSG) in Berlin.

Moritz Neujeffski

Since October 2018 Moritz Neujeffski is a research fellow of the Center for Civil Society Research. Within the project "Regional Parliaments Lab I REGIOPARL" (in cooperation with Stiftung Forum Morgen), Moritz examines how financial transfer systems between European regions are becoming politically contested. Growing regional inequalities and the perspectives of new populist movements are thereby also taken into account. Previously Moritz worked as a project manager at the School of Data Germany, an educational project by Open Knowledge Foundation Deutschland e.V.. He has worked in the Unit Inequality and Social Policy and from July 2017 to September 2018 in the President's Project Group as a research assistant. He studied Public Policy and Human Development (M.Sc.) and European Studies (B.A.) at Maastricht University.

Justus Schönlau

Justus Schönlau is political advisor to the Party of European Socialists (PES) group in the Committee of the Regions, supporting PES members on climate and energy, as well as on issues of European governance, citizenship and migration. He graduated from the universities of Edinburgh and the Central European University, Budapest, and holds a PhD from the University of Reading, UK (2002). His thesis was published as "Drafting the EU Charter: Rights, Legitimacy and Process" in 2005 (Palgrave-Macmillan). He has previously worked as assistant for a member of the European Parliament and as post-doctoral research fellow at the University of Exeter. Recent publications include "Shaping EU Policy from Below – EU Democracy and the Committee of the Regions" with Simona Piattoni, 2015, and "Beyond mere 'consultation': Expanding the European Committee of the Region's Role" (JCER 2017). He has regular teaching contracts (Lehrauftrag) at the University of Bielefeld, Germany, on EU environmental policy and decision making.

Claire Wallace

Claire Wallace is Professor of Sociology at the University of Aberdeen. She previously worked at the Institute for Advanced Studies in Vienna and was President of the European Sociological Association between 2007 and 2009 as well as Editor of its flagship journal "European Societies". She co-ordinated a project ENRI-East "The Interplay of European, National and Regional Identities on Europe's Eastern

Borderlands" for the EU Framework Programme between 2008 and 2011 on which she draws for this talk. Claire Wallace is a member of the Academy of Social Science.

Ulrike Guérot

Prof. Dr. Ulrike Guérot is Professor at the Danube University in Krems, Austria and head of the Department for European Policy and the Study of Democracy. Moreover, she is the founder of the European Democracy Lab in Berlin, a think-tank dedicated to the idea of an European Republic. Prior to that Ulrike Guérot has worked in several international think-tanks in Paris, Brussels, London and Washington. Her first book "Why Europe needs to become a Republic! A political utopia", was published in 2016. Her latest Work "The new civil war – the open Europe and its enemies", became a bestseller in Germany.

Urszula Roman-Kamphaus

Dr. Urszula Roman-Kamphaus is affiliated to Business School, Edinburgh Napier University. Dr. Urszula Roman-Kamphaus is currently providing services as Lecturer. Dr. Urszula Roman-Kamphaus has published numerous publications in various national and international peer-reviewed journals and presented scientific papers across the world. Her expertise and academic interest oscillates mainly around the EU policies, multi-level governance and cross-border cooperation. She holds a PhD from the University of the West of Scotland that investigated the impact of the EU Cross-border Cooperation Programmes on the Central Eastern European borders.

Social Sciences

kollektiv orangotango+ (ed.)
This Is Not an Atlas
A Global Collection of Counter-Cartographies

2018, 352 p., hardcover, col. ill.
34,99 € (DE), 978-3-8376-4519-4
E-Book: free available, ISBN 978-3-8394-4519-8

Gabriele Dietze, Julia Roth (eds.)
Right-Wing Populism and Gender
European Perspectives and Beyond

April 2020, 286 p., pb., ill.
35,00 € (DE), 978-3-8376-4980-2
E-Book: 34,99 € (DE), ISBN 978-3-8394-4980-6

Mozilla Foundation
Internet Health Report 2019
2019, 118 p., pb., ill.
19,99 € (DE), 978-3-8376-4946-8
E-Book: free available, ISBN 978-3-8394-4946-2

All print, e-book and open access versions of the titles in our list are available in our online shop www.transcript-verlag.de/en!

Social Sciences

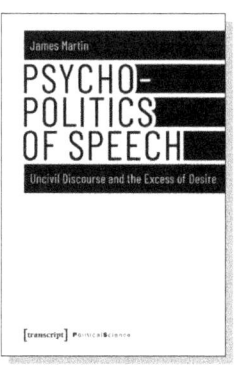

James Martin
Psychopolitics of Speech
Uncivil Discourse and the Excess of Desire

2019, 186 p., hardcover
79,99 € (DE), 978-3-8376-3919-3
E-Book: 79,99 € (DE), ISBN 978-3-8394-3919-7

Michael Bray
Powers of the Mind
Mental and Manual Labor
in the Contemporary Political Crisis

2019, 208 p., hardcover
99,99 € (DE), 978-3-8376-4147-9
E-Book: 99,99 € (DE), ISBN 978-3-8394-4147-3

Iain MacKenzie
Resistance and the Politics of Truth
Foucault, Deleuze, Badiou

2018, 148 p., pb.
29,99 € (DE), 978-3-8376-3907-0
E-Book: 26,99 € (DE), ISBN 978-3-8394-3907-4
EPUB: 26,99 € (DE), ISBN 978-3-7328-3907-0

**All print, e-book and open access versions of the titles in our list
are available in our online shop www.transcript-verlag.de/en!**

GPSR Authorized Representative: Easy Access System Europe, Mustamäe tee
50, 10621 Tallinn, Estonia, gpsr.requests@easproject.com

www.ingramcontent.com/pod-product-compliance
Lightning Source LLC
Chambersburg PA
CBHW070042040426
42333CB00041B/1960